D0756933

St. Louis Currents
The Fifth Edition

Edited by
Andrew J. Theising
Southern Illinois University Edwardsville
and
E. Terrence Jones
University of Missouri–St. Louis
Managing Editors:
Heather Birdsell and Hugh Pavitt
SIUE Institute for Urban Research

© 2016 The Board of Trustees of Southern Illinois University, Edwardsville, IL
All Rights Reserved. No portion of this book or its illustrations may be reproduced in any form without the expressed written permission of the copyright holder, except by a reviewer, who may use brief quotations and images.

Library of Congress Control Number: 2015954891

ISBN: 978-1-68106-019-4

Photographs by Paul Groenier ©2016, unless otherwise identified. Used by permission and protected by copyright.

SIUE Institute for Urban Research Staff:
James Hanlon, Ph.D., Director
Hugh Pavitt, MPA, Senior Research Fellow
Heather Birdsell, Office Support Associate
Jonathan Thurston, MPA, Graduate Research Assistant
Justin Huff, MPA, Graduate Research Assistant

Table of Contents

IN BOOKS LIES THE SOUL
OF THE WHOLE PAST TIME:
THE ARTICULATE AUDIBLE
VOICE OF THE PAST.
THOMAS CARLYLE

ST. LOUIS
CURRENTS

Acknowledgments

The editors gratefully acknowledge the financial support and production assistance of the SIUE Institute for Urban Research in the preparation of this volume, especially Director Jim Hanlon and Associate Provost Jerry Weinberg. Special recognition goes to the managing editors of this volume, Heather Birdsell and Hugh Pavitt, whose management of the day-to-day activity was essential to the project. The editors are also grateful to Josh Stevens, Barbara Northcott, and the staff of Reedy Press for guidance and patience in the production process. Jonathan Thurston and Justin Huff provided substantial technical assistance. The editors are grateful for the additional helpers at SIUE and UMSL, who made this work possible.

Introduction

St. Louis recently concluded celebration of its 250th anniversary, and this is an appropriate time to look back at the issues that shaped the region and to consider the issues facing it in the decades to come. *St. Louis Currents* provides both that thoughtful look back and mindful consideration of the future. From the very first issue of *Currents* in 1986, the book has been an important resource for civic leaders in our community.

The St. Louis region is home to some wonderful assets— social, economic, and political. The area has a wonderful diversity that reflects a long and vibrant history. It has been an economic engine that played a pivotal role in the national economy's development and continues to showcase cutting-edge technology and unbridled creativity. The region is home to major institutions, such as Scott Air Force Base and the Federal Reserve Bank, that shape the quality of life here and abroad. The magnificent Gateway Arch stands over the Mississippi River as a memorial to those brave women and men who settled the western expanse of the country. St. Louis has long served as a testament to their vision and success.

The issues raised by the events of Ferguson, Missouri, remind us that there is much work to be done. This region, like other major metropolitan centers, still grapples with social inequality, zones of economic distress, and questions of institutional performance. The challenges facing the area are great, but the creativity and resilience shown by the people of the region over time give hope that we can meet these challenges for the benefit of all.

Southern Illinois University Edwardsville is pleased to join with FOCUS St. Louis and the St. Louis Metropolitan Research Exchange to help produce this latest volume of *St. Louis Currents*. This new volume provides insightful perspectives on critical issues that have shaped the region's historical experience and will direct the path before us. The essays in this volume were chosen carefully to illustrate key perspectives on a variety of issues—some long familiar and some less so. Taken together, they provide an interesting and educational examination to inform our region's citizens and leaders.

Universities have an important role to play in metropolitan areas. Universities are centers of thinking and knowledge, and are important threads in the metropolitan fabric. SIUE is proud to have called the St. Louis region home for nearly sixty years and is also proud to be preparing area leaders for the twenty-first century and beyond.

Julie Furst-Bowe
Chancellor, Southern Illinois University Edwardsville

ST. LOUIS CURRENTS

About the Sponsor

Julie A. Furst-Bowe, Ed.D., served as the eighth chancellor of Southern Illinois University Edwardsville (SIUE) from 2012 to 2015. Dr. Furst-Bowe is recognized nationally and internationally for her expertise in systems thinking in higher education and has authored several articles and edited a book on this topic, *Quality and Performance Excellence in Higher Education*. In 2012, she edited a book on advancing STEM education and serves as editor of the *International Journal of Excellence in Education*. For more than a decade, she has served as a quality improvement consultant for numerous colleges and universities across the United States and has shared her experience with educators in sixteen countries throughout North America, Europe, Asia, and the Middle East.

Dr. Furst-Bowe has been appointed by the U.S. secretary of commerce to serve on the Board of Overseers for the Malcolm Baldrige National Quality Award, an award that provides the highest level of national recognition for performance excellence that a U.S. organization can achieve. She is also a founding board member of the National Consortium for Continuous Improvement in Higher Education and serves as higher education chair for the American Society for Quality.

ST. LOUIS
CURRENTS

ST. LOUIS CURRENTS

Introduction

FOCUS St. Louis is pleased to share the fifth volume of *St. Louis Currents*, a series that has provided insight on the region for three decades. FOCUS and its predecessor organizations have always been in a unique position to assemble this regional perspective because the organization always has used its diverse voice to speak on issues important to the greater St. Louis region.

Regionalism has only grown in importance over the last three decades. More and more, it is difficult to survive in a competitive environment alone. There is so much good to offer on both sides of the river that it makes sense to team up and celebrate our successes together. City and suburb, urban and rural, Illinois and Missouri all have shown the ability to come together at critical junctures. FOCUS St. Louis has been proud to have facilitated some of these partnerships and prepared some of the leaders making these important decisions.

The St. Louis region has weathered many storms. In the last great recession, the St. Louis region saw the closure of three automobile assembly plants (the two Chrylser plants in Fenton and the Ford plant in Hazelwood), yet the St. Louis region did not see unemployment rates much different than the national average. While this was painful for the region, lesser regions would have been devastated beyond recovery by such a loss. The St. Louis region absorbed the hit and was able to see recovery over time, albeit slow. This is a testament to the region's diversification of its economy, its ability to shift from traditional economic roles to new ones. No single jurisdiction made this happen. There was no single agency, no single industry, no single elected official able to take responsibility. It was a cooperative effort of public, private, and nonprofit over the years that worked for the benefit of all.

This new issue of *Currents* offers an opportunity to visit key issues facing our region and to understand them from new perspectives. Some of these are new looks at familiar issues from our past, some are identifying critical decisions that we will have to make in the years to come. All of these issues represent our collective experience and the choices we have for our collective future. As regional citizens, we have a duty to understand the many pieces of our past and use them wisely to shape our future.

I hope you enjoy the fifth volume of *St. Louis Currents*. If you feel moved to action by what you read, please remember that there is a seat at the table for you at FOCUS St. Louis.

Yemi S. Akande-Bartsch
Executive Director, FOCUS St. Louis

About the Sponsor

Yemi S. Akande-Bartsch, Ph.D., is the executive director of FOCUS St. Louis. Dr. Akande-Bartsch has been with FOCUS for two years; prior to assuming her current position, she was the vice-president, Leadership and Alumni program. Before FOCUS, Dr. Akande-Bartsch was managing partner at YsA Group, a leadership training and development company based in Cleveland, Ohio. Previously, she served as senior director of civic education for the Cleveland Leadership Center and program director for the Cleveland Executive Fellowship. She was also a lecturer at The Boler School of Business and assistant professor of Communications and Theatre Arts at Ohio's John Carroll University. Dr. Akande-Bartsch holds a doctorate in Communications from the University of Oklahoma, as well as two master's degrees: in Human Relations and Organizational Development; and in Public Relations, Journalism, and Mass Communications. She earned her bachelor's degree in Speech Communications from Southwest Baptist University in Bolivar, Missouri. Dr. Akande-Bartsch serves on the board of directors of The Sheldon Arts Foundation and is a member of the Association of Leadership Professionals and International Leadership Association. Dr. Akande-Bartsch and her husband, William "Bill" Bartsch, reside in Chesterfield, Missouri.

ST. LOUIS CURRENTS

Introduction

ST. LOUIS CURRENTS

As scholars we rarely have the opportunity to eavesdrop on a conversation a region is having about itself. But the fifth volume of *Currents* provides exactly this. Since the first *Currents* in 1986, there have been close to a hundred thought-provoking essays by some of our region's best minds reflecting the hopes, dreams, and fears that have gripped the region for the last thirty years.

The overwhelmingly dominant topic in this conversation has been a pre-occupation with the size of the region's population and the decline in its relative rank. St. Louisans have been consumed with this decline; with what others have thought about our supposed demise; and with what we can do about it.

In the 1986 volume, George Wendel, Saint Louis University's preeminent urbanist, noted that the region's population rank had fallen to 12th in the 1980 census and wondered if this trend might not be reversible. While most of Volume I's authors felt St. Louis would be able to turn things around, the tenor drastically shifted from hope to foreboding in the 1992 edition. The 1990 census showed that St. Louis had fallen to 17th place and Volume II authors were fixated on the region's daunting challenges that included political fragmentation, infrastructure decay, financial shortfalls, racial polarization, environmental concerns, and the lack of effective leadership.

In Volume III, published in 1996, the sense of angst about the region's decline became even more pronounced. Again acting as our demographer-in-chief, George Wendel pointed out that the region had continued its downward movement, dropping to 18th place. What concerned Wendel more was the freefall in the city of St. Louis's population. As he noted: "St. Louis is the most extreme case of proportional central city population decline in the United States," having shrunk by 54% between 1950 and 1990.

There was no 2004 edition of *Currents* (the region was well-analyzed during that anniversary year already), so more than a decade would pass before the next publication of *Currents* in 2009. By then the region had fallen to 18th place, with its forfeiture of being a second-tier metropolis a foregone conclusion. In "W(h)ither St. Louis?" Mark Tranel, director of the Public Policy Research Center at UMSL laid out St. Louis's predicament in undeniable terms: "For the past 50 years," he wrote, "there has been an outsized set of both absolute and comparative indicators generally showing a withering trend." Between 1950 and 2000, the region had shrunk from 10th to

ST. LOUIS CURRENTS

From the Editors

Welcome to the fifth edition of *St. Louis Currents*. This most recent volume sets the stage for the coming years by giving fresh perspective on the past and new understanding for the future. The essays in this volume each bring a perspective that has not been seen, from voices that may not be familiar beyond their certain professional circles.

St. Louis Currents has been an important guidebook for the region for three decades now. Though the issues remain familiar over time, the region's approach to them has changed, and in some cases, has even improved. In other cases, the region still struggles.

Residents move, leaders change, institutions come and go, but the issues remain the same. Education, economy, race, and quality of life are perennial topics on the region's agenda. *St. Louis Currents* provides insightful analysis on these key matters and informs the next generation of leaders who will be making vital decisions.

St. Louis is not all that unique among major metropolitan areas. Every major region has millions of people spread across many jurisdictions. Every major region grapples with unequal distribution of wealth. Every major region faces a challenge in public education. Every major region has created institutions to address economic development, environmental controls, and service delivery. These are basic issues of human need and government purpose.

What is unique is St. Louis's particular mix of leaders and the specific decisions that *we the people* choose to make for ourselves. As the region climbs out of the Great Recession and processes the lessons of Ferguson, the decisions made by the people ultimately will define the region's successes and struggles. The essays in this volume will help prepare citizens and leaders alike for action on some of those matters, and hopefully start some important discussions that will carry the region forward.

The Editors
Andy Theising
Senior Research Fellow, The Institute for Urban Research, Southern Illinois University Edwardsville

Terry Jones
Founders Professor of Political Science and Public Policy Administration and Dean Emeritus of Arts and Sciences, University of Missouri-St. Louis

About the Editors

Andrew J. Theising, Ph.D., is an associate professor and chair of the Political Science Department of Southern Illinois University Edwardsville, where he teaches courses in urban politics and public administration. He is also a senior research Fellow at the Institute for Urban Research. Dr. Theising is an author and editor of several books, including the fourth edition of *St. Louis Currents*, which focused on urban planning. His research has been used by media nationwide, including the *New York Times* and the PBS *NewsHour*. He is active on the governance boards of the Head Start Program serving St. Clair County and the East St. Louis Charter High School.

E. Terrence (Terry) Jones, Ph.D., is founders professor of political science and public policy administration at the University of Missouri-St. Louis. He has authored three books (*The Metropolitan Chase: Politics and Policies in Urban America, Fragmented by Design: Why St. Louis Has So Many Governments,* and *Conducting Political Research*), co-edited *St. Louis Metromorphosis: Past Trends and Future Directions,* and published over fifty professional articles, book chapters, and technical reports. He has served as a consultant to more than seventy governments and nonprofit organizations in the St. Louis metropolitan area.

ST. LOUIS
CURRENTS

Hub City

St. Louis's regional economy began as a colonial outpost that brought together traders of all backgrounds. Over time, it developed across time and space. The place went from serving a colonial purpose to serving a domestic purpose, and always responding to technological changes.

Lindenwood University's Jeffrey Smith explores the St. Louis region as an economic hub, not just locally but nationally. Smith captures the story of how a small trading center boomed into one of the country's leading centers of commerce and then chronicles its decline from that apex.

The economics of the region did much more than shape how well people fared commercially. It shaped the role of government, it defined new expectations for St. Louisans, it created new infrastructure, and it attracted new populations.

So many components seen in the St. Louis of today were part of the region's hub function many years ago. Smith's essay provides an insightful look back to help us understand the region we live in today.

ST. LOUIS
CURRENTS

ST. LOUIS
CURRENTS

St. Louis as Historical Hub

Jeffrey E. Smith, Ph.D.

In May 2011, the Missouri legislature adjourned without passing an economic stimulus bill that included an "Aerotropolis" at Lambert Airport in St. Louis. The idea behind it was to create a hub for international trade, particularly with China, through a series of tax credits for those forwarding goods to foreign destinations and incentives for those building the facilities to support that commerce.[1] On the surface, it seemed like a bold innovation to connect Missouri, located in the center of the United States, with the global trade far from its borders by envisioning St. Louis as a "gateway zone" for goods. This new concept is not very new at all—St. Louis was founded on much the same premise and has continued to build around this "hinge economy" connecting regions, the nation, and the world. Since its inception, Missouri's economy has been an international one; indeed, the region's greatest economic growth had strong foundations in the efforts of public-private partnerships to nurture Missouri's role in international markets and commerce. And, as with the aerotropolis proposal, government played a role in the development of the Missouri economy and its directions.

The Fur Trade and the International West

The story of St. Louis as an international trade hub starts in New Orleans in 1763. At the time, France controlled (or at least claimed) all the lands drained by the Mississippi River and its tributaries, thanks to a grandiose claim made by Rene-Robert La Salle in 1682, naming the huge swath of land "Louisiana" for the reigning French monarch, Louis XIV. Over the next eight decades after La Salle's tour, the French focused much of their energies in North America on the lucrative fur trade with Native American tribes. At the end of the French and Indian War in 1763, officials in New Orleans rewarded local merchant Gilbert Antoine St. Maxent with an exclusive charter to trade with the tribes on the Missouri River for his service as a colonel in the militia. He joined Pierre Laclede Liguest, with whom he had served in the war, to create Maxent, Laclede, and Company. Laclede set off with his stepson Auguste Chouteau the following July to build a trade fort and establish new commercial relations with the tribes on the lower Missouri. The North American fur trade connected producers of raw materials (pelts) with markets as distant as Europe and East Asia; by the time of Missouri statehood, John

Jacob Astor had become the leader in the lucrative business of selling furs in China to exchange for tea and silk. The French gave the company an exclusive charter, not unlike a license granting a sort of monopoly on that commerce in that region. Conceptually, St. Louis began as an "aerotropolis," complete with government support.

What Laclede, Chouteau, and the others did not realize when they first established the trade fort was that they were no longer living under the French flag, but rather the Spanish one. France lost the French and Indian War to Great Britain, but in order to keep all of Louisiana out of British hands, France had signed the secret Treaty of Fontainebleau in late 1762 with the Spaniards ceding its North American holdings to Spain.[2] Meantime, St. Louis grew based almost entirely on commerce in furs with native tribes. Each year traders traveled north and west, and every spring tribes traveled to St. Louis with piles of pelts to exchange with Europeans for myriad goods—blankets and tools, hoes and axes, kettles and tobacco, gunpowder and ribbons. The value of this trade was immense; trade with just one tribe, the Sac and Fox, was $60,000 per year by 1804.[3] Spanish government officials required licenses to trade with the tribes—perhaps the area's first public-private partnership—and they were easily acquired by compensating local officials, so the fur trade quickly came to be in the hands of a few large traders like the Chouteau family and Manuel Lisa.[4] So successful was this business that St. Louisans found it more lucrative to focus their energies there and importing food from downriver, earning the village the moniker "paincourt"—short of bread. The problem was not that they could not produce foodstuffs, but that it made economic sense to focus energies on commerce and import food.[5]

Even after farming began in the St. Louis area, the village became a central clearinghouse for the fur trade. Spain proved unable to supply the burgeoning demands of the fur trade by the end of the American War of Independence, but Great Britain was more than able to fill the void. Britain ran its fur trade in Canada primarily through two chartered joint stock companies, the Hudson's Bay Company and the North West Company, which had made Britain the largest fur dealer in the world.[6] As a rapidly industrializing power (and the first to experience the Industrial Revolution) financed by its mercantilist-based global system of colonies (including the thirteen on the Atlantic coast of North America), Britain was in prime position to address the demand for furs in both Europe and East Asia as well as to fuel the growing commerce with native tribes. By the late eighteenth century, the British were the largest buyer of furs from native tribes in the Mississippi Valley and Great Lakes.

St. Louis remained a center for the exchange of goods going to the far reaches of the globe. Anxious to divert British trade, Spain reopened the Mississippi River to American shipping in 1789; despite having to pay duties to Spanish officials, American merchants and farmers became part of the same network of goods as St. Louisans.[7] Spanish officials managed the Indian trade in much the same way as other Europeans, by granting licenses to traders and giving individuals or joint stock companies trade rights with specific tribes, often along the Missouri or Mississippi rivers and their tributaries. Spain endorsed a new concept to trade with tribes farther up the Missouri with the Mandan in present-day North Dakota in 1794, but meager profits from several expeditions slowed interest in the region until the United States acquired Louisiana.

Thomas Jefferson clearly understood the pivotal role of the region in a broader global commerce in which the fur trade was central. Jefferson expanded the Indian factory trade system, an early public-private partnership that started under the Washington administration. As originally conceived, these trade "factories " (so named because they were managed by men called factors) were embedded in army forts as places where regional tribes could exchange their goods, primarily furs, for an assortment of goods that would, Americans thought, help them become more "civilized." President George Washington saw the promise of such commerce and goods as giving Native Americans the "blessings of civilization" that would transform them into Christian, English-speaking, land-owning farmers who would contribute to the national economy. The number of trade factories, trading for furs with Indians and selling them at auction to fund the factory system, more than doubled under Jefferson, the most under any president.[8] Even before the Louisiana Purchase was complete, Jefferson expanded on his views regarding a western public-private partnership in the fur business; in early 1803, he sent Congress a confidential message saying that the region "is inhabited by numerous tribes, who furnish great supplies of furs & peltry to the trade of another nation [i.e., Great Britain]," and suggested a route connecting the United States to the Pacific (and, by extension, China and India) "traversing a moderate climate, offering according to the best accounts a continued navigation from it's [sic] source, and, possibly with a single portage, from the Western ocean."[9] Jefferson was even clearer in his instructions dated June 20, 1803, to Meriwether Lewis, co-commander of the Corps of Northwest Discovery commissioned to traverse the route from St. Louis to the Pacific: "The object of your mission is to explore the Missouri river [sic], & such principal stream[s] of it . . . [that] may offer the most direct & practicable water communication across this continent for the purposes of commerce."[10] Captains Lewis and William Clark conveyed these sentiments to the tribal leaders they met on their expedition, telling chiefs that they were not there as traders, but others would follow with more goods and, the captains said, the new "Great Father" (that is, Jefferson) expected that those traders would be treated well.[11] Although supported with public funds, Lewis and Clark were clearly to advance private enterprise, including the fur trade from St. Louis.

By the start of the War of 1812, St. Louisans still saw their city as an epicenter of the fur trade. A group of leading fur traders and government officials, including Auguste Chouteau, Manuel Lisa, explorer-turned-Indian-Agent William Clark, and territorial governor Meriwether Lewis's brother Reuben, pooled resources in 1809 to form the St. Louis Missouri Fur Company. However, the company was eventually driven out of business by John Jacob Astor's American Fur Company, which held a virtual monopoly on the American fur trade by the 1820s. St. Louis thus became only one part of a large network within Astor's network that acquired furs in the West, which it then exchanged for silk, tea, and other products in China. Thus, furs that passed through St. Louis ended up as part of a web of commerce that stretched to western Europe and the coastal trade ports in China.

The national fur business declined starting in the 1830s due to competition from the Hudson's Bay Company in Canada, declining supplies, and changing styles, and that downturn included St. Louis. During the 1880s, however, the fur business in St. Louis experienced a renaissance; local fur receipts increased almost fivefold during the decade, and continued to grow into the early twentieth century.[12] Furs from Alaska, Canada, and the United States continued to flow into St. Louis, making it the leading market for raw furs by the early 1900s. By the 1912—1913 fur-harvesting season, for example, furs sold in St. Louis were valued at some $12 million—an increase by a third in less than a decade.[13]

A series of federal laws and policies helped secure St. Louis's place as a global fur center in the 1910s. The fashion for fur coats, with fur on the outside of the coat rather than as a lining and collar, grew during the Gilded Age, with sealskin furs being particularly popular. By 1910, fur-bearing seals were approaching extinction.[14] The federal government responded with the Fur Seal Act of 1910, placing Pribilof seals under regulatory control of the Department of Commerce's Bureau of Fisheries and signing the North Pacific Fur Seal Convention in 1911 with Great Britain and Japan whereby all agreed to a temporary moratorium on harvesting seals heading south on annual breeding migrations. St. Louis fur magnate Philip Fouke, president of Funsten Brothers, convinced federal officials in 1913 to sell the now-regulated harvests of furs through St. Louis rather than London, making St. Louis a global leader in fur sales, especially with its contract two years later to become the exclusive seller of government furs.[15] When World War I ended, St. Louis was flooded with furs and fur dealers from Europe, making the newly formed St. Louis Fur Exchange created in 1916 immensely profitable.[16] In 1920, following two record-breaking auctions, the St. Louis Fur Exchange built its new seven-story exchange in downtown St. Louis near the waterfront. Its display rooms, storage facilities, and auction room allowed it to declare itself "the world's largest raw fur exchange."[17] After a brief downturn, the fur auctions resumed in 1934 and continued profitably until the Fouke Fur Company (successor to the St. Louis Fur Exchange) ceased auctions there in 1956.

Steamboats, Commercial Growth, and the Global Hinge Economy

With so many furs of such great value being exported, it meant that there was much imported as well. St. Louis evolved quickly into a commercial center. Because it was the gatekeeper to the Missouri River, Missouri also became a key transfer point for goods and people. Location was key to this development. From the standpoint of the early twenty-first century, it seems counterintuitive that a state in the center of the nation would be a hub for international commerce, but for much of the state's first century, Missouri was at a critical juncture with foreign commerce that shaped the early business community. As with the value of real estate, a central tenet to the early development of the Missouri economy, and especially that of St. Louis, was location.

Early river commerce was central to the fur trade since the Missouri and Upper Mississippi rivers and their tributaries were the main thoroughfares for connecting tribal regions with the new United States. Yet St. Louis remained on the edge of the frontier until the arrival of the first steamboats. Swift currents and shallow waters meant that steam-powered river craft on the western rivers required a different design with a shallower draft and different engine configuration. When the first steamboat, *Zebulon Pike*, arrived at the wharf in St. Louis in 1817, and on the Missouri two years later, it ushered in a revolution in transportation for Missouri. Previous craft had to rely on the current and wind for power going downriver, and had an arduous trip back up against the swift currents. That all changed with new transportation; even the earliest steamboats traveled from New Orleans upriver to St. Louis in just ten days, as compared to more than ninety for unpowered flatboats and keelboats. In 1849, the record for the same trip was three and a half days.[18] By the time of Missouri statehood in 1821, the St. Louis riverfront was a beehive of activity with steamboats parked along its wharf in front of the present-day Gateway Arch grounds.

Steamboats facilitated the rapid growth of the St. Louis economy in the state's first decades. When St. Louis was chartered as a city in 1822, the city's first mayor, William Carr Lane, immediately called for public funding of an enhanced levee on the Mississippi River to facilitate expanded steamboat trade. This public-private partnership was successful; by 1832, just fifteen years after the arrival of the *Zebulon Pike*, some 532 steamboats docked at the St. Louis wharf, unloading and reloading goods from not only North America but also Europe, coastal Africa, India, and China. The number of steamboats almost quadrupled by 1845, and grew another 50 percent within just a few years. Not only were there more steamboats on the rivers, but they were bigger, so tonnage grew almost fourfold between 1834 and 1844, and doubled again ten years later. Even when shipping and travel rates doubled during the 1850s, commerce continued undeterred.[19] Each of those 3,000 steamboats carried between 300 and 400 passengers and 700 tons of freight, all stopping in St. Louis for people to spend money and for goods to be bought, warehoused, financed, and sold. St. Louis's location as the main port near the divide between the Upper and Lower Mississippi River and between the points where the Ohio and Missouri Rivers flowed into the Mississippi made it an ideal connector location. Goods from overseas came up the Mississippi via New Orleans, pork and precut houses from Cincinnati, furs from the Upper Missouri and the Great Lakes, and tobacco from Missouri plantations all converged on the St. Louis waterfront.

Commerce and Western Trade

Westward expansion, starting with Mexican independence in 1821, also contributed to the rapid growth of the Missouri economy in the 1820s and 1830s. Spanish policy had ensured that the Americans were kept out of the lucrative trade with Santa Fe, its northernmost important settlement, but the newly independent Mexican government opened the city. Almost immediately, William Becknell led a group along the six-hundred-mile trek from Franklin, Missouri, to open this new market, supplying furs, silver, and mules with standard returns on investment between 20 and 50 percent. Within the next few years, the starting point for the Santa Fe Trail moved westward to the new Westport (later Kansas City), further enhancing the region's importance as an exchange center for distant goods. As with steamboats, wagons on the Santa Fe Trail grew as commerce demanded. Murphy wagons, which were manufactured in St. Louis and assembled in Westport, required six yoke of oxen to haul in caravans as large as twenty five wagons.[20] This role of St. Louis and Missouri as an economic exchange point lessened the impact of the Panic of 1837 in the state. The flow of goods into the state's economy and specie into the State Bank of Missouri, existing through a charter granted by the Missouri legislature, kept currency stable; migration kept money coming to the state as well. St. Louis's population doubled during the 1820s and again during the 1830s, with many immigrants bringing money with them to invest in new businesses.[21]

This westward movement of people and goods created additional opportunities for new and existing businessmen with the aid and support of government. This was particularly true when settlers began moving west to the Oregon Territory. Migration started slowly in the 1830s,[22] picked up in the 1840s, but exploded starting in 1849.[23] By the first part of that year, word had traveled back east of gold discoveries at a mill owned by John Sutter in California, which had just been acquired by the United States in its war with Mexico. Between 1849 and 1854, more than fifty thousand people moved to California annually in search of easy wealth. The great majority of them went overland on the Oregon and California Trails, which started in western Missouri. Most of these argonauts—typically young, male, and single with little intention of remaining in California—had read at least one of the standard "emigrant's guides," sort of the Fodor's of the western trails, which advised them to purchase needed supplies in St. Louis rather than carry or ship them from home in places like New York or Ohio (the states sending the most argonauts west, besides Missouri). This was a boon to the St. Louis economy, since thousands of men were passing through the city each spring, all looking to purchase the same list of goods from guidebooks by Lansford Hastings or Joseph Ware. Prices for coffee, hardtack, salt pork, gold pans, floppy hats, horses, wagons, and other essentials skyrocketed; indeed, every diarist of the Gold Rush who commented on St. Louis decried the high prices and (often) low quality of the goods.[24] Other cities and towns upriver soon expanded as suppliers as well, with outfitters emerging in places like Independence, Westport, and St. Joseph.[25]

The Role of Bridges and Railroads

As a river-based transportation hub, St. Louis grew and flourished. Having said that, a river-based economy had its problems. Rivers are not easily crossed and they do not always flow everywhere people, goods, and products need to go. In Missouri as elsewhere, railroads and bridges, starting with the Illinois and Missouri Bridge (later named the Eads Bridge for its chief engineer), were the solutions. By the early 1830s, railroads were the cutting-edge technology; just ten years after John Stevens showed his steam-powered locomotive on a circular track in New Jersey in 1825, some sixty-four delegates attended a statewide railroad convention in St. Louis and proposed construction of two roads to connect the two regions producing export products to St. Louis, the largest shipping and warehousing city in the state—one westward to Fayette in the heart of the state's tobacco plantation country, the other southwest to the mineral mining counties.[26] Typically, eastern states like Pennsylvania, Ohio, Maryland, and New York were heavy investors in such costly infrastructure during the period, but Missouri was different. With neither sufficient private capital nor state or federal underwriting, the proposals languished during the Panic of 1837.

But with hopes of becoming the eastern terminus of a national rail line that would connect east and west, St. Louisans hosted a national railroad convention in 1849. It was one of several held by cities at the time. Both Chicago and Memphis, for example, had similar aspirations and held such conventions. Among its speakers was Missouri senator Thomas Hart Benton, one of the Senate's great orators and a noted proponent of expanded rail lines and commerce. In his speech, Benton called on the United States to complete the vision that started with Christopher Columbus and build a route to East Asia with a new sort of public-private partnership. For Benton, his home state of Missouri was the key hinge point between the developed United States and the lucrative trade in Asia; it could be the place of exchange where exotic goods from the east mixed with those of Europe and the United States. Appropriately enough, the statue of Benton in Lafayette Park (sculpted by Harriet Hosmer in 1868) faces west, inscribed with Benton's quote from the convention, "To the East, to India."

Railroad investment was somewhat slow in Missouri during the decade before the Civil War, particularly after the disastrous Pacific Railroad's Gasconade Bridge collapsed in November 1855, leaving thirty-one dead. The state legislature started a program of state aid for construction in 1851, and the federal government gave the state alternating sections of public land along the route of the Hannibal & St. Joseph and Pacific Railroads.[27] Although about eighty percent of the stock sold in the Hannibal & St. Joseph was to private individuals (many of whom were in eastern cities like New York and Boston), this was not the general trend with antebellum railroads in Missouri; overall, during the 1850s, individuals purchased only about a third of the stock sold in railroads.[28] Public opposition to state operation and construction of railroads meant that the state resorted to financial aid to these start-up companies, which often managed the money poorly and defaulted during the 1860s.[29]

During the Civil War, state government facilitated migration to the state through agents and advertising in the eastern United States, Canada, and even Europe. Thanks to offers of free or cheap transport and promises of homesteads in "one of the richest and healthiest agricultural and pastoral regions on this continent," the Hannibal & St. Joseph had sold some five hundred thousand acres of land mostly to individual farmers rather than speculators, increasing the state's population by as much as one hundred thousand by 1870.[30] However, the Hannibal & St. Joseph was the only railroad completed across the state at war's end, with a combination of eastern capital and a $3 million loan from the state, leaving the state government, now under a new constitution written in early 1865, faced with the possibility of railroad connections to some regions of the state bypassing cities like St. Louis and connecting to railroads that went straight to Chicago. Pressures from around the state after the war compelled the state legislature to actively facilitate completion of roads crisscrossing the state by absorbing railroad debts, releasing some roads from liens, and offering financial incentives for completing roads to key points and penalties for failing to do so. Despite the cloak of suspicion of bribery of state officials, three east-west roads and another north-south one were completed by the early 1870s.[31]

Cities and towns after the war invested heavily in bringing the railroad to their communities. As in other states, town fathers knew that rail connections were critical to their town's growth, and that being bypassed would leave them an economic backwater. Between 1867 and 1872, Missouri governmental entities invested more than $17 million in intrastate railways and another $1 million in connector lines outside the state.[32] Completion of the Pacific Railroad to Kansas City spurred rapid growth of the old Santa Fe Trail hub as a processing point for the commodities from the emerging West, most notably processing cattle and milling flour. With an economy resting on "bread and beef," it also experienced growth in the smaller industries to support its burgeoning population, which grew some eightfold in the 1860s.[33] In all, railroad investment worked. The areas with new rail connections grew far faster than others, and Missouri manufacturing trebled in the decade.[34] By 1880, Missouri had more almost four thousand miles of railroad track—double the miles just a decade before.[35] Only three counties (Dallas, Douglas, and Ozark) had no rail connections by 1904.[36]

Essential to the successful transformation of the Missouri economy through railroads was crossing the Mississippi River. Until after the Civil War, ferrying companies facilitated crossing large rivers. At St. Louis, the Wiggins Ferry Company had a virtual monopoly on ferrying railroad cars, cargo, and people across the Mississippi at St. Louis. For companies like Wiggins, ice was a major hazard; in the three years after the Civil War, for example, the Mississippi was closed to ferry traffic no fewer than sixty days.[37] The first bridge over the Mississippi at St. Louis (completed in 1874) connected Illinois with a system of tunnels running beneath the streets of downtown St. Louis. Although designed by James Buchanan Eads, the bridge construction was contracted to the Keystone Bridge Company, whose vice president Andrew Carnegie, helped organize the financing for the bridge; a third of the investment funding for the bridge came through Carnegie's contact with Junius Morgan (J. P. Morgan's father) in London.[38] Bridge operations suffered economic woes, and eventually two more bridges were built across the river to circumvent high tolls on the Eads.

It would be difficult to overstate the transformative impact of railroads on the St. Louis and Missouri economies. After 1870, more trunk lines were built with a growing number of feeder lines that connected more and more people to cities and, therefore, to burgeoning global markets. St. Louis in particular was a center for goods both domestic and international, with its role as a hinge center for river and rail transport; people in rural communities now had access to those goods through the middlemen, wholesalers, and transporters based in St. Louis.

The railroad transformed the lives of rural Missourians in fundamental ways. Not only did they have access to goods from distant places that had once been impossible luxuries, but they also conducted business differently. The combination of transportation and mechanization meant that farmers in the Great West, including Missouri, raised more commercial crops on more acres than ever; railroads contributed by giving them ways to ship those agricultural commodities to eastern markets. By 1880, there were markedly more farmers cultivating more acres than just ten years previous.[39] Herein lies the crux of the fundamental transformation in western agriculture of which Missouri farmers were a part. More acres came under cultivation thanks to the use of new farm machinery, which was expensive, increasing the debt carried by farmers. It also meant that farm commodities were increasingly part of a global marketplace, so that prices for, say, Missouri wheat might be shaped by the wheat harvests in other parts of the world. Exacerbating the problem was the growth of agricultural output nationally, which meant that supply rose faster than demand, driving down prices. Small wonder that western farmers in places like Missouri started to support national monetary policies that were inflationary, such as printing paper money (advanced by the Greenback Party) and increasing money supply through monetizing silver as proposed by the People's Party or the populists. So prominent was this region that the populists held their convention to nominate William Jennings Bryan for president in St. Louis in 1896.[40]

St. Louis remained the great transportation and manufacturing hub of the state in the Gilded Age, though. Transportation connections combined with raw materials (lead, zinc, and coal, primarily) and agricultural commodities (wheat, corn, and cotton) from the state to transform the city into a manufacturing center. The value of manufactured goods from St. Louis mushroomed fourfold between 1870 and 1880, and doubled again ten years later; capital invested in manufacturing and industrial establishments both more than trebled in the 1880s.[41] Even as late as the 1970s, the St. Louis riverport was the nation's largest; the port's docks processed more than 24 million tons of goods in 1979, including coal being shipped to the Gulf of Mexico.[42] During the 1880s and 1890s, St. Louis boosters actively solicited business with interests in Mexico, and even sent to Mexico City several hundred copies of *St. Louis Through a Camera*, an illustrated booklet published in 1892 designed to promote the city.

The Transformative Effect of Cupples Station

The tunnels constructed in the 1870s were the foundation for an innovation in the Gilded Age that became a prototype for cities across the country—and a sort of "aerotropolis" for railroads on the outskirts of downtown St. Louis that became the origin of ideas about air hubs and shipping industrial parks in the twentieth century. As Cupples Station was constructed and expanded over three decades, it successfully made St. Louis a rail-shipping hub. The last third of the nineteenth century was a period of rapid and profound industrial growth in the United States. As manufacturing grew, so too did the need to transport, sell, and redistribute these manufactured goods. Just as manufacturing centralized and grew into large companies, so too did the concept of the merchant into a network of wholesalers, jobbers, and distributors who acquired goods from manufacturers and sold them to retailers and customers elsewhere. By their very nature these middlemen were located in places that could serve as hubs with transportation spokes stretching throughout the region. However, the transportation component was not as efficient as it might seem on the surface. These wholesalers had to rely on local drayage and transportation to move goods from their points of entry to warehouses, then again when shipped out to different places.[43] Cupples Station changed all that.

The brainchild of Robert Brookings (vice president of Cupples Woodenware Company, the largest woodenware company in the United States), Cupples Station stood between the mouth of the Terminal Railroad Association tunnel (adjacent to present-day Busch Stadium) and the tracks that connected to all the main rail lines on both the Missouri and Illinois sides of the Mississippi. Under Brookings's leadership, Cupples Station became a complex of warehouses (mostly seven stories) with rail spurs connecting them to main lines. Within six years after completion of the first warehouse at Seventh and Pine Streets, ten warehouse buildings stood in the complex. Now wholesalers did not have to move goods from the railroad tracks to warehouses and back again when shipping goods out to customers. The warehouses were designed with efficiency and safety in mind.[44] By the turn of the century, Cupples Station handled more than one thousand tons of freight every day, making it the largest and busiest rail freight station in the United States.[45]

For wholesalers, this innovation could not have come at a better time. By the late nineteenth century, manufacturers of a growing number of consumer goods started marketing products directly to consumers, which altered a series of relationships in the chain of distribution. Direct marketing of brand-name products to consumers also carried with it responsibility for delivery and quality control, so a growing number of manufacturers of everything from flour to shortening, soda pop to beer, crackers to canned soup, along with catalogue houses like Sears and Montgomery Ward, moved into the distribution business. Therefore, wholesalers like those in St. Louis specializing in nonbrand products were under increased pressure to cut costs and operate more efficiently than ever before. A centralized warehousing and distribution center was the answer to the question of managing goods coming into and leaving St. Louis; Cupples Station became the model for other distribution cities by the early twentieth century. In many ways, Cupples Station was also a rail-based prototype for both industrial shipping centers such as Earth City and the aerotropolis proposal of 2011.

Air Transport: Economic Déjà Vu

Rail and river travel continued to be the principal modes of transporting both goods and people well into the twentieth century, but new technologies contributed to the role of the St. Louis region as an economic hub. St. Louis played an early role in air transportation as well. Within less than a decade after the Wright brothers made their historic flight at Kitty Hawk, Archibald Huxley took former president Theodore Roosevelt on a plane ride at Kinloch Field in St. Louis, making him the first president to fly in an airplane.[46] Former Olympic golf star and pharmaceuticals manufacturer Albert Lambert became so enamored with flight that he purchased 550 acres northwest of the city to operate as an airfield. The year after Charles Lindbergh left Lambert's field in his *Spirit of St. Louis* to start a journey that ended in Paris in May 1927, Lambert sold the land to the city of St. Louis to operate as an airfield.

The new terminal at Lambert Field was dedicated in 1930, and completed three years later.[47] Regional population growth and increased air traffic for both shipping and passenger travel meant that the region was rapidly outgrowing its airport. So great was interest in the future of air transportation that noted city planner Harland Bartholomew called for more than thirty airports and heliports scattered around the metropolitan area in his 1947 St. Louis city plan.[48] The new Lambert International Airport, designed by the architectural firm Hellmuth, Yamasaki and Leinweber, was completed in 1957.

Despite several additions to Lambert over the next decade or so, there was much public debate in the late 1960s and early 1970s over airports and their locations. More runways were needed, and Lambert appeared to be landlocked. Some called for a new regional airport across the Mississippi River in Illinois, and the state of Illinois offered substantial financial support for it. Critics of the Illinois plan wanted to keep the airport—and its jobs, business, and tax revenues—on the Missouri side. The *St. Louis Post-Dispatch* stridently advocated for a Missouri airport at an expanded Lambert; in 1977, the Missouri congressional delegation led by Sen. Thomas Eagleton convinced Transportation Secretary Brock Adams to put federal funding into expanding Lambert.[49]

Perhaps the most interesting aspect of the aerotropolis proposal and the economic incentive bill was not that Missouri sought to be an innovator, but rather that it stood on the shoulders of its history spanning to the days when St. Louis was not even part of the United States and Missouri did not even exist. The notion of government and private industry working together to facilitate economic growth—a series of public-private partnerships—by capitalizing on international commercial connections seems new and foreign to some, but it is not. It is the story of the decades of our greatest economic growth.

About the Author

Jeffrey Smith, Ph.D., is chair of the History and Geography Department at Lindenwood University in St. Charles, Missouri. He is also editor of *The Confluence*, a peer-reviewed regional studies journal published by the Lindenwood University Press.

Smith has written and spoken on a range of regional topics for scholarly conferences and popular publications alike. He is author of "'Turning the World Upside Down': (2010), *Seeking A Newer World: The Journals and Letters of George C. Sibley, 1808-1811* (2003), *Gold Rush: The Overland Diary of Samuel A. Lane, 1850* (1984), and numerous articles. His primary interest and study have focused on Jacksonian America and the Gilded Age-Progressive Era, largely in St. Louis. He is completing a social history of Bellefontaine Cemetery in St. Louis between its founding in 1849 and 1920, due for release in Fall 2015.

ST. LOUIS CURRENTS

Race and Health Care

Race and health care are both issues of tremendous importance today in the region and the nation. St. Louis was a segregated city from its earliest days. Its schools were segregated, its restaurants and theaters were segregated, and for many decades so were its hospitals. Taylor Desloge has prepared a brilliant analysis of the Homer G. Phillips Hospital experience.

Politics were intimately involved in both the creation of and closing down of Homer G. Phillips. African Americans cherished the hospital and its staff, and the building and its surroundings still evoke powerful feelings of community.

The Fight for Homer G. Phillips Hospital
and the Making of Health Care Politics

Taylor Desloge

> *If you want to treat us as well as you treat yourselves take us . . . into your city hospital. If you don't and we have to have our own segregated hospital, let us go off where we won't have to observe the differences . . . I am against segregation . . . and never lose a chance to say so, but if the white laws of this state order segregation, then those who want it ought to pay for it. It's your luxury, not ours. – Fannie Cook, "Black Liberty"*

When prolific St. Louis author and social welfare activist Fannie Cook sat down in 1940 to write a fictionalized tribute to her close friend and fellow St. Louis League of Women Voters member, Carrie King Bowles, she tellingly chose to center it on a single moment—a tense meeting of the St. Louis Community Council's Interracial Committee over the location of a long-promised new "colored hospital" on a steamy July night in the early 1930s. White doctors, politicians, and social workers hoped to save money by building the new hospital as an extension to the existing white hospital. Much to their befuddlement, they faced an African American community nearly united in opposition. In the story's cinematic climax, "Mrs. Adams" (a "middle-aged, neatly dressed . . . colored clubwoman" clearly based on Bowles) rises to her feet, stands down a white crowd "lined up in opposition," and delivers a powerful critique of segregation, demanding a separate, black-run hospital as a remedy—however imperfect—to the problem of inadequate health care for black people in St. Louis.[1]

Cook's account of the struggle to build a new black hospital in Depression-eraSt. Louis was fictionalized. Yet it was based in real experience. A new "colored hospital"—what would become the now-iconic Homer G. Phillips Municipal Hospital—originally was devised through the persistent efforts of local lawyer Homer G. Phillips, as part of an $87 million civic improvement bond issue in 1923. The hospital was delayed for nearly a decade due to a debate between black and white doctors, politicians, and social welfare activists—a debate which would ultimately ensnare the public at large—over whether to build the structure as a separate institution in the Elleardsville neighborhood or as an extension to the existing (white) City Hospital No. 1 in a largely white section of the city. The city administration believed that building the hospital as an extension made good economic sense; doing so would expand the beds available to black patients with "large savings in initial investment and annual savings in operating cost." Yet for African Americans, the issue was laden with racial meaning; as Homer G. Phillips himself explained to Mayor Victor Miller in 1927, "to change the site . . . would mean 'segregation with humiliation.'" The hospital controversy spoke to the political goals, hopes, and fears of the St. Louis African American community as few other issues had. It fueled protests among the black professional class over the potential loss of a new economic and cultural anchor for black life in St. Louis, worries over the career prospects of black doctors in a white-dominated hospital, and even age-old fears of medical experimentation on black patients at the hands of unscrupulous white doctors. Most of all, however, as Fannie Cook's story demonstrates, it helped mobilize a new political movement that viewed the problem of health as inseparable from the problem of racial inequality, one which was deeply invested in the larger interwar project of undermining biological and advancing social and economic explanations for racial inequality.[2]

Homer G. Phillips Hospital—a modern, 7 story, 685-bed Art Deco-style complex that at one time trained up to a third of black doctors in the United States—is "considered by many to be the most tangible achievement of St. Louis' black community" and perhaps its "most widely known symbol." As the city's "colored hospital," the structure embodied a nearly never-ending battle for black control, from the struggle over the right of black doctors to practice at City Hospital No. 2 (the "colored" city hospital that preceded Homer G. Phillips Hospital), to the fight over the building's location, to later pushes to ensure equal employment opportunity and even the vigorous debate over its closing in the late 1970s. However, beyond its immediate historic significance as a place of employment or an iconic local institution, Homer G. Phillips Hospital was the product of a profound reconceptualization in African American political thought during the interwar years, of the nature of racial inequality in general and the links between health and social and economic inequality in particular.[3]

Many historians have emphasized the pioneering role played by interwar scientists and social scientists in revising long-held assumptions about race. Historians of public health argue that, beginning in the 1920s, medical professionals increasingly rejected wholly biological explanations for racial health disparities.[4] Social scientists challenged biology as the basis for racial difference as well. As historian Daryl Michael Scott writes, "culture and social environment replaced biology as means of explaining black behavior." In response to problems of urbanization, modernization, and immigrant assimilation, they constructed an environmentalist paradigm for understanding human behavior. Racial inequality was a problem resulting from cultural adjustment and "damage" inflicted by negative white attitudes toward African Americans. The Chicago School, championed by sociologists like Robert Park and Charles Johnson, advanced the view that, "blacks could be assimilated into the mainstream of American life."[5]

Social science played a key role in shaping the ideological contours of many forms of black activism. In his study of the Urban League during the first half of the twentieth century, Touré Reed argues that the league's "uplift" philosophy was powerfully shaped by the theories of urban adjustment advanced by Chicago School sociology, particularly those of social organization and disorganization and urban ecology.[6] Historians have likewise credited interwar social scientists with establishing the groundwork for a postwar racial liberalism that, ultimately, produced legal victories like *Brown v. Board of Education*.[7]

Few have examined the effects of this intellectual, social, and political transformation on African American health politics: in spite of the fact that scholars have long recognized that black doctors, coming from a marginalized position themselves, have historically emphasized the roots of disease in social and political inequality far more than their white counterparts.[8] Indeed, many have characterized black health-care politics in this era as a continuation of the service-oriented and institution-building approach to health championed by philanthropic organizations like the Rosenwald Fund and the Rockefeller Foundation in the 1920s. In this understanding, first private organizations and then, during the New Deal, the federal government funded a dramatic expansion of medical facilities for African Americans to improve dismal black health statistics, assuage white fears of contagious disease, address the political demands of increasingly influential black voters, and provide vital training opportunities for black medical professionals. Karen Kruse Thomas's study of the growth of black hospitals in the South between the 1920s and 1950s, for instance, argues that African American leaders made an accomodationist "devil's bargain" with white southern liberals, setting aside the question of racial equality in favor of a colorblind language of "Southern uplift" that channeled public resources to Jim Crow hospitals in a "needs-based calculus."[9]

At first a product of the service-oriented health-care politics of the 1920s, Homer G. Phillips Hospital played a key role in the forging of a new black health-care politics that took segregation as its target and viewed health as inextricably connected to the problem of black inequality. New social scientific understandings of racial inequality, which gradually filtered down to the grassroots level of urban politics, provided the ideological framework for a growing and parallel movement. This framework challenged, and ultimately upended, a 1920s consensus that conceptualized black health as primarily a problem of service provision and, by necessary extension, political patronage. For African American activists, Homer G. Phillips Hospital provided an opportunity to redress the social and economic inequalities, embodied most potently in the frail forms of the diseased, produced by the system of segregation. Defying both the contemporary criticism of integrationist outsiders in the national black press and the strict divide between integrationism and separatism that, until relatively recently, dominated the historiography of black politics, advocates for a separate black hospital were laying the foundations for the decidedly integrationist ideology of "racial liberalism" that would dismantle legal barriers in the postwar era.

Yet if the eventually triumphant story of Homer G. Phillips Hospital speaks to the success of the new black health-care politics, it also demonstrates its limits as a remedy for inequality. While the dominant racial politics to emerge from the New Deal era provided an important ideological ground for attacking biological understandings of racial inequality and the legal system of segregation they supported, it proved incapable of addressing the problem of class inequality in an industrial society.

The Great Migration and the "New Public Health" of the 1920s

Over 1.5 million African Americans migrated from the rural South to urban centers across the country in search of better jobs, more freedoms, and greater security in the decades between Reconstruction and the Great Depression. Many chose to settle in St. Louis, where, between 1900 and 1956, the black population increased by 561.7%—from 35,516 to 235,000—essentially doubling between 1900 and 1920 and then doubling again between 1920 and 1940.[10] As in other cities, these new migrants found themselves at the bottom of the socioeconomic order. Barred from high-paying union jobs and coerced into artificially expensive housing in crowded, segregated, and often unsanitary neighborhoods through violence, intimidation, and exclusionary legal mechanisms, black migrants paid for inequality with their health as well as their wealth. An American Public Health Association survey of the city conducted in 1927 presented a dismal picture of black health. Death rates for African Americans were startlingly high, standing at 23.91 per 1,000 people in 1925 compared to only 13.49 for whites. African American migrants were particularly menaced by tuberculosis, suffering at five times the rate of white St. Louisans.[11]

Partially in response to the influx, the St. Louis Department of Public Welfare embraced the strategies of the New Public Health movement of the 1920s, which sought to manage contagious disease through city-funded bacteriological laboratories, patient surveillance, clinics, and educational programs. The results were often more stigmatizing than helpful to African American city dwellers, as these new programs often emerged out of racial fears that framed black migrants as inherently diseased.[12]

Adherents of New Public Health expressed a deep faith in medicine's ability to attack disease "without disrupting the social order," often leading them to downplay or even ignore the social and economic causes of disease and older priorities like environmental sanitation in favor of investing in expanded services to treat the sick. Perhaps reflecting Fannie Cook's astute observation that

St. Louis has historically been "a Northern city with a Southern exposure," St. Louis combined New Public Health's stigmatizing approach to minority communities with a relatively strong commitment to expanding health services for African Americans. In 1923, St. Louis made headlines around the nation both for becoming the first city to set aside public funds for the construction of a "modern Negro hospital" and for forcibly vaccinating all African American migrants arriving from the South—nearly three thousand a day at one point in the early 1920s—at Union Station. [13]

New Public Health's emphasis on expansion of services made it particularly adaptable to the machinations of local politics. For one, service provision and patronage played a key role in keeping black voters behind the GOP ward machine that dominated the city for most of the first few decades of the twentieth century. [14] For another, black churches, political organizations, and philanthropic groups pushed the city to expand health services considerably throughout the 1920s. As the St. Louis Urban League stated in the late 1920s, they were determined to "not only be confined to Negro groups" but to "work with health agencies, institutions and with the Department of the City engaged in health programs" to expand social services. [15] the groundwork was laid in the 1910s, when a committee of seventeen black physicians—rebuffed in their attempts to open the City Hospital to black interns—convinced the city to purchase the Barnes Medical College building at Lawton and Garrison Avenues in North St. Louis to create a new black hospital. City Hospital No. 2, a 177 bed institution, opened in 1919 as a stopgap measure until a larger, better-equipped hospital could be built. [16] Throughout the 1920s, organizations like the League of Women Voters, the St. Louis Tuberculosis and Health Society, and the Urban League frequently published surveys on St. Louis health resources and services open to African Americans, often pressuring the city government to build new clinics in black communities, create new education programs, and expand beds for indigent black patients in local hospitals.

The original push for Homer G. Phillips Hospital emerged, in part, out of the same confluence of local politics and social service provision. Indeed, it began as a quintessential political deal. The man who sought to fulfill the city's promise to build a permanent black hospital was local lawyer Homer Gilliam Phillips (1880—1931), now a legendary—if somewhat enigmatic—figure in St. Louis history. In 1922, he "reactivated" the committee of seventeen black physicians who had originally pushed for City Hospital No. 2. A year later, he struck an agreement with Mayor Henry Kiel to include a new "colored hospital" as part of an $87 million bond issue that provided funds for a new municipal stadium, street widening and improvement, the future Gateway Mall, and the St. Louis Soldiers Memorial. Kiel needed black voters to ensure passage of the bond issue, the largest called for by any city to that date. [17]

Phillips proved an ideal spokesman for the new hospital. The orphaned son of a Sedalia, Missouri, Methodist minister, his life offers a powerful success story in the midst of what is often referred to by historians as the "nadir of American race relations." After graduating from Howard University School of Law in Washington—where he boarded in the home of celebrated poet Paul Laurence Dunbar—Phillips established a law firm in St. Louis in 1904. As a lawyer, he was an expert in fraud cases. On one occasion, Phillips successfully defended a local life insurance company against a fraudulent claim by hauling the "dead" man's coffin into the courtroom and revealing it to be full of cement. Yet he is most remembered as a civil rights leader and towering figure among the black cultural elite of the era. Judge Nathan Young, an activist and newspaper publisher in St. Louis during the same time period, described him as "an inspiration to his people" and "an inspiring speaker and social reformer who stood down the virulent racism spreading through the city and the nation." From the battle against a 1916 referendum mandating residential segregation to the hospital controversy, Phillips was involved in nearly all of the civil rights causes taken on by the local African

American community for twenty years until his tragic shooting death—at the hands of two still-unidentified assailants—at a Delmar and Aubert Ave. streetcar station in 1931.[18]

He found strong support for at least the idea of a new hospital. From the standpoint of the service-oriented health politics of the 1920s, including the new "Negro hospital" in the civic improvement bond issue was not controversial. Indeed, even as the campaign for the new hospital simmered throughout the 1920s and foundered in the "location controversy," social welfare advocates and local government officials on both sides of the color line found common ground in publicizing the need for better facilities, wherever their location. It was clear to all involved that City Hospital No. 2 was not up to the task of providing decent care to the city's black community. As one doctor put it in 1928, it was "inexcusable" to have so few beds open to black patients in a city "of more than 90,000 negro[e]s" and a black "death rate higher than its birth rate."[19] A flyer released by the League of Women Voters for a 1933 bond campaign to provide additional funds for completion of the hospital framed the issue in much the same way and even played to white fears of disease. Quoting the city hospital commissioner ("an adequate number of hospital beds for Negroes is absolutely essential if the high incidence of disease among this section is to be improved"), it warned voters that "the health . . . of the entire city is at stake."[20]

Moreover, City Hospital No. 2 was widely perceived to be an additional threat to the health of black St. Louisians. Known as the "firetrap" and "the slaughterhouse," the hospital had an infamous reputation for overcrowding, scarce funding, and deplorable sanitary conditions. Doctors frequently expressed frustration with the facility's lack of modern medical tools, a problem widely publicized when a doctor died after being electrocuted by a faulty X-ray machine at the hospital in 1930. Priscilla Dowden-White notes that black St. Louisans expressed a widespread dread of hospitalization during the 1920s and 30s, often preferring to treat even the most serious illnesses at home. She quotes one black St. Louisan, "If I go to City Hospital # 2, I'll come home in a box."[21] Dr. Haven Emerson, a New Yorker who surveyed St. Louis medical services in 1927, found that "sanitary conditions for the animals at Forest Park Zoo are better than those at the Negro Hospital." He declared it an "outrage and disgrace" that "should be closed as soon as possible." [22] A 1933 campaign flyer for a second bond issue to build a new hospital reported that not only was the building a dangerous firetrap that exposed patients—including pregnant mothers—to heat as high as "102 degrees" on hot summer days but that it only had one toilet available for every fifty to sixty patients.[23]

Nonetheless, little action was taken. The Board of Aldermen, supported by the Public Welfare Department, passed a condemnation ordinance for a site on Goode Avenue in the Elleardsville ("the Ville") neighborhood in 1925.[24] However, opponents of the measure—a coalition of white doctors, cost-cutting bureaucrats and (white) real estate interests in the Ville—argued that the bond issue had not promised a separate hospital and pushed for the bond money to be spent on renovating Deaconess Hospital, an old hospital adjacent to City Hospital No. 1, as an extension to the white hospital. In 1927, Republican mayor Victor Miller joined their cause and attempted to repeal the ordinance.[25] The St. Louis Bureau of Municipal Research endorsed his position in a comprehensive study of the sites in Elleardsville and City Hospital No. 1. After examining both sites from the perspective of economic feasibility, ambulance response time, and nearness to the black population, the bureau concluded that "facilities of equal character could not be provided for the Negro Hospital on a separate location."[26]

The Controversy Begins: Professional Opportunity and Community Health

Opposition from black leaders, led once again by Homer G. Phillips, was immediate. For African Americans, it was the beginning of a larger break from the public health consensus of the 1920s and a rethinking of the role played by health in politics. The first great volley was fired on behalf of black doctors and nurses. "A formidable and representative group of colored citizens," led by Phillips, went before the Public Welfare Committee of the Board of Aldermen in July 1927. Phillips "forcibly explained why the new institution should be located" in the Ville, emphasizing the professional development needs of black doctors and nurses.[27] It was a theme continued throughout the extended conflict. "I have not yet been convinced," Urban League secretary John T. Clark wrote Fannie Cook in May 1930, "that the matter of location is not the most important in the controversy . . . . The development of our medical leaders will have its least chance for success if the Negro hospital becomes an appendage of Hospital #1."[28]

The record of black/white relations in St. Louis health care and a longer, nationwide history of exclusion and condescension had given black doctors ample grounds to mistrust whites in both medicine and social welfare. Black doctors faced segregation on an institutional level in medicine in the North and South, severely limiting their opportunities for professional development. They were barred from joining the St. Louis Medical Society[29]—and the American Medical Association at large—and were consequently forced to form their own organization, the Mound City Medical Society. In the wake of Abraham Flexner's professionalization and standardization campaigns in the 1910s and early 1920s, only two medical schools in the country served the black population—Meharry Medical College in Nashville and Howard University in Washington, D.C.—while Northern medical schools like Harvard, Yale, Temple, and the University of Chicago admitted a token number of African Americans annually, graduating a *combined* total of ten a year during the 1930s. Internships, vital for medical training, were highly limited as well: blacks were generally barred from working in white hospitals and only fourteen black hospitals nationwide were accredited for internships before 1940.[30]

Within the segregated system, black doctors faced condescending attitudes—personal slights, questioning of competence, refusal to delegate responsibility—that surely contributed to their desire for a separate hospital. Many white doctors viewed black physicians as incompetent and even dangerous risks. City Hospital No. 2, staffed by white doctors from the medical schools of Washington University and St. Louis University, relegated black doctors to associate positions. Dowden-White cites one particularly humiliating incident faced by a black doctor working at the black City Hospital No. 2 in the 1920s from a letter written to the dean of the St. Louis University Medical School. Such treatment must have been, if the statements of the Mound City Medical Society are any indication, all too common:

> I have been working under Dr. Elz in the Eye Department and up to this time he hasn't let me assist or do anything in the nature of operation. I spoke to him today about it and he said he is not going to be responsible for my work in the hospital. I am a graduate of Manhattan Eye, Ear, Nose and Throat Hospital and I have done every operation I have seen done at anytime in this department. Kindly give this matter your car[e]ful attention and inform me if this condition can not be adjusted.[31]

Much of the fight over Homer G. Phillips Hospital was about professional opportunity. The segregated hospital system, the APHA had found in a survey of St. Louis hospitals in 1927, afforded few opportunities for black doctors. Dr. Haven Emerson of New York decried the "meagre provision for professional advancement" provided to black doctors in St. Louis and the promises that have been made "that these would be corrected, only to be broken." Moreover, he continued, even those limited opportunities available to black doctors were in "institutions falling far short of the best facilities that can be provided for modern diagnostic and treatment procedures."[32] In a statement released to the Community Council's Race Relations Committee in March 1930, St. Louis black doctors called on the existing hospital and the new one—whatever its location—to allow "colored physicians [to] be appointed to serve on the visiting staff . . . . A Negro superintendent of Nurses . . . Negro laboratory technicians" and "Negro personnel in all administrative positions." The hospital, they noted, "offers the major opportunity for practice in general diagnosis and surgery to colored physicians."[33]

For black doctors, professional opportunity went hand-in-hand with the imperative of improving community health. The black doctors of the Mound City Medical Society emphasized this point in a statement to the Community Council's Race Relations Committee in 1930, declaring that "the development of skill and technique of colored physicians and nurses is of primary importance in improving the health of the colored population."[34] Philanthropic organizations involved in black public health like the Rosenwald Fund and the Rockefeller Foundation had recognized this fact by the 1930s. Training black doctors was a central part, for instance, of the Rosenwald Fund's program for improving Southern black health.[35] Outside observers of St. Louis health care recognized the connection as well. In a finding often touted by African American community leaders, the American Public Health Association counted just eighty black physicians in the city in 1927 and declared that as the "chief reliance of the colored sick of the community, the professional opportunities open to them for increasing their skill and keeping abreast of the developments in diagnosis and treatment" will "in a large measure determine the quality of the medical services for negroes."[36]

Nonetheless, most of the white doctors, philanthropists, and public health officials involved in the debate did not seem to recognize a connection between the professional goals of black doctors and the health of the black community at large. As Fannie Cook wrote in "Black Liberty," on the issue of the hospital, "white doctors who habitually sacrificed their personal advantage in order to extend courtesies to their colored confreres" were just as blind to the barriers put up against black doctors as "white doctors who thought all colored men should be porters."[37] Indeed, Cook herself showed just such a lack of understanding in 1930 when she declared in a letter to the rest of the Race Relations Committee that the black doctors' demands for professional opportunities "did not place sufficient emphasis upon the fact that this group of doctors was primarily interested in service to the patient, rather than in their own professional opportunities."[38]

Those who did see a link between public health and professional opportunity often paternalistically substituted their own judgment for that of their African American colleagues. Even Dr. Haven Emerson's survey, which called for more training opportunities for black doctors, carried a tone of condescending paternalism. Emerson reported that local white doctors felt that "there is not yet sufficient experience among the colored physicians as a group to handle such a large undertaking" as a separate hospital. "White persons who have given thought to the subject," he wrote authoritatively, believed that the new hospital should be "adjacent to city hospital number one and an integral part of that institution" both to save costs and to supervise black physicians. Ultimately, a hospital "conducted entirely by negro physicians would be a calamity for the colored sick and for

However, for its advocates, the hospital was more than merely a political football; it spoke to an evolving political critique of racial inequality among African American professionals, politicians, and social welfare activists and more than a few interested whites, which placed health at its center. Indeed, the hospital debate played a key role in the local forging of what political scientist Preston Smith, in his study of public housing in postwar Chicago, calls a "black civic ideology" of "racial democracy." Racial democracy, which framed racial inequality as largely a problem of white attitudes and the law, served as a powerful mobilizing force in bringing down barriers to full black participation in American life.[52]

To be sure, outsiders—and even a few locals—looked upon the sight of black St. Louisans rallying around a Jim Crow hospital with incredulity. The *Pittsburgh Courier*, a premier African American newspaper, warned that "separate but equal" would never be equal. The "probability of a white and black standard in necessary appropriations for the care of the city's sick" would hurt black health in the long run, making any "Jim Crow hospital" a "menace not only to the segregated negroes but the entire community."[53] A small minority of older black physicians in St. Louis agreed, and a few even spoke out against the hospital as a capitulation to segregation.[54]

The fight for the new black hospital was inseparable from the fight against segregation. The issue of job opportunities for black doctors had been inescapably about segregation. Fannie Cook had given voice to the problem well through the character of Mrs. Adams in "Black Liberty." Advocates for the hospital rarely missed an opportunity to speak out against the root cause of the problem. John Clark, for instance, bitterly attacked the confused and inconsistent logic of segregation when he went before the Board of Aldermen on the issue of the hospital, "Why not save money by moving [white] Central and [black] Sumner High Schools adjacent to [white] Soldan or [black] Vashon. . . . [have] one heating plant? One set of laboratories? . . . the principle is the same." Black St. Louisans, he stated forcefully, were less willing to rely on the "fair play" of whites than "ever before."[55]

More than simply a problem of legal inequality, the hospital issue cut to problems of economic and social inequality. The controversy coincided with some of the earliest local critiques of segregation from a public health standpoint, critiques that only grew louder throughout the 1930s. In 1928, Dr. Park J. White, a pediatrician and faculty member at the Washington University School of Medicine, published a damning report—and call to arms—on segregation. Drawing from his own findings on infant mortality in St. Louis and statistics on disease, mortality, and life expectancy from around the country, he argued against the notion of inherent racial predisposition to ill health. In his understanding, African Americans faced a health crisis because "community health is largely a matter of money and education." Segregation, for him, was the root cause because it was at heart "the denial of opportunity" for "material and cultural advancement." Clearly influenced by the debate over the new black hospital, White called for greater opportunities for black doctors and nurses, who must "make heroic sacrifices to get their professional training in the North and East." Moreover, he concluded that doctors must call for a "lifting of the restrictions" barring black Americans from opportunity as "the facts presented leave little doubt that those who would deny negroes the right to material and cultural advancement would, however unwittingly, deny them the right to life itself."[56]

Black physicians joined the critique. Throughout the Depression years, for instance, doctors were at the forefront of efforts to publicize the unhealthy living conditions created by segregation. "Most of the old buildings . . . in which negroes are forced to live because there is no other residential outlet available for them," the African American doctors of St. Louis's Mound City Medical Society declared in 1937, "are not fit for man or beast." They charged that the "poorly lighted and badly ventilated, damp, old, termite, bedbug and rat-eaten apartments and buildings where the great mass of St. Louis' negroes must live" led to the "tearing down of healthy bodies."[57]

This new health awareness reflected—and was often directly informed and framed by—a national discussion among social scientists on the nature and roots of racial inequality. Samuel K. Roberts notes a "growing body of social science, much of it authored by African American statisticians, economists, sociologists, and health experts connected to the local and national politics of the New Deal" cited doctors and scientists operating "within the new environmentalist" paradigm for understanding disease.[58] W. E. B. Dubois increasingly incorporated health into his wider attacks on racial inequality, writing in one article, "The susceptibility of Negroes to Tuberculosis . . . shows not any lack of 'racial' resistance, but the result of people who are poor and live in poor surroundings."[59] Urban League researcher Ira De A. Reid wrote a similar critique of St. Louis housing conditions in 1934, arguing that "[the fact that] Atlanta, Birmingham and Memphis with less adequate facilities and more stereotyped attitudes of racial adjustment should curb the high Negro mortality moreso than does St. Louis is a distinct reflection on the City's adjustment program and policies in the field of public health."[60]

Health played a key role as well in Chicago School models of urban sociology. In a 1932 report on black housing, embraced as a model for a series of reports on the "Industrial Status of Negroes in St. Louis," Charles Johnson approached the problem of poor conditions in black neighborhoods from the perspective of Chicago School sociology. Low wages, high rent, and racial segregation, he argued, have forced "negro population[s] . . . into the most deteriorated residence sections of the city" and precipitated a health crisis among urban African Americans. Unlike white ethnic groups, however, they could not reach the Chicago School's coveted goal of assimilation through adjustment as the "negro of the Fourth generation [since migration] is just as easily identified as 'a negro' by people who do not wish to live near negro[e]s as is a negro just from the canebrakes." They remain "trapped" within an "evil social environment."[61]

The solutions proposed hinged on community development and organization, not as a means of retreat or black separatism—as many would argue—but as a means of gaining equality, essentially defined as assimilation and parity with whites, through diligent, self-reliant political action. The Urban League, the central player in the fight over Homer G. Phillips Hospital, offers a good example. In line with Chicago School sociology, the Urban League believed that equality—and eventual assimilation—would be achieved through improvement of the "social organization" of the St. Louis black community, a process which required drawing black migrants into a strong, rooted community life and continual efforts to incorporate African Americans into the wider economic and social structure of the city. John Clark summed up this strategy well in his annual address to the League's board of directors in 1937, in which he stated that "the negro . . . is learning the value of collective thinking and organizing on industrial and civic matters, the value of intelligent political action, the importance of creating goodwill among a wide circle of white citizens."[62]

Institutions like Homer G. Phillips Hospital served as hallmarks of this philosophy of organization. As Joseph Heathcott writes, "Over the course of a half century, the black community was forced, by necessity, to develop an array of institutions, capacities, and networks of interdependence in order to compensate for the vast spatial, physical and emotional distortions of segregation." Within them, he argues, African Americans forged a "civic culture" centered on "democracy and resistance."[63]

The new hospital's proposed location in Elleardsville (the Ville") is an important indication of the meaning it held for St. Louis's African American community as well as the strategy African Americans had for advancement. The Ville is the historically African American neighborhood just northwest of downtown St. Louis and west of Grand Avenue—apart from the majority of the city's black population then in the Mill Creek Valley area—that became known for its well-to-do families and prominent institutions.

Its elite image emerged, in part, out of an interwar strategy for black advancement that prized the development of a strong civic culture as a counter to the inequalities imposed by segregation. The Ville became the nexus of that strategy. It had been one of the scattered areas across the city that housed black St. Louisans since the end of the nineteenth century. By the early twentieth century, it had attracted a small community of elite African Americans and it became home to Sumner High School. It truly made its transition into an African American neighborhood in the 1920s, when the St. Louis Real Estate Exchange conceded to a black demand for housing west of Grand Avenue by agreeing to expand property sales around the neighborhood's small existing black population. The neighborhood flipped from majority white to majority black in less than a decade: In 1920, African Americans comprised 8 percent of the neighborhood's population; by 1930 they made up 86 percent of a population that had dropped by over 50 percent, to 10,577.[64]

The black professional elite actively sought to make the Ville a center for the black middle class. Indeed, the Ville's "elite" image emerged, in part, out of an effort to create an alternative vision of black community life. The Urban League took particular interest in shoring up the middle class community in the Ville in the 1920s. Its late 1920s papers show that the organization was engaged in helping black homebuyers in blocks around the Ville, including around Vandeventer Ave. on its eastern edge and Cote Brilliante and Cora Street on its western edge. The League was eager to help "ambitious . . . Colored families" of a "very high type" on the expanding edges of the Ville who were often "ordered to vacate" because the "titles of most of their property have a clause restricting the former white owners from selling to colored owners."[65]

Black institutions relocated to the Ville along with the black elite. During the 1920s and 30s, the Ville grew to be an almost legendary center of institutional life. It became home to not just Sumner High in the early part of the twentieth century but three black elementary schools, a teacher's college, a beauty college run by black millionaire Annie Malone, a children's home, a black bank and home loan service, and important pillars of black religious and political life in St. Louis like Antioch Baptist Church. Homer G. Phillips Hospital promised to strengthen the economic and cultural life of the neighborhood by serving as an anchor for a growing professional class.[66]

Racial Politics and the Problem of Class

Yet the hospital's location in the elite Ville neighborhood, an elite community of black professionals, suggests the institution stood in a complicated relation to black civic ideology. If the Homer G. Phillips Hospital controversy spoke to a new political understanding of inequality, it was one founded, fundamentally, on an argument that largely obscured class differences among black St. Louisans. The interwar social welfare activists who struggled for Homer G. Phillips Hospital operated out of an ideological framework that viewed racial inequality as an issue of white attitudes rather than a larger problem built into the American political economy. Moreover, the institution-based politics of racial uplift which they endorsed to counter segregation also played the dual role of boosting the middle class identity of St. Louis's black professional elite, and largely neglecting the culture and economic struggles of the black working class.

In recent years, historians have re-evaluated the tenets of mid-twentieth-century racial liberalism and the social science basis on which it was founded. In particular, many have argued that its narrow focus on civil rights, white attitudes, and assimilation into white American society co-opted the formation of a broader, class-based black politics. Moreover, interwar social scientists' essential acceptance of the political economy of American capitalism—and preoccupation with the culture of the poor—prevented them from approaching the problem of race from a structural perspective. As Touré Reed writes in his study of the Urban League, Chicago School sociology proved to be a powerful tool against biological racism but in its emphasis on assimilation and social organization it "accepted the hegemony of industrial capitalism, leading it to focus on problems of social adjustment rather than political economy."[67]

More than just ignoring the problem of class in the black community, the new social science-based activism of the interwar era often exacerbated it. Indeed, Preston Smith argues of a similar push by black cultural elites for "racial democracy" in postwar Chicago, "as much as racial democracy constituted a racial politics, it also represented a class politics masked by the equation of racial progress with normative middle-class achievement." Interwar social science served much the same purpose. Touré Reed contends that the Urban League's essential acceptance of the social and economic order of industrial America and its emphasis on "mutually beneficial contact between the races" ultimately "required the organization to discipline black workers and separate the deserving from the undeserving poor."[68]

Nowhere is this dynamic clearer than in the self-conscious creation of a new black community life in the Ville. Fannie Cook provides a particularly revealing description of the neighborhood in the opening pages of her 1946 novel, *Mrs. Palmers Honey*. Cook described the Ville as a "model of Christian respectability," comparing it favorably to the conditions in which lower class African Americans lived. She wrote that "few white people ever thought of at all," believing that "St. Louis had but one colored district, the be-taverned crisscross of shabby streets near Union Station." Yet the Ville was a different kind of place, where houses "were low" with "suburban trees . . . and suburban fences around the small front lawns." The Ville, as she described it, served as a model for a kind of racial uplift centered on black institutions, a "Negro high school, a Negro grade school, a school for doubly handicapped children . . . a Negro teacher's college, a Negro city hospital." As such, it spoke both for and against the city's wider African American community. As Cook wrote in her account, to the people of the Ville, "the black folks near Union Station were 'immigrants' . . . their ways slowed the climb for other Negroes. Because of that [T]he Ville bore them a grudge."[69]

It is hardly a coincidence, then, that all of the addresses listed for members of the Colored Committee of the League of Women Voters in a membership roster from the late 1920s are in the Ville area. This includes chairwoman Carrie King Bowles (1873—1942), who lived at 4528 Kennerly Ave., in the heart of the Ville.[70] Much like Cook's image of the Ville itself, Bowles built her self-image around the principles of "respectability" and "uplift," long embraced by the black elite. Bowles wrote Cook frequently throughout the late 1930s as Cook prepared to write a profile of her for a national political magazine focused on social justice issues. Her letters reveal an activism shaped heavily by social science literature—Bowles sent Cook a reading list for a book club she had founded, boasting that W. E. B. Dubois himself had once visited her group—and her own identity as a woman raised by "forebears" of "the best stock" with "high intellectual and moral standards."[71] In keeping with the philosophy of middle class African American clubwomen dating to the late nineteenth century, Bowles celebrates the "Negro woman's . . . deep maternal feeling for all unfortunates," her service as the "back bone of Negro churches," and her "passionate love of home, family and race." All of which, she writes, have contributed to the advancement of the "Negro people" and their standard of living.[72]

Many residents of the Ville sought to not merely model middle class values to the black poor but, implicitly, to define themselves against them and claim the privileges they believed their class position accorded to them. The black elite were keenly aware of the fact that the conditions of the neighborhoods inhabited by African Americans—something fundamentally outside of their control—often served as a judgment on them. As Urban League researcher Ira De A. Reid wrote in a 1934 report on social conditions in black St. Louis, "the Negro section invariably and inevitably conjures up an impression of poor living conditions, usually the worst the city affords." Here, again, the assimilationist bent of interwar social science played into a distinct class politics. The Urban League's housing policy, for instance, was heavily geared toward creating spaces for the black middle class and facilitating their transition—key to the Chicago School's models of urban ecology—away from the slums. One Urban League researcher suggested in a report on black housing, "Emphasizing to white house owners and agents that there are different kinds of Negroes just as there are different kinds of whites, and that some of the Negroes are among the most desirable tenants obtainable." Another argued that "An attractive Negro block or neighborhood is the best argument possible in convincing a white owner or agent that all Negroes are not shiftless or irresponsible, an easy generalization into which lazy-minded individuals incline to fall."[73]

While the issue of the hospital itself did not appear to trigger a class-based political divide among St. Louis's African Americans, it did play into a broader politics of black advancement that catered heavily to the identity and political demands of the black middle class. In some sense, this is symbolized most clearly by the construction of the hospital itself. Ultimately, black social welfare activists won the battle to locate Homer G. Phillips Hospital in the Ville, but only thanks to a 1931 court decision, which declared that the original bond issue had required funding for an independent hospital. Ironically, however, the hospital—like many prominent St. Louis black institutions—was built by segregated, all-white unions; the city refused to hire skilled black labor for work on the hospital. In the end, the fight for Homer G. Phillips Hospital opened one door for the black professional class while slamming another shut for the black working class.[74]

Conclusion: A Broader View of Black Health, a Narrower Terrain for Black Politics

After nearly two decades of struggle, two bond issues, and additional WPA funds, Homer G. Phillips Hospital opened on February 22, 1937, at a final cost of $3,160,000. The opening ceremony was an elaborate day of parades, music, and speeches attended by Mayor Bernard Dickmann, Governor Lloyd C. Stark, Senator Bennett "Champ" Clark, and Interior Secretary Harold C. Ickes. It spoke to the meaning that black social welfare activists—and, to some extent, the black community as a whole—had vested in the site in the long struggle for the hospital. In the words of Ickes himself, "Its [the hospital's] real significance is that . . . it symbolizes the just demands and needs of our Negro citizens . . . to achieve your rightful place in our economic system." For over forty years, the modern hospital was the pride of the Ville, and was perhaps the most important black teaching hospital in the United States.[75]

More than simply a victory for black autonomy, the completion of Homer G. Phillips Hospital represented the culmination of a profound shift in black health-care politics during the 1930s. What began as a matter of expanding the number of hospital beds available to black St. Louisans became a battle over professional opportunity, political power, health, economic development, and, ultimately, racial inequality itself. By speaking so powerfully to the disempowered status of black St. Louisans, the "location debate" facilitated the development of a black critique of racial inequality, specifically the institution of segregation, from a political, economic, and social standpoint that would help lay the foundations for postwar, racial liberal ideology. Yet, both the narrow social science basis of that critique and the hospital's role in the class politics of the city's black professional elite served to limit its possibility and ultimate impact. Much like mid-century racial liberals, advocates of the hospital viewed inequality as fundamentally a problem of race rather than class. As a result, while they played a vital role in building a "civic ideology" that would ultimately succeed in bringing down legal segregation, advocates of the hospital failed to develop a broader politics with which to challenge the many other mechanisms through which racial inequality operates.

Endnotes

1. "Black Liberty," unpublished short story, Fannie Cook Papers, Missouri History Museum Archives, Box 24, Folder 4 (Bowles is referred to under the pseudonym "Mrs. Adams" in the story"; Fannie Cook, "Carrie King Bowles," *Common Ground*, September 1941: 58—62.

2. "Hospital Fight Is Waging," *Pittsburgh Courier*, July 2, 1927; Dowden-White, *Groping Toward Democracy*, 170; Qtd. in American Public Health Association, *A Study of the Health Activities of St. Louis, Missouri*. (St. Louis: Community Council of St. Louis, 1927), 78; Qtd. in "Hospital Fight is Waging," *Pittsburgh Courier*, July 2, 1927.

3. United States Department of the Interior, Heritage Conservation and Recreation Service, National Register of Historic Places nomination form: Homer G. Phillips Hospital, Missouri Historic Preservation Program, St. Louis, MO, June 1982. http://www.dnr.mo.gov/shpo/nps-nr/82004738.pdf

4. See Samuel K. Roberts, *Infectious Fear: Politics, Disease, and the Health Effects of Segregation* (Chapel Hill, N.C.: University of North Carolina Press, 2009).

5. Daryl Michael Scott, *Contempt and Pity: Social Policy and the Image of the Damaged Black Psyche* (Chapel Hill, N.C.: University of North Carolina Press, 1997), 19; Touré Reed, *Not Alms but Opportunity: The Urban League and the Politics of Racial Uplift, 1910—1950* (Chapel Hill, NC: University of North Carolina Press, 2008).

6. Reed, *Not Alms but Opportunity*, 20.

7. Michael Klarman, *From Jim Crow to Civil Rights: The Supreme Court and the Struggle for Racial Equality* (Oxford: Oxford University Press, 2004)

8. Edward Beardsley, *A History of Neglect: Health Care for Blacks and Mill Workers in the Twentieth-Century South* (Knoxville, TN: University of Tennessee Press, 1987).

9. Karen Kruse Thomas, *Deluxe Jim Crow: Civil Rights and American Health Policy*, 1935-1954 (Athens, GA: UGA Press, 2011); see also Vanessa N. Gamble, *Making a Place for Ourselves: The Black Hospital Movement, 1920-1945* (Oxford, UK: Oxford University Press, 1995) and David McBride, *Integrating the City of Medicine: Blacks in Philadelphia Healthcare, 1910-1960* (Philadelphia, PA: Temple University Press, 1989).

10. St. Louis NAACP, "To the general membership of the St. Louis NAACP for the year ending December 31, 1956," Annual Report for 1956 in Olin Library, Washington University St. Louis.

11. American Public Health Association, *A Study of the Health Activities of St. Louis, Missouri* (St. Louis: Community Council of St. Louis, 1927), 26—30.

12. Samuel K. Roberts, *Infectious Fear: Politics, Disease, and the Health Effects of Segregation* (Chapel Hill, N.C.: University of North Carolina Press, 2009); Natalia Molina, *Fit to be Citizens? Public Health and Race in Los Angeles, 1879—1939* (Berkeley, CA: University of California Press, 2006); Nayan Shah, *Contagious Divides: Epidemics and Race in San Francisco's Chinatown* (Berkeley, CA: University of California Press, 2001); Tera Hunter, *To 'Joy My Freedom: Southern Black Women's Lives and Labors after the Civil War* (Cambridge, MA: Harvard University Press, 1997).

13. Quoted in David Rosner, "The EXODUS of Public Health: What History Can Tell Us About the Future," *American Journal of Public Health* 100, no. 1 (2010): 54-63; Negro Health Auxiliary of the Tuberculosis and Health Society of St. Louis, "Health Service Review: 1929," Series 1, Box 7, Urban League of St. Louis Records, Washington University Archives; St. Louis Department of Public Welfare, Division of Health, *Annual Report of the Health Commissioner for the Year 1923*, by Max C. Starkloff, M.D. (St. Louis, MO: Department of Public Welfare, 1923), 16; "St. Louis Over," *The Baltimore Afro-American*, November 9, 1923.

14. Joseph Heathcott, "Black Archipelago: Politics and Civic Life in the Jim Crow City," *Journal of Social History* 38, No. 3 (spring 2005) and Priscilla Dowden-White, *Groping toward Democracy*.

15. Negro Health Auxiliary of the Tuberculosis and Health Society of St. Louis, "Health Service Review: 1929," Urban League of St. Louis Records, Series 1, Box 7.

16. http://www.dnr.mo.gov/shpo/nps-nr/82004738.pdf

17. Mark Tranel, *St. Louis Plans: The Ideal and the Real St. Louis* (St. Louis: Missouri Historical Society Press, 2007), 90.

18. Quoted. in "Homer G. Phillips: A St. Louis Martyr? Lifetime Fight for Civil Rights Ended in Shooting Death on City Streets," *St. Louis Post-Dispatch*, February 27, 1994; Edward T. Clayton, "The Strange Murder of Homer G. Phillips," *Ebony*, September 1977, 160.

19. "Medics Face Scathing Criticism of Lax Conditions in St. Louis Hospital," *Pittsburgh Courier*, January 28, 1928.

20. "St. Louis Voters Are Asked to Support New Negro Hospital," St. Louis League of Women Voters Papers, Box 54, Folder 715.

21. Quoted in Dowden-White, *Groping Toward Democracy*, 166.

22. "Medics Face Scathing Criticism of Lax Conditions in St. Louis Hospital," *Pittsburgh Courier*, January 28, 1928.

23. "21 Outstanding Facts You Ought to Know Regarding City Hospital Number 2," Urban League of St. Louis Records, Series 1, Box 5.

24. Dowden-White, *Groping Toward Democracy*, 170.

25. "Hospital Fight Is Waging," *Pittsburgh Courier*, July 2, 1927.

26. "The Location of the New Negro Hospital," February 8, 1928, St. Louis League of Women Voters Papers, Box 54, Folder 715.

27. "Hospital Fight Is Waging," *Pittsburgh Courier*, July 2, 1927.

28. John T. Clark to Fannie Cook, Box 4, Folder 2, Fannie Cook Papers, Missouri Historical Society Library and Archives.

29. Whenever the St. Louis Medical Society is mentioned in the Fannie Cook papers.

30. *Deluxe Jim Crow: Civil Rights and American Health Policy*, 208, 214.

31. Quoted in Dowden-White, *Groping Toward Democracy*, 164–165.

32. American Public Health Association, 77

33. "Needs for Hospital No. 2 in the Interest of Efficient Service: Submitted by Committee of Negro Physicians," Fannie Cook Papers, Box 4, Folder 7.

34. "Needs for Hospital Number 2 in the Interest of Efficient Service: Submitted by Committee of Negro Physicians," Fannie Cook Papers, Box 4, Folder 7.

35. McBride, *Integrating the City of Medicine*, 75.

36. Survey of St. Louis Public Health Activities, 1927, 78, St. Louis Public Library.

37. "Black Liberty," Fannie Cook Papers, Box 24, Folder 4.

38. Fannie Cook to Race Relations Committee, May 23, 1930, Fannie Cook Papers, Box 4, Folder 2.

39. APHA Survey of St. Louis Public Health, 78, St. Louis Public Library.

40. "Hospital Fight is Waging," *Pittsburgh Courier*, July 2, 1927.

41. Fannie Cook to unspecified recipients, May 21, 1930, Fannie Cook Papers, Box 4, Folder 2.

42. John Clark to Fannie Cook, May 29, 1930, Fannie Cook Papers, Box 4, Folder 2.

43. Bertha Howell to Fannie Cook, June 23, 1930, Fannie Cook Papers, Box 4, Folder 2.

44. Fannie Cook to Dr. Tinsley, no date, Fannie Cook Papers, Box 4, Folder 2.

45. "Why the Change of Heart—Mayor Miller?," *St. Louis Argus*, December 14, 1927.

46. Colored Committee of the St. Louis League of Women Voters to the Executive Committee of the St. Louis League of Women Voters, February 20, 1928, St. Louis League of Women Voters Papers, Box 54, Folder 715.

47. Quoted in Dowden-White, *Groping Toward Democracy*, 170.

48. John Clark to ministers, November 23, 1928, Urban League of St. Louis Records, Series 1, Box 7, "Tuberculosis and Health Society 1926–1942," Washington University Archives.

49. Joseph Heathcott, "Black Archipelago: Politics and Civic Life in the Jim Crow City," *Journal of Social History* 38, No. 3 (spring 2005); Clark to ministers, November 23, 1928, Urban League Urban League of St. Louis Records, Series 1, Box 7, "Tuberculosis and Health Society 1926–1942," Washington University Archives.

50. "Petition and Recommendation from the Federation of Block Units," undated, Series 8, Box 4, "Federation of Block Units—Petitions," Urban League of St. Louis Records.

51. "Another Miller Blunder" and "Remember the Hospital," *St. Louis Argus*, December 7, 1927; see *St. Louis Argus*, November 2, 1928, for a good example.

52. Preston Smith, *Racial Democracy and the Black Metropolis: Housing Policy in Postwar Chicago* (Minneapolis, MN: University of Minnesota Press, 2012).

53. "One Fruit of Segregation," *Pittsburgh Courier*, February 4, 1928.

54. Dowden-White, *Groping Toward Democracy*, 173.

55. Quoted in Dowden-White, *Groping Toward Democracy*, 171.

56. Park J. White, M.D., "Segregation and the Health of Negroes," *Hospital Social Service Association of New York City* 17 (1928): 224–228.

57. "Better Housing Fight Continues Strong," *Kansas City Call*, April 28, 1937.

58. Roberts, *Infectious Fear*, 65.

59. W. E. B. Dubois, "The Health of Black Folk." *The Crisis* (February 1933).

60. Ira De A. Reid, "A Study of the Industrial Status of Negroes in St. Louis, 1934," 8, Health and Welfare Council of Metropolitan St. Louis, the State Historical Society of Missouri, Series 3, Box 10, Folder 274 ("Social Conditions, 1934–1935").

61. Charles S. Johnson, *Negro Housing: Report of the Committee on Negro Housing* (Washington, D.C.: National Capital Press, Inc, 1932), 2. http://archive.org/stream/negrohousingrepo00presrich/negrohousingrepo00presrich_djvu.txt

62. "Verbal Report—1937," Series 1, Box 3, Urban League of St. Louis Records, University Archives, Department of Special Collections, Washington University Libraries (St. Louis, Mo.).

63. Joseph Heathcott, "Black Archipelago: Politics and Civic Life in the Jim Crow City," *Journal of Social History* 38, No. 3 (spring 2005)

64. Dowden-White, *Groping Toward Democracy*, 34-35.

65. "Housing- Cote Brilliante Ave., June 16, 1927," Urban League of St. Louis Records

66. Dowden-White, *Groping Toward Democracy*, 37.

67. Touré Reed, *Not Alms but Opportunity: The Urban League and the Politics of Racial Uplift, 1910–1950* (Chapel Hill, N.C.: University of North Carolina Press, 2008), 192–193. See also Nikhil Pal Singh, *Black Is a Country: Race and the Unfinished Struggle for Democracy* (Cambridge, MA: Harvard University Press, 2005); Alice O'Connor, *Poverty Knowledge: Social Science, Social Policy and the Poor in Twentieth-Century US History* (Princeton: Princeton University Press, 2002); Daryl Michael Scott, *Contempt and Pity: Social Policy and the Image of the Damaged Black Psyche* (Chapel Hill, N.C.: University of North Carolina Press, 1997).

68. Reed, *Not Alms but Opportunity*, 7.

69. Fannie Cook, *Mrs. Palmer's Honey* (New York: Doubleday and Company Inc, 1946), 1–2.

70. Membership Roster, no date (probably late 1920s), St. Louis League of Women Voters Papers, State Historical Society of Missouri Library at UMSL, Box 54, Folder 715.

71. Carrie Bowles to Fannie Cook, February 24, 1941, Box 18, Folder 6, Fannie Cook Papers.

72. Carrie Bowles, "The Negro Woman's Contribution to American Life," Box 18, Folder 6, Fannie Cook Papers.

73. Ira De A. Reid, "A Study of the Industrial Status of Negroes in St. Louis, 1934," 8, Health and Welfare Council of Metropolitan St. Louis, the State Historical Society of Missouri, Series 3, Box 10, Folder 274 ("Social Conditions, 1934–1935").

74. Dowden-White, *Groping Toward Democracy*, 174- 176.

75. Quoted in United States Department of the Interior, Heritage Conservation and Recreation Service, National Register of Historic Places nomination form: Homer G. Phillips Hospital, Missouri Historic Preservation Program, St. Louis, Mo., June 1982. http://www.dnr.mo.gov/shpo/nps-nr/82004738.pdf

ST. LOUIS
CURRENTS

About the Author

Taylor Desloge is a third-year graduate student in history and American studies at Washington University in St. Louis and a 2011 graduate of Princeton University with a degree in history and urban studies. He studies late nineteenth and early twentieth-century American urban history, with a focus on Progressive and New Deal era city planning ideology and urban reform movements. Through Taylor's past work on the early historic preservation movement, he has also developed a strong interest in architectural history. His developing dissertation, on public health work in St. Louis during the interwar era, explores the interrelationships between public health ideology, racial attitudes, and philanthropic and government health programs in African American neighborhoods. His project will seek to understand public health work's role in shaping and maintaining racial segregation and the reasons behind its failure to improve housing conditions in black neighborhoods.

Race and Entertainment

For decades, the East Side of the region has been home to clubs and adult entertainment. The East Side was the place where closing times were rarely enforced and the party would go on into the wee hours.

The entire St. Louis region partook of the hopping nightlife in East St. Louis and throughout St. Clair and Madison Counties. However, over the years those establishments closed, moved on, or, in a few cases, carried on under new names or management. Some of the greatest names in music played these clubs.

Anthony Cheeseboro has documented the African American experience in the entertainment venues of the East Side. The artistry and creativity of the night scene helped shape deep social bonds in the greater East St. Louis area and enriched the region's cultural history.

Leisure and Entertainment in Greater East St. Louis, 1950–1995

Anthony Cheeseboro, Ph.D.

Although communities are often defined by their economic base, the natures of leisure and entertainment options in a community tell an observer a great deal about a place. They also have a huge effect on how residents perceive their community. Anybody who has been recruited for a job or a school knows that entertainment and leisure opportunities are always mentioned, often very prominently, by recruiters. Leisure and entertainment are mentioned so much because they are excellent barometers of the quality of life in a given area. A community with a clean cineplex, beautiful parks, and an outdoor theater gives an entirely different impression than a town with three bars and a massage parlor.

In this project, I am looking at how the nature of leisure and recreational activity changed in the area of greater East St. Louis between 1950 and 1995. I define "greater East St. Louis" as East St. Louis, Brooklyn (Lovejoy,) Centreville, Washington Park, Venice, and Madison, Illinois. With the exception of Madison, all of these towns are majority African American, and all except Madison and Venice are in St. Clair County. All except Washington Park have old black communities that were established in the nineteenth or early twentieth centuries. As of 2012, all of these communities are quite poor and generally lack a significant number of jobs and commercial infrastructure. It is important to note that this area had initially attracted large numbers of African Americans because it offered significant employment opportunities in a number of industries. As the economic dynamics of the region have shifted, resulting in major deindustrialization, whites and the majority of upwardly mobile have moved away to other cities. The African American poor have been left behind.

At the beginning of the period, African Americans were drawn to the greater East St. Louis area by the large number of jobs that were available. East St. Louis was first and foremost a railroad center where numerous lines converged along north-south and east-west routes. Directly related to the importance of the railways was the development of stockyards and meat processing in East St. Louis (National City). In addition to these two major sources of employment, there were steel mills in Granite City that provided jobs for African Americans, and there was the Alcoa aluminum mill, which had begun to integrate its workforce during the World War I era. Compared to other northern cities, it would appear that greater East St. Louis offered a lower percentage of high-wage jobs than many other industrial regions of the Midwest during this period. The result was that East St. Louis was always a city with a large poor urban African American population.

Despite the high levels of poverty, this area did have a large, employed working class. The availability of regular employment is the primary difference between the world of the Black urban environment of 1950–1970 and contemporary deindustrialized inner cities. This working class is important because it was able to support a varied entertainment infrastructure. Most of the musicians who worked in clubs had day jobs in various industries or in education. The school system of the East St. Louis area, like that of all of Illinois south of Springfield, was segregated. This actually provided additional opportunities for advancement and upward mobility for African Americans. Unlike those blacks who emigrated to northern cities that had integrated schools, college-educated blacks in the greater East St. Louis area were able to work in areas for which they were trained and their children could reasonably aspire to the sorts of professional jobs that were typically open to people of their race at that time in southern communities.

East St. Louis, from its very origins, supported a spirited nightlife that offered both legitimate and illegal forms of pleasure. It appears that black nightlife in East St. Louis picked up in the period after World War I, while Brooklyn established itself as an entertainment destination in the late nineteenth century. Due to its location by the Mississippi River, the St. Louis region naturally drew on the blues and jazz, both traditions that developed in the Mid-South along the Mississippi River. In the nineteenth century, St. Louis attracted a number of musicians who supported themselves in establishments on the Missouri side of the river. Both Scott Joplin and W.C. Handy spent time in St. Louis.[1] This is very important in terms of the history of African American music because W.C. Handy was instrumental in the creation of the blues as a distinct musical form that would influence all black music that has come since its creation.[2] Joplin was a key figure in the development of ragtime, the form of African American music that would reach the greatest popular audience before the evolution of jazz. Joplin would eventually make St. Louis his home, and Handy found inspiration to write the *St. Louis Blues* while he was in the area.[3] At this early time, East St. Louis had a very small African American population, but the musical tradition on the Missouri side would go on to influence the music that was produced in greater East St. Louis.

The African American presence in the greater East St. Louis area has its origins with the initial western settlement of the area. As Sundiata Cha-Jua and others have documented African Americans began to settle in what is now Brooklyn by the 1830s.[4] Similarly, African Americans accompanied Edward Coles when he first began his occupation of Madison County in the 1810s.[5] By the 1870s, East St. Louis had an African American population of 300.[6] By 1890, the population had grown modestly to 350 out of an overall population of 15,169.[7] The African American population of East St. Louis consisted overwhelmingly of unskilled laborers in the nineteenth and early twentieth centuries.[8] The majority of women were listed as laundresses and domestics.[9] The men had a variety of jobs: hod carriers, teamsters, hostlers, cotton compress operators, and various railroad related jobs.[10] Interestingly, even as early as 1889, several men were listed as having skilled jobs, at least two were firemen, two were carpenters, three were bricklayers, and one was a butcher.[11] There were also a number of ministers in the African American community too. The oldest church in the African American community was the church that would eventually come to be known as Macedonia Baptist Church, which was founded in 1871.[12] Of course there were much older churches in Brooklyn and other communities, but Macedonia was the oldest to actually be in East St. Louis itself. It is important to note that the first school for black children in East St. Louis was located in Macedonia Baptist Church.[13]

Given the current reality of East St. Louis, what is really striking about the directories from the early twentieth century is the diversity of jobs held by black East St. Louisans from the World War II era onward. After the foundation of working class people was established, a community of professionals like lawyers, physicians, dentists, and others were able to provide services to the African American population. By 1918, Officer Funeral Home (operated by the family that would eventually spawn Carl Officer, one of East St. Louis's most colorful mayors) had been founded.[14] Funeral homes are of particular importance to African Americans because these businesses tend to be very resistant to integration, and they supply a great deal of capital to their owners. Another famous professional who established himself in East St. Louis was Dr. Miles Dewey Davis, the father of jazz trumpeter Miles Davis. By the late 1920s his office in East St. Louis was open and it would continue to function until the early 1960s.[15] By 1930, East St. Louis had an African American population of six thousand out of a total population of eighty thousand.[16] At that time, African Americans mainly lived around Bond Avenue. This fairly compact distribution of African Americans made it easy for a diverse selection of businesses, that catered to African Americans to establish themselves. By 1930, the African American community could count among its businesses two cinemas, the Broadway and Lincoln, twenty-six restaurants, three coal delivery services, three cleaners, a real estate agency, and six physicians.[17] In addition to these businesses there were ten pool halls and an indeterminate number of nightclubs.[18] The essential point to be made here is that despite the devastating effects of the Great Depression, the economic foundation of black East St. Louis was completely different from what now exists in what has been an all African American city for the last forty years. The 1930s was a period of intense industrial activity and there was a large demand for labor that in turn allowed professional services and businesses to develop that could serve the working class. Of course, the key factor in the growth of the service-oriented businesses in the black community was the hard reality of segregation. Black people had to be entertained, fed, or buried by their own since there was no access to the larger white world.

Although the African American working class was crucial to the development of black business, perhaps the single largest section of the African American professional/middle class that depended directly on them was educators. As mentioned earlier, schools for the African American community began in Macedonia Baptist Church in 1871; however, it was not long before the number of students was too large to be accommodated in a single church building. The school was then moved to a blacksmith shop on Collinsville Avenue, a building that was still too small to accommodate the student body.[19] According to the testimony of Miss Lucy Mae Turner, a teacher who started working in East St. Louis in 1911, the black community was able to secure a proper school through rather creative means. Miss Turner stated that under the leadership of a Captain John Robinson (a Civil War veteran), Morton Hawkins, and a Mr. Beasley, the children of the black school marched to the Clay School on Collinsville, Avenue, where the black children came in and sat down beside the white children, apparently catching the administration of the Clay School completely off guard. The outcome of this protest was that the city quickly agreed to build a school for African American children, and that school, built in 1886, became known as Lincoln.

By the 1940s the black school system was well established and it supported dozens of African American teachers and administrators. By 1938, there were just under one hundred African American teachers, and at least seven principals, in the East St. Louis school system.[20] There was an additional body of teachers in Brooklyn and several surrounding cities like Venice. Teaching was very important to the African American community on multiple levels. It was a viable occupation that could be had with a college degree. It was steady, state-supported work. Teaching provided economic independence and social respectability for African American women. It also meant that a significant number of educated and employed role models were in regular contact with the youth of the black community. Because of segregation in housing, African American teachers lived in the same neighborhoods as their students, and they were well known to the general community. In terms of leisure and entertainment, teaching was important because it provided an example of respectable middle class employment for musicians in the case of music teachers, and the work schedule of teachers, which included fairly long holidays and no summers, was ideal for educators who sought additional money as gigging musicians.[21]

Since area musicians tended to be well educated, they were able to work a wide variety of styles and gigs.[22] As music styles changed, local players were able to move from swing to bebop to R&B with ease, although it would appear that most local musicians were jazz artists at heart.[23] Although musicians easily crossed genres, it appears that the clubs themselves tended to favor one style of music or another. The Blue Note, for instance, was clearly a jazz club, blues musician David Dee said that there was a network of clubs in East St. Louis that featured blues artists.[24] That said, East St. Louisans enjoyed all of the music and visited the variety of clubs that were available.

As was said earlier, 1950–1960 was the height of economic development in the East St. Louis area. The railroads and stockyards were at their height, and would soon begin to decline.

With the exception of Chuck Berry, major figures in East Side R&B were not natives of the area. A much higher percentage of jazz musicians were born in the area. R&B artists who came to the St. Louis area included Ike Turner, Tina Turner, Albert King, Luther Ingram, and Johnnie Johnson; those born in St. Louis included Fontella Bass, Chuck Berry, Leo Gooden (Centreville Blue Note Club, L.G. Records, Leo Gooden Five, and Leo Gooden with Strings).

Clubs in East St. Louis were above all small businesses. The Manhattan Club was a very famous club in East St. Louis that was well known for featuring legendary musicians. On July 4, 1955, the owner was listed as Richard Allen, a resident of Gaty Avenue who was born in Butler, Alabama.[25] Shortly afterward, the owner was listed as Brooker Merritt along with his wife.[26] They owned the club throughout the 1970s. Looking at newspaper clippings, the thing that is most striking about the Manhattan Club is how much it was targeted by local criminals. A short search of local archives showed that the club had been reported robbed or burglarized seven times between 1955–1975.[27] Without any evidence to prove it, I suspect that it was subjected to theft many times without being formally reported to the police. It is also notable that crime occurred frequently in and around the club. A quick search of Manhattan Club citations in local papers between 1955–1962 shows ten victims of assault with deadly weapons including guns, knives, and brass knuckles.[28] In addition to theft, the Merritts also suffered from tax problems. In 1960, the IRS placed a lien on the club for back taxes in the amount of $4,453.[29] The bottom line was that the Manhattan was a small business that catered to a poor and working class clientele. This reality meant that the club was often treated as a nuisance by the local authorities.

In August 1961, the club was shut down by the police over reports of illegal gambling and the beating and assault of a participant in a game.[30] It is striking that this black club suffered from basically the same problems that have been reported in East St. Louis clubs in the media during 2012. This is an indication that the clubs are not a symptom of decline, but merely reflect ongoing strife and friction among the poor. Although it seems clear that owners like the Merritts allowed illegal gambling to take place in their establishments, it seems that the criminal activity that went on in these clubs was not enough to drag down the city. Instead of attacking clubs, the city fathers could have made a legitimate argument that it was in the interest of the community to aid club owners in creating a safe environment for their patrons and wider communities, the same way the city would aid other small business owners.

Similar to the issues of gambling in the Manhattan Club, Garrett's Lounge in Brooklyn was also a site of illegal gambling. The Garrett family, who have run clubs in Brooklyn, Venice, and Madison for several generations, are a very interesting example of how clubs can fit into a community. In 2012, the Garrett family ran Garrett's Tavern in Madison, Illinois, and the Pink Slip, a strip club, in Brooklyn. At one point, the Garretts actually had a national profile because of a book by Elin Schoen, *Tales of an All Night Town* (1979), which told the story of a shootout between the police chief of Brooklyn and an auxiliary officer in the early 1970s.[31] The shootout and much of the action that led up to it took place in Garrett's Lounge, which is now the Pink Slip.[32] Looking at articles from the *Metro Journal* newspapers, it is clear that Garrett family establishments had significant issues with gambling. In 1965, *Metro Journal* assistant city editor, Charles O. Stewart, investigated the Garrett family because reports of gambling activity in their clubs came to the attention of the Illinois Crime Commission.[33] The year before, Madison "Slugger" Garrett II was arrested at the Venice Garrett's Tavern for running an illegal dice game.[34] Stewart would become the victim of a stabbing outside the Blue Haven nightclub in Brooklyn in December 1965.[35] As a result of the 1964–65 investigation, the mayor of Madison, Stephen Maeras, suspended the operation of Garrett & Sons as well as Young Lounge.[36] In addition, the license of Garrett's Brooklyn Club, the Blue Haven, was placed under review by the Illinois Liquor Commission.[37] Early in 1966, clubs run by the Garretts in Madison and Brooklyn, as well as other clubs such as the Harlem Club and Paramount Club of East St. Louis were also closed for gambling.[38] Despite the serious attention that the club came under in 1965, the gambling culture apparently continued because ten years later the club was raided and people were arrested for gambling once again.[39]

During the 1960s, another notable club owner was Leo Gooden, the proprietor of the Blue Note in Alorton along with Otis Blue. While live music was a staple of clubs until the 1980s and a number of artists with national profiles regularly worked in greater East St. Louis clubs, the Blue Note, along with Brooklyn's Harlem Club, arguably had the best reputation for music and was known as a classy entertainment venue. Although shootings and other violent incidents occurred in the vicinity of the club, the owner was noteworthy for his efforts at establishing a record company and his role in local Democratic Party politics.

Leo Gooden was a St. Clair County sheriff's deputy in the 1950s and he was also a member of the Paramount Democratic Club in the East St. Louis Southend.[40] In 1959, he organized a run for city commissioner with a slate of African American candidates who sought to improve conditions in the traditionally black neighborhoods of East St. Louis.[41] He was not successful in his bid for office, and he eventually lost his appointment as a deputy supposedly because he refused to accept a transfer to Belleville.[42] At the same time Gooden was involved in politics and law enforcement, he was also involved in some "hustles" that clearly existed on the margins of legality. In 1957, he apparently received money from a fortune teller who was also running a gambling operation during a carnival.[43] By the end of the 1950s, Leo Gooden and Otis Blue were listed as the owners of the Blue Note in newspapers and telephone directories. By 1962, both Gooden and Blue were having tax lien issues not unlike those of the Merritts described earlier.[44] By 1964, Gooden had launched L-G records, which was a very impressive operation and was quite well executed.[45] Although the music recorded by L-G seemed to lean more toward jazz than the soul sounds that came to dominate the 1960s, the music being produced was good enough that L-G possibly could have survived as a specialty label for a long time had he not died in 1967. At least three recordings from L-G records are still in print and can be ordered online.[46]

The mixture of styles in Gooden's music is a great example of the kind of genre mixing that is at the heart of the musical culture of East St. Louis, a place where the greatest of musicians like Miles Davis and Hamiet Blueitt have deep roots in the pop music of their day. Once again, even among musicians who possessed world-class talent, there was little sense of disdain for playing popular music. Certainly, part of this attitude stemmed from the craftsman's attitude of simply doing the work that was available, but it is also clear that the majority of musicians who worked in the area appreciated the blues and R&B, as well as jazz. The degree to which differences in appreciation and levels of respect were accorded to different music tends to be reflected in the music that East

St. Louis jazz musicians produced. No matter how abstract or avant garde, the music always maintained a base in the blues and popular culture of the region.

As mentioned earlier, gambling was an integral part of club life in East St. Louis. According to former police officer and alderman Percy McKinney, the underground gambling action in the clubs was very fast and usually in much larger amounts than the gambling that was legally established in the St. Louis area during the 1990s.[47] He said it was not usual for gamblers to win and lose upwards of $10,000 within minutes. Gambling was a powerful draw for men, both workers and those who sustained themselves through the informal economy. Although it has not been discussed in this paper, an important aspect of the informal economy was the sex trade. In the wake of deindustrialization, the legal form of sex trade, "exotic dancing" (or stripping), would come to be an economic mainstay in some of the towns on the periphery of East St. Louis.[48]

During spring 2011, I interviewed Madison Garrett III, the current proprietor of the Pink Slip, the former Garrett's Lounge in Brooklyn.[49] He told me that the club was converted to a strip club in 1991 because it was no longer making money as a club that featured music.[50] Currently, the Pink Slip is exceptional in that it is the only black-owned strip club of any significance in Brooklyn. The others are corporate clubs that are parts of networks that offer erotic entertainment nationwide.

Strip clubs seem to have undergone an interesting evolution since they became common in the 1990s. Initially, they attracted a large number of local women, many of whom got involved in drugs, according to an interview I had with the police chiefs of both Brooklyn and Washington Park.[51] Currently, the clubs tend to bring in out-of-town dancers who work the weekends and go back to any number of cities within a few hours of Brooklyn, like Memphis or Kansas City. At the time, I was told that this work was quite lucrative with young women making up to $9,000 on a profitable weekend. Not unlike the dancers themselves, the customers who patronize these clubs tend to be from outside the local community. What is noticeable to anyone who looks at the license plates of the cars in strip club parking lots is that a very large number of them are from Missouri.[52] Once again, the Metro East serves as the place where St. Louis situates its entertainment of questionable morality. With the exception of Sauget, all of the cities that feature strip clubs are the predominately black communities that ring East St. Louis.

The transformation to strip clubs was similar in most of the cities that ring East St. Louis except for the story of Washington Park. Washington Park had virtually no black community in the decade after World War II. The 1950 census showed a black population of two men and no women. The city was solidly white until it suddenly became majority black in the 1980 census. According to federal magistrate Donald Wilkerson, the catalyst behind the transformation of Washington Park was the establishment of a housing project in the city limits during the 1970s.[53] Washington Park, which had always been a modest, working class community, quickly changed into a poor, majority African American village. In the process of this change, city officials from the "old regime," including a former police chief, became involved in the strip club business. Once again, national corporations, including Larry Flynt's Hustler corporation, would eventually come to dominate erotic entertainment. Washington Park has been noteworthy in its open acquiescence to the strip club culture. Many people in the region still make light of the fact that the mayor of Washington Park gave Larry Flynt the key to the city because he bought busses for the village's school children.[54]

Brooklyn mayor Marcellus West was credited with beginning the process of adult entertainment in the city in 1987.[55] As mentioned earlier, the majority of clubs in Brooklyn are part of national corporate chains, but one club is locally run by African American entrepreneurs. That club is the Pink Slip, which is run by the Garrett family. According to Madison Garrett III, the Brooklyn branch of Garrett's Lounge was converted to a strip club in 1991 because of declining profits. In all likelihood, the old Garrett's Lounge floundered because Brooklyn's population shrank dramatically after 1970. This was probably directly connected to the decline of the packing industry in adjacent National City. As the black working class died, the need for a neighborhood bar disappeared also. The great advantage of erotic entertainment was that it could attract patrons from outside the village of Brooklyn since this sort of leisure activity was not available in an appealing form in Missouri, and was limited mainly to struggling Metro East towns like Brooklyn that had no great advantage over one another. As mentioned earlier, when clubs were initially brought to their communities, a large number of dancers came from the local community. This was especially true for an establishment run by a local businessman named Everette Baker, who ran the Fantasyland complex of clubs in Brooklyn.[56] Baker concurrently ran legal sexually oriented businesses like strip clubs and adult book-stores, while his massage parlors were fronts for prostitution.[57] Baker was never a target of local law enforcement, but he was eventually convicted of using credit cards and ATMs to accept payment for prostitution since those acts violated federal money laundering and conspiracy statues.[58] He was convicted in 1998, and received a fifteen year sentence in prison. He was also forced to forfeit $7.5 million dollars of proceeds from his activities.[59] While Baker was running his business, he employed a large number of local women, including two daughters of the chief of police.[60] In addition to hir-ing local women, among others, he also provided "massages" (sex) to city of Brooklyn employees as Christmas bonuses.[61] The Everette Baker story is interesting in that although he clearly operated a criminal enterprise that exploited women, among some people there is also a sense that his financial success made him the focus of prosecutors that a less successful purveyor would not have been. In fact, I personally remember being told by an older white man who claimed to know Baker that he told him to stop depositing so much money in a Granite City bank. In his words, a black man putting that much money in a bank will get the attention of federal authorities in a way that a white businessman doing such a thing would not.

The phenomenon of strip clubs is worth mentioning although the participants are often not local women. Although local women are less active in greater East St. Louis clubs than when the clubs first opened, many women still continue to work as exotic dancers. As mentioned earlier, exotic dancing is legal and lucrative to a degree that simply cannot be matched by most jobs available to young workers of either gender. This is doubly true for women with low levels of formal educa-tion. Within the African American community, the popularity of hip hop and the glorification of strip club culture, especially in southern crunk rap, has made stripping and the sexualization of the body a casual matter among young black women. Simply put, there is very little stigma attached to exotic dancing from the mid-1990s onward. The acceptability of stripping combined with the disap-pearance of living wage jobs for working class black men has made strip club work a rational choice. This was especially true in Brooklyn, a neighbor of National City, which had been the site of the nation's largest hog processing facility in 1959. Between 1959 and 1986, all of the meat processing facilities in National City had closed and the railroad facilities that transported the meat had cor-respondingly been downsized.[62] It should be no wonder that by 1987, Brooklyn leaders had reached out to adult entertainment to maintain some sort of economy for their village.

In spring 2012, a public argument broke out between the whip of the United States Senate, Dick Durbin, a native of East St. Louis, and Alvin Parks, then mayor of East St. Louis.[63] In the sev-eral months prior to the disagreement, there had been a number of shootings in and around clubs in East St. Louis, as well as a number of shootings in other parts of the city that apparently were related to disputes that originated in East St. Louis clubs. Senator Durbin, while promising more money for public housing in East St. Louis, also called for the nightclubs to be closed at an earlier time. East St. Louis clubs are of course famous or notorious for being open all night long with liquor being served until 6:00 a.m. In response to Senator Durbin's demands, Mayor Parks has noted that the clubs are a significant source of tax dollars in a town that is noteworthy for its paucity of taxable businesses. At times Parks has shut down clubs earlier, but these measures have always been temporary because the city needs the money. It is also important to note that the clubs are owned by local African American business people, and that they are a source of employment for about four hundred in a city of maybe twenty thousand that suffers chronic high unemployment, especially among black males.

The question of the clubs has drawn opinions from many sides, but Reverend Jesse Jackson probably made the most important observation. He was recently quoted as saying that many cities have late-night or all-night clubs—New York and Las Vegas being two prominent examples—but that those cities do not have the moribund economy that afflicts the residents of East St. Louis. In other words, too many unemployed young men with guns and grudges are the source of the problem, not all-night parties. On June 2–3, 2012, a regional police force of local and state police raided several clubs in East St. Louis and arrested at least three people. There is no doubt that a police raid on any given night will turn up violations in East St. Louis clubs, but that is certainly true of other areas too, including places that suffer from much lower levels of violent crime. In many ways, the discussion of the clubs in East St. Louis that took place during the spring of 2012 reflects almost all discussion of this small, former industrial suburb: it focuses on spectacular and horrible events while failing to look deeply into the factors that have created the dysfunctional community that East St. Louis is seen to be by the majority of people in the St. Louis metropolitan area and the nation in general.

Black clubs are an attractive target because they tend to reinforce stereotypes of African Americans. Clubs are a place where people seek pleasure and engage in activities that go against the sober work ethic that is held up as the ideal of responsible middle and working class Americans. It is easy to cast the women who frequent clubs as "easy," or immoral, and the men as unattached to the regimen of work at minimum, and frankly dangerous at worst. The African American club also has a lurid hold on the imagination of white America because the African American club is the place where one can experience the heart of current black popular culture, and Black popular culture has long been the engine that has driven American popular culture in general. For roughly a century, going back to the era of Prohibition and the birth of Jazz, the African American club has been known to the general culture as the place where one could hear the latest music, learn the newest dances, and develop the hippest vocabulary. Mainstream fashion has also taken cues from the African American nightclub. The number of whites who have spent time in African American clubs is almost too long to mention, but includes everyone from glamorous movie stars during Prohibition, to conservative firebrand Pat Buchanan, who frequented jazz clubs in East St. Louis during the early 1960s when he was a young reporter working for the *St. Louis Globe-Democrat*.

Given this history, it is easy to see why Dick Durbin could gain traction by arguing for improvement in East St. Louis by focusing on the city's nightclubs and the violence that has been connected to them. The idea that East St. Louis would be a better place if the shiftless, hedonistic, blacks were made to sober up and go to bed at a decent hour fits in easily with overriding conservatism of our society that focuses exclusively on personal failures while ignoring systemic problems, especially when it regards minority communities that have long suffered from problems of unemployment and crime. That said, Mayor Parks spoke a fundamental truth when he noted that the nightclubs of East St. Louis are important to the city's economy as employers and as sources of tax revenue. The importance of entertainment and hospitality should be self-evident to anyone with even a passing knowledge of the East St. Louis economy, because the Casino Queen has certainly been the largest single employer and source of revenue for the city since it reached an advanced level of deindustrialization in the 1970s. Similarly, African American clubs have been the backbone of black entrepreneurial activity in the city since the African American population began to expand around the time of World War I. African American clubs in East St. Louis very much reflect the history of that city's African American population. When industry was strong in East St. Louis and there were plenty of jobs and segregation was firmly entrenched, the city and its neighbors Brooklyn, Madison, Venice, Washington, Centerville, and Alorton, all had a wide variety of entertainment venues that catered to African Americans of all socioeconomic backgrounds. These establishments went all the way from hole-in-the-wall juke joints to "respectable" music and supper clubs. East St. Louis, like all northern industrial towns, attracted African American entrepreneurs who followed African American workers to the cities. In the 1960s, the city's most industrious young businessmen, like politician/club owner Leo Gooden, made their marks owning nightclubs. Similarly, young white artists like Bonnie Bramlett of Delany and Bonnie traveled to the Manhattan Club in order to learn R&B at the feet of the genre's masters such as Ike and Tina Turner, Little Milton, and Albert King.

East St. Louis today is a city that is nearly a fourth of the size it was in 1950, and almost all of the industry that made it a favored destination of Southern migrants fifty years ago is gone. Instead of being exciting and exotic to non–African Americans, the city's clubs now appear to be simply dangerous and reflective of the hopelessness that they see in the city's population. The research done for this paper suggests that the personal violence and robberies around clubs are nothing new and even existed when greater East St. Louis had a much more prosperous black working class. This sort of crime, as terrible as it is for its victims, is symptomatic of much greater problems in the society, not the cause of the area's decline. In fact, it can be argued that the level of state response to violence around the clubs is greater now than it was when the area was more prosperous. Quite possibly, this change is a response to the fact that these areas are now controlled by the African American population, and their complaints cannot be ignored by public officials like the mayor or Senator Durbin, the way their predecessors did in earlier times. Unspoken, but secretly acknowledged in the minds of both blacks and whites, is the idea that closing East St. Louis's nightclubs could be the first step in forces from outside the city returning and reclaiming empty prime real estate. The problem with this picture is that the African American poor who now are the overwhelming majority of the population of East St. Louis and its environs will not simply disappear. The fact that the black poor will not disappear is the fundamental truth behind the idea that violence associated with the cities nightclubs is simply a manifestation of a much greater problem that has unfolded over most of the last century. As other scholars of East St. Louis such as Jennifer Hamer, author of *Abandoned in the Heartland* have noted, the deindustrialization that has undermined East St. Louis now devastates the country as a whole. Going to bed early and staying sober won't give the new poor jobs.

Endnotes

1. Dennis Owsley, *City of Gabriels: The History of Jazz in St. Louis*, 1895–1973 (St. Louis: Reedy Press, 2006).
2. Pg. 7.
3. Ibid.
4. Sundiata Keita Cha-Jua, *America's First Black Town: Brooklyn, Illinois*, 1830–1915 (Urbana:
5. University of Illinois Press, 2000).
6. Pg. 3.
7. Cha-Jua, Pg. 4.
8. Reginald Petty, "Black History Tidbits," an unpublished manuscript of information from East
9. St. Louis city records. Pg. 1.
10. Ibid.
11. Reginald Petty, "East St. Louis African American Directory, 1889–1890." Unpublished, pgs. 1–6.
12. Ibid.
13. Petty, "East St. Louis African American Directory, 1889–1890". Pgs. 1–6. Date according to Reginald Petty's direc-
    tory. The church website, eslmacedoniabaptistchurch.com, says 1863.
14. Petty, "Black History Tidbits" www.officerfh.com.
15. Miles Davis & Quincy Troupe, *Miles: The Autobiography*. (New York: Simon and Schuster, 1989).
16. Reginald Petty, "East St. Louis African American Directory, 1930." Unpublished.
17. Reginald Petty, "East St. Louis African American Directory, 1938." Unpublished.
18. Ibid.
19. Petty, 1889–1890 Directory, Pgs. 1–6.
20. Petty, 1938 *Directory*.
21. Phone interview, Rick Perkins, October 10, 2010.
22. Interview, Eddie Randall Jr., October 20, 2010.
23. Interview, James Thomas, October 20, 2010.
24. Interview, David Dee, August 2012.
25. *Metro East Journal*, July 4, 1955.
26. Ibid, October 19, 1955.
27. Ibid, March 19, 1975.
28. *Metro-East Journal*, October 19, 1955; August 4, 1957; October 9, 1957; January 16, 1958; May 18, 1958; June 20,
    1958; September 16, 1958; February 6, 1959; May 5, 1959; August 13, 1969; September 11, 1959; November 17,
    1959; March 31, 1960; May 31, 1960; April 10, 1961; June 6, 1961; August 1, 1961; August 2, 1961; June 26, 1962.
29. Ibid, March 31, 1960.
30. Ibid, August 1 and 2, 1961.
31. Elin Schoen, *Tales of an All-Night Town* (New York: Harcourt, Brace, Jovanovich, 1979).
32. Ibid.
33. *Metro-East Journal*, December 1 and 6, 1965.
34. Ibid, June 12, 1964.
35. Ibid, December 4, 1965.
36. Ibid, December 5, 1965.
37. Ibid.
38. Ibid, January 7, 1966.
39. Ibid, June 12, 1975.
40. *Metro-East Journal*, February 6, 1959.
41. Ibid, February 8, 1959.
42. Ibid, January 2, 1959.
43. Ibid, May 3, 1957.
44. Ibid, September 11, 1962.
45. Ibid, February 23, 1964.
46. "Leo Sings With Strings" (1963), www.discogs.com; "Leo's Five Direct from the Blue Note (1963), www.cduniverse.
    com.
47. Interview, Percy McKinney, December 12, 2011.
48. Scott Eden, "Fantasies Made Fresh," *Maisonneuve Magazine*. December 2004,
49. Interview, Madison Garrett III, March 30, 2011.

50. Ibid.

51. Interview, Police Chiefs of Brooklyn and Washington Park, Illinois, April, 2011.

52. Eden, "Fantasies Made Fresh."

53. Interview, Donald Wilkerson, January 2011.

54. *All Things Considered, National Public Radio*, June 11, 2003.

55. Bruce Rushton, "Welcome to Brooklyn," *Riverfront Times*, www.riverfrontimes.com, June 5, 2000,

56. 56. 227 F.3d 955 (7th Circuit 2000) Everette O. Baker Appeal, N. 99-3840, in the United States Court of Appeals for the Seventh Circuit. Argued May 19, 2000, decided September 20, 2000.

57. Seventh Circuit, pg. 1.

58. Ibid, pg. 2.

59. Ibid, pg. 2.

60. Ibid, pg. 3.

61. Ibid. pg. 2

62. Ellen Nore, *St. Louis National Stockyards Company: East Side Story, 125 Years of Service*, St. Louis, Mo., 2000.

63. CBS, KMOX St. Louis, "Durbin Repeats Call for East St. Louis Action on Clubs," March 5, 2012.

The Problem of Regional Exclusivity: The "High School" Question and Its Implications

Sarah VanSlette, Ph.D., with Kiley Herndon, B.S.

Introduction

On June 9, 2013, critically acclaimed author and St. Louis transplant Curtis Sittenfeld wrote an op-ed for the *New York Times* about her difficulty getting acclimated to St. Louis. While the title of the op-ed is *Loving the Midwest* and she ends the essay by proclaiming that she now feels like a true St. Louisan, she spends a good portion of the article talking about all the ways in which St. Louis and St. Louisans made her feel like she didn't belong. Some criticisms she offers of the city and its natives included its conservative politics, its love of provel cheese, and that she "will never satisfactorily answer the question natives here ask one another on meeting, which is where they went to high school." After describing her general complaints about St. Louis, she leveled her harshest criticism: "But the ultimate affront in St. Louis wasn't politics or food; it was that my husband and I struggled to make friends. I am not exaggerating when I say that in 2008, we held a Super Bowl 'party' to which zero guests showed up."[1]

St. Louisans are accustomed to defending Imo's Pizza and its use of provel cheese (actress and St. Louis native Jenna Fischer had this debate with Jimmy Kimmel on the nationally syndicated show, *Jimmy Kimmel Live*).[2] St. Louisans are also proud of the way in which the question "Where'd you go to high school" functions as a secret handshake between natives.[3] But what place does a secret handshake have in a city that hopes to attract new residents? This study explores the relationship between transplants' (like Sittenfeld) perceptions of St. Louis and the high school question.

Transplants and Regional Reputation

After living away from St. Louis for ten years, I moved back home as an outsider (a "transplant") and began to view the city and its culture in a different light. After a few conversations with people who were either newly returned natives or nonnative transplants to St. Louis, I noticed that many were finding it hard to break into the long-standing social circles made up of people who had been friends since high school. The transplants were puzzled (some annoyed) after being asked where they went to high school. Being a native, and also having friends who I met in high school, I understand that the intent behind "the high school question" isn't to ostracize or to embarrass transplants, but the intent behind the question is not clear to transplants. St. Louis natives will defend the question as a means to get to know someone better and find commonalities, whereas a transplant will see it as a way to identify outsiders and to potentially determine personal demographic information, such as socioeconomic status and religious affiliation.

I began an informal ethnographic investigation of the way other transplants feel about living in the St. Louis Metropolitan Statistical Area (MSA) in fall 2011. I went to social gatherings where the majority of attendees were transplants, had in-depth discussions with friends who were transplants, and started searching the web to see what resources existed for people who were new to St. Louis. It is through this informal ethnographic research that the scope of St. Louis's "PR problem" of being unwelcoming to transplants became clear; in particular, many transplants wondered why natives were always asking where they went to high school. Asking the traditional St. Louis ice-breaker question, "Where did you go to high school?" tells natives a lot about a person's socioeconomic status and friends. Unfortunately, this preoccupation with high schools left some transplants feeling left out, unwelcome, and eager to move away from the St. Louis metro area (taking their skills and businesses with them). As Kristen Hare, reporter for the *St. Louis Beacon*, stated, "The high school question might be seeking to make connections or to peg people, but for people not from here, it also can create a sense of otherness."[4]

St. Louis does not have a sterling image to begin with, so we cannot afford to alienate those who choose to move here from other cities. In 2011, the East-West Gateway Council of Governments wrote about the reputation of the MSA:

> St. Louis often is criticized as stodgy, not open to change, too insular, and not up-to-date. Image-wise, it sometimes is viewed as unattractive to people looking for a high energy, fun, robust metro area.[5]

If we hope to attract young, educated, culturally diverse people to our city, we must do our best to make them feel welcome and to make St. Louis a place that feels open to new people and new ideas.

This study is an attempt to collect qualitative and quantitative data to help understand non-natives' opinions of St. Louis, and to discern if the aforementioned criticisms of the MSA are justified. As a public relations scholar, I understand the importance of reputation and image, even if they are based solely on the opinions of outsiders. The MSA's reputation among nonnatives is important, especially when one considers the consequences of population loss. Enrico Moretti (2012) points out that between the 2000 and 2010 censuses, St. Louis City's population loss rate was the seventh highest in the nation (at 8%), behind New Orleans, Detroit, Cleveland, Cincinnati, Pittsburgh, and Toledo.[6] Moretti underscores the negative implications of such big drops in population: "It is as if year after year Rust Belt cities keep being hit by their own Hurricane Katrina."[7]

If natives' lack of openness could potentially make young, well-educated transplants want to leave the MSA, corporations and the local governments should be invested in studying this problem. The negative impression St. Louis is making on transplants is disheartening, and the economic implications are depressing as well.[8] The MSA has no problem drawing people to the area, but does need to improve population retention.[9] In a nationwide study of urban population growth between 2000–2009, the city of St. Louis experienced the fastest rate of growth of any major metropolitan area of college-educated adults between the ages of 25 and 34 (87%).[10] The city is drawing thousands of college-educated newcomers every year, and in 2012 *Forbes* named St. Louis "The best city for job-seeking college grads…in terms of overall career happiness in conjunction with the average cost-of-living-adjusted salary."[11] Certainly our ability to draw young college graduates is something to be proud of. Even with the influx of these new, young, college-educated residents, they couldn't make up for the incomes lost by those who are leaving the MSA. Between 2001–2010, the city of St. Louis lost $760 million and St. Louis County lost $3.41 billion in resident adjusted gross income due to migration.[12] The MSA should be focused on retention of the young professional transplants for both social and economic reasons.

A few local organizations have risen up to counteract this issue. One is St. Louis Transplants,[13] a social group for dues-paying members who are new to the MSA. Another local company called Acclimate describes itself as "a high-touch personal network that creates a positive whole-life experience for new hires moving to St. Louis and their families; ensuring higher talent retention for employers."[14] These new companies are trying to fulfill a need and help transplants build a network and a social foundation from which they can grow more comfortable in the St. Louis area. Thus, the infrastructure to assist transplants is starting to grow, but prior to this study, no one had reached out to transplants to more formally investigate how they felt about St. Louis, its residents, and the famous "Where did you go to high school" question. The intense response I received from the regional media and from MSA residents when I announced my intention to study this subject in February 2012 is further proof of the public's interest in this subject and the need to look closely at the implications of the data collected.

The primary aim of this research is to evaluate the effect of St. Louis's "Where did you go to high school?" culture and its implications for nonnatives, with a focus on reputational effects. The study revolves around the following thesis: St. Louis's age-old high school question is having a detrimental effect on transplants in the region because transplants view it as a social barrier and associate it with a lack of openness among natives, and the question diminishes the ability of transplants to develop affinity for the region.

Methodology

I generated an initial pool of 37 survey items,[15] which included natives' openness, employment experience, demographics, and affinity toward St. Louis. The online survey received 313 responses, 3 interviews, and 3 in-depth questionnaires. Due to feasibility, cost, and time constraints, a non-probabilistic sample of approximately 1,080 people were invited to participate in the study via Facebook, Twitter, and an email to the employees of Southern Illinois University Edwardsville. The survey was conducted online starting on February 15, 2012, and ending on February 15, 2013. Only transplants (nonnatives) were asked to complete the 37-item survey (among the 313 respondents, 52 were excluded because they were not transplants). After the survey, a random selection of 22 people was invited for interviews and in-depth questionnaires.

We then cross-tabulated the results of the survey questions with the questions I asked about the transplants' intentions to stay in St. Louis and the transplants' overall opinions of the MSA and its native residents. Finally, the qualitative comments in the survey, the interview transcripts, and the extended questionnaires were all analyzed using a careful textual analysis and themes were identified.

Results and Discussion

See the appendix for Table 1, which summarizes the average response on key survey questions related to the four concepts of interest: employee experience, natives' openness, the high school question, and affinity for St. Louis. Most respondents indicated that the primary reason for being in St. Louis was focused around two concepts, opportunities and family. There were 188 respondents who came to St. Louis to start a job, for a job opportunity, or for school; family was the second most cited concept, with 121 respondents indicating that family, a spouse, or love interest was the primary reason for moving. The average respondent of this survey was a 41-year-old married, white woman with a graduate degree, working in an education, training, or library job. Specific results follow.

Most transplants came to St. Louis for a new job. The majority of survey respondents came to St. Louis because they were starting a new job, and the second most popular answer was that they were following a spouse who was starting a new job. Most respondents (78) currently work in the education, training, or library field. The other most common answers to the occupation question, in order of prevalence, were student or other, management occupations, business and financial operations occupations, and arts, design, entertainment, sports, and media occupations.

St. Louis employers do not acclimate transplant new hires to their new city. Only 18% of transplants had employers that offered an orientation to St. Louis. One transplant interviewee was very disappointed that there was no orientation to St. Louis or a more formal acclimation program. When asked if she felt welcome by her fellow employees, she said:

> No. I didn't know what to expect. I've never relocated. . . . Then I go down here and there's nothing. It sucked. It's so like pocketed in the corporation. You have to find your own way to join the pride groups and women's business movements. There is nothing for relocated people.

However, most fellow employees welcomed the newcomer to St. Louis and many (58%) invited the transplant to a party or gathering outside of work. The same interviewee that said she was disappointed by her corporation's lack of orientation program, has started her own informal group to welcome new employee transplants.

> There's like five or six of us that have relocated. . . . We will go do happy hour or something like that. We go a little rogue. . . . You know, we did tours with them. "This is not gonna be your corporate tour, we're gonna go here." We went to the Loop. We did fun stuff like that. We know what we like. In a corporate tour, you don't get that kind of personalization.

The high school question 3 4. In a transplant's first year in St. Louis, he or she will be asked the *high school* question 4 times on average. Certainly there were some transplants who have never been asked the question (16%), but 51% of respondents were asked the question 10 or more times since they moved to St. Louis, with 23% being asked where they went to high school more than 10 times in their first year here.

Transplants don't like being asked the high school question. With a mean score of 2.42 (5 being most positive) transplants' feelings toward being asked the high school question are generally negative. One interviewee had this to say about how she felt about being asked the high school question: "I feel like I witnessed a secret society of crazy people. Yes . . . For me, it's about where you went to college. What you went to college for. Not what high school you went to." Another transplant interviewee also wondered why people weren't asking where he went to college instead:

> I first got asked the infamous St. Louis question. . . . and it was like, "so what school did you go to?" I was like, went to college here, and went to grad school here. No high school. And I looked at the person very quizzically. Because I haven't heard about this whole . . . infamous St. Louis question yet. I look at this person quizzically like ummm . . . I'm from California, and at the time, high school was ten years ago. And so why are you asking? It's confusing and kind of weird quite honestly.

After she was asked the high school question for the first time, another interviewee thought it was a joke until someone later gave her an explanation for it: "Then someone told me, 'No, that's how they decide what kind of person you are. What kind of upbringing. What kind of class medium you come from depends on where you went to high school.' That is not at all like Minneapolis. It's definitely a St. Louis thing."

Reactions from natives not positive to those who didn't go to high school in St. Louis. If when answering the high school question a transplant indicated that "I am not from here," most reactions were neutral, but there were far more negative reactions than positive. If a survey respondent got a negative reaction from a native when they found out they didn't go to high school here, that transplant will be less likely to recommend St. Louis to others (4.13 promoter score on a 5-point Likert scale for those who got a positive response from natives after telling them they didn't go to high school here, versus a 2.37 promoter score for those who got a negative response from natives). After getting negative responses when she said she did not go to high school in St. Louis, one long-term St. Louis transplant said, "In the early years it would hurt my feelings. But now I think . . . I feel sad for them. They're just missing so much. So much. So many really grand people." Another interviewee said that some transplants get defensive if they ask you the high school question and you tell them you aren't from St. Louis: "A couple of times, they've been defensive about it. Like why they're asking that. It's like, 'Oh we ask that because, people go to different schools. It's kind of like a rivalry thing.' And all that. It's interesting to me."

Transplants think natives could be more open. Sixty percent of survey respondents view native St. Louisans in a positive light and nearly 80% of transplants had been invited to a native's home. However, when asked to characterize natives' feelings about transplants, the average was "somewhat negative." Those respondents who believe natives are not open to transplants are also less likely to recommend St. Louis to others (4.27 net promoter score on a 5-point Likert scale for those who think natives have positive feelings toward transplants, versus a 1.58 net promoter score for transplants who think natives have negative feelings toward transplants). One questionnaire respondent described St. Louisans this way: "My personal feeling is that they are neither standoffish nor welcoming. I think, if they have friends already, they forget what it's like to be the outsider." When asked what she thought about native St. Louisans, another transplant interviewee had this to say: "I think taken one by one, they are nice people. If they stop to think about you and what your situation is, and where you come from, everything is fine. But I sort of think they're provincial." One respondent to the questionnaire believes that St. Louisans may be friendly, but already have enough friends and family that take up their time:

> Most people here have family in the area and they are VERY connected to family. Good luck finding people to spend the major holidays with if you are not a native. There are many people who have families who have been here for generations so their local roots run deep. As Seinfeld once quipped, they're "not in the market for new friends right now, but if anyone dies or moves and they have an opening they'll certainly give you a call."

Most transplants are satisfied with St. Louis. The average survey responses to all the questions related to St. Louis affinity ranged between 3.17 and 3.75 on a 5-point Likert scale, where 5 always represented positive feelings about St. Louis and 1 represented negative feelings about St. Louis. One transplant interviewee said, "I think St. Louis natives don't appreciate enough of what this area has to offer. There are a surprising number of cool things to do here. I was pleasantly surprised by that." Another interviewee said that she feels at home in St. Louis: "Oh we love it here. I'm a Midwestern girl at heart. It was an easy, easy move. An easy adjustment for me to come back. I love the change in seasons. There are a lot of wonderful things to do around here. Family oriented."

Transplants that are unhappy with St. Louis plan to leave in 4 years. However, if they are happy with St. Louis, they are open to staying for 9 years, on average.

Limitations of the Study. Beyond limitations inherent in all survey research, we note two specific limitations of this study. First, the net participant response rate remains unknown. No practical mechanism exists to identify the actual number of transplants in the St. Louis MSA. Accordingly, we resorted to a self-identification process, which may have led to a selection bias. Collection of emails included social media channels, email collection at events for transplants, along with traditional television and radio appearances by the principal investigator. Those who felt compelled to participate in the study may have felt very strongly about being asked "Where'd you go to high school." Conceivably, the respondents were different in systematic ways from non-respondents but it is unlikely that non-respondents would have felt worse about the St. Louis question than respondents. Second, the common demographic profile of respondents on the basis of job description, gender, and education limits the generalizability of the findings. However, the themes found in the responses seem to be corroborated by the informal conversations I've had with a broader sample of transplants in the past, so I believe they are valid.

Conclusion

Despite the limitations of this pilot study, St. Louisans should care about the opinions and perspectives reflected in the survey responses. These perspectives and perceptions may be surprising to some natives, especially the natives (many of whom have contacted me to express this view) who strongly believe that the high school question is a harmless ice-breaker question intended to find commonalities with the other person. What those natives need to remember is that when it comes to the transplants' perceptions of the question, the natives' intentions behind the question do not matter. It seems that many transplants have either been told or have decided that the high school question is used to determine someone's socioeconomic status or to stereotype them some other way. This perception could have negative consequences for the city and its ability to draw more transplants.

Our study found that transplants who believe a native responded negatively when they said they did not go to high school in St. Louis are less likely to recommend St. Louis to others. Our data also shows that transplants who believe that natives are not open to transplants are also less likely to recommend St. Louis to others. Perhaps the most important finding from this survey is that, put simply, transplants don't like being asked "the high school question." If transplants don't like being asked the question, and many feel that they are getting negative responses from natives when they answer the question, natives should carefully consider the consequences of the question before they ask it.

I was once part of a discussion on Twitter about "the high school question," and Courtney Sloger, then marketing & communications director at FOCUS St. Louis, created the hashtag #changethequestionSTL and asked people to tweet new questions that could replace the famous "Where'd you go to high school?" Her question drew a lot of responses, all using the hashtag #changethequestionSTL. Some suggestions included, "What brought you to St. Louis?" "What do you like about St. Louis?" "What city (or town) are you from?" These new questions would seem like obvious ice-breaker questions, but changing habits (and the culture of a city) can be difficult. It is encouraging that more people are thinking critically about the question St. Louis takes for granted and asking whether it is a cultural artifact worth holding on to.

Acknowledgments. The authors wish to acknowledge with appreciation the support received from the SIUE Institute for Urban Research, Dr. Andrew Theising, Hugh Pavitt, and Monica Brooks. Thanks also for support received from Jessica Bock of the *St. Louis Post-Dispatch*, the SIUE Speech Communication department Dr. Isaac Blankson, Jeffrey VanSlette, and Lisa Nettlehorst.

References

Blythe, J. (1947). Can public relations help reduce prejudice? *Public Opinion Quarterly, 11*(3), 342–360.

CEO's for Cities (2011). Young and restless 2011. Retrieved on August 16, 2012, from http://www.ceosforcities.org/pagefiles/Young_and_Restless_2011.pdf

Dilthey, W. (1976). *Selected writings* (H.P. Rickman, trans.). Cambridge: Cambridge University Press.

East-West Gateway Council of Governments (2011 November 18). Born in the MSA: Most people who live in St. Louis were born here. In other metros—not so much. Retrieved August 16, 2012, from http://www.ewgateway.org/blogs/rtr/index.php/2011/11/18/born-in-the-msa/

Finley, T., and T. Joachims (2005). *Supervised clustering with support vector machines.* Paper presented at the Annual International Conference on Machine Learning in Bonn, Germany.

Guba, E.G. (1990). *The paradigm dialogue.* Newbury Park, CA: Sage.

Hare, K. (2011, August 19). That high school question. *The St. Louis Beacon.* Retrieved on August 16, 2012 from
https://www.stlbeacon.org/#!/content/15435/that_high_school_question

Hartigan, J.A., and M.A. Wong (1979). Algorithm AS 136: A K-means clustering algorithm. *Journal of the Royal Statistical Society, Series C (Applied Statistics), 28* (1): 100–108.

Hastie, T., R. Tibshirani, and J. Friedman (2009). *The elements of statistical learning: Data mining, inference, and prediction.* New York: Springer.

Husserl, E. (1931) *Ideas: General introduction to pure phenomenology.* London: Allen & Unwin.

Lindlof, T.R., & B.C. Taylor (2011). *Qualitative communication research methods (3rd Ed).* Thousand Oaks, CA: Sage.

Long, J.S. (1997). *Regression models for categorical and limited dependent variables.* Thousand Oaks, CA: Sage.

Merrigan, G., & C.L. Huston (2008). *Communication research methods (2nd Ed).* Belmont, CA: Wadsworth/Thomson Learning.

Mertens, D.M. (1998). *Research methods in education and psychology: Integrating diversity with quantitative & qualitative approaches.* Thousand Oaks, CA: Sage.

Miller, L. (2012, December 20). Jenna Fischer talks favorite St. Louis foods with Jimmy Kimmel, he calls Imo's the worst pizza ever. *The Riverfront Times.* Retrieved from http://blogs.riverfronttimes.com/gutcheck/2012/12/jenna_fischer_jimmy_kimmel_live_st_louis_foods_imos_pizza_pappys_smokehouse_ted_drewes.php

Moretti, E. (2012). *The new geography of jobs.* New York: Houghton Mifflin Harcourt Publishing Company.

Moskop, W. (2012 May 29). St. Louis County losing people, resident income. *The St. Louis Post-Dispatch.* Retrieved on August 16, 2012, from http://www.stltoday.com/news/local/metro/st-louis-county-losing-people-resident-income/article_94d9d3e5-1086-559a-b8e2-4bcbde756325.html#ixzz1wOtLpMT1

Schutz, A. (1967). *The phenomenology of the social world.* Evanston, IL: Northwestern University Press.

Silverman, D.A. (2011 September 6). Guest post: The importance of ethics to the PR industry.

Sittenfeld, C. (2013 June 8). Loving the Midwest. *The New York Times.* Retrieved from http://www.nytimes.com/2013/06/09/opinion/sunday/loving-the-midwest.html?_r=0

Appendix

Survey Responses

5 = Highly Favorable, Much Better, Very Likely, Highly Satisfied, Positive; 4 = Favorable, Better, Likely, Satisfied, Somewhat Positive; 3 = Neutral; 2 = Unfavorable, Worse, Unlikely, Unsatisfied, Somewhat Negative; 1 = Highly Unfavorable, Much Worse, Very Unlikely, Highly Unsatisfied, Negative

Concept	Item	Rating	Missing
Affinity	How long do you plan to live in the St. Louis region? (in years)	7.89	107/261
	What is your opinion of the St. Louis region?	3.75	1/261
	Think of other cities you've lived in before moving to St. Louis. How does St. Louis compare to those cities? St. Louis is . . .	3.17	2/261
	How satisfied are you with your quality of life in St. Louis?	3.73	2/261
	If your friend from out of town was considering moving to a new city, how likely would you be to recommend St. Louis?	3.43	0/261
High School Question	Has a St. Louis native ever asked you where you went to high school?	83.9% (219/261)	0/261
	How would you characterize your feelings about being asked where you went to high school?	2.42	0/219
	When you tell St. Louis natives that you did not go to high school in St. Louis, how would you characterize their response?	2.64	0/219
	How many times have you been asked "Where did you go to high school?" since moving to St. Louis? (count)	10.07	0/219
Natives' Openness	What is your opinion of the people of the St. Louis region?	3.58	1/261
	Think of other cities you've lived in before moving to St. Louis. How do the people living in St. Louis compare to the people living in those cities?	2.98	0/261
	How satisfied are you with the amount of friends you've made since moving to St. Louis?	3.26	1/261
	How many of your friends are St. Louis natives?	2.84	0/261
	Has a St. Louis native ever invited you to their home for a meal or party?	79.5% (206/259)	2/261
	Has anyone ever given you a housewarming gift or another gift to welcome you to St. Louis?	30.77% (80/260)	1/261
	How would you characterize St. Louis natives' feelings about transplants (nonnatives)?	2.74	0/261

Employee Experience	What brought you to the St. Louis region? (reporting job)	66.67% (174/261)	0/261
	How often do you consider quitting your job?	2.25	11/261
	Did your employer do anything to acclimate you and other new employees to the St. Louis region?	18.3% (46/252)	9/261
	At your job, did fellow employees welcome you as a newcomer?	74.2% (184/248)	13/261
	At your job, did fellow employees invite you to social gatherings outside of work?	57.8% (144/249)	12/261

Endnotes

1. Sittenfeld, para. 4.
2. Miller, 2012.
3. Hare, 2011.
4. Hare, 2011, para. 47.
5. East-West Gateway, 2011, para. 2.
6. Moretti, 2012, 23.
7. Moretti, 2012, 23.
8. Moskop, 2012.
9. Moskop, 2012.
10. CEO's for Cities, 2011.
11. Smith, 2012, para. 2.
12. Moskop, 2012.
13. See the website http://www.stltransplants.com.
14. See the website http://www.acclimatestl.com/.
15. The questions on the survey were as follows:

1. I have read the consent statement above and agree to participate in the survey.
2. I understand that only St. Louis transplants (people who moved to St. Louis after they graduated from high school) are invited to participate in this survey. I characterize myself as a St. Louis transplant.
3. I am 18 years or older (all participants must be 18+ years).
4. How long have you lived in the St. Louis region?
5. How long do you plan to live in the St. Louis region?
6. What is your opinion of the St. Louis region?
7. Think of other cities you've lived in before moving to St. Louis. How does St. Louis compare to those cities? St. Louis is . . .
8. What word or phrase best describes St. Louis?
9. What brought you to the St. Louis region? (check all that apply)
   a. Starting new job
   b. Job opportunities/Looking for job
   c. Spousal career move
   d. To be near family
   e. To be near friends
   f. Attending a local university or college
   g. Life Transition (Divorce, Death in the family, Retirement)
   h. Romantic Interests
   i. Regional attractions (sports teams, museums, shopping, parks, art, etc.)
   j. Regional services (medical care, school systems, social services, etc.)
   k. Other (please specify)
10. What is your opinion of the people of the St. Louis region?
11. Think of other cities you've lived in before moving to St. Louis. How do the people living in St. Louis compare to the people living in those cities? St. Louisans are . . .
12. What word or phrase best describes the people of the St. Louis region?
13. How often do you consider quitting your job?
14. How satisfied are you with the amount of friends you've made since moving to St. Louis?
15. How many of your friends are St. Louis natives?
16. How many of your friends are fellow transplants to St. Louis (i.e. non-natives)?
17. How satisfied are you with your quality of life in St. Louis?
18. Did your employer do anything to acclimate you and other new employees to the St. Louis region?
19. At your job, did fellow employees welcome you as a newcomer?
20. At your job, did fellow employees invite you to social gatherings outside of work?
21. Has a St. Louis native ever invited you to their home for a meal or party?
22. Has anyone ever given you a housewarming gift or another gift to welcome you to St. Louis?
23. Has a St. Louis native ever asked you where you went to high school?
24. How would you characterize your feelings about being asked where you went to high school?
25. When you tell St. Louis natives that you did not go to high school in St. Louis, how would you characterize their response?
26. How would you characterize St. Louis natives' feelings about transplants (non-natives)?
27. How many times have you been asked "Where did you go to high school?" since moving to St. Louis?
28. If your friend from out of town was considering moving to a new city, how likely would you be to recommend St. Louis?

29. Would you be willing to answer more questions related to this study at a later date, perhaps in an interview or with a more extended questionnaire?

30. If you consent to be interviewed at a later date, please provide your first name and email address in the space below.

31. Are you male or female?

32. Are you now married, partnered, widowed, divorced, separated, or never married?

33. How old are you?

34. In what ZIP code is your home located? (enter 5-digit ZIP code; for example, 63108 or 63122)

35. What is your ethnicity?

36. What is the highest level of school you have completed or the highest degree you have received?

37. What type of job do you have?

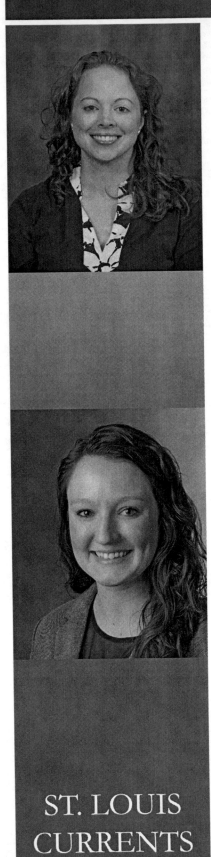

About the Authors

Sarah VanSlette, Ph.D., is assistant professor in the Department of Applied Communication Studies at Southern Illinois University Edwardsville. She is a St. Louis native who earned her undergraduate degree in communication and English at Saint Louis University. She earned her M.A. and Ph.D. from Purdue University in public relations. Dr. VanSlette teaches courses in public relations, social media, and public speaking. Her research interests include public relations pedagogy, social media in public relations campaigns, and corporate reputation management. She approaches her study of public relations and strategic communication from a rhetorical perspective. Her work has been published in *Communication Quarterly* and she is the author of several book chapters. Her continuing research on "the high school question" has been featured in the *St. Louis Post-Dispatch*, the *Riverfront Times*, and other local and national media.

Kiley Herndon is a graduate of Southern Illinois University Edwardsville, where she gained he B.A. in English and a B.S. in applied communication studies. Ms. Herndon describes herself as a lover of reading, social media, and traveling the world as a curious, constant student.

ST. LOUIS
CURRENTS

A Failing Grade in Education

The challenges that confront weak educational performance in parts of the region's K-12 population are not new. Today's problems have evolved over decades, even a century, into what is now a seemingly intractable problem.

Mark Tranel offers his insight on the current state of regional education, with ideas on how the region arrived at this situation and suggestions for improvements. The correlation between poverty and educational performance is sad. Tranel provides considerable data to demonstrate the point.

Solutions are difficult but not impossible. Certainly there are ideas that can improve the classroom setting, but some of the most important improvements may lie outside the school building.

Poor Education

Mark Tranel, Ph.D.

The promise of our educational system as the great equalizer appears more myth than reality today as the gap in outcomes between the poor and non-poor continues to grow in conjunction with the increasing divergence in incomes and wealth. Poverty and Education: Finding the Way Forward, 2013

The 1986 *St. Louis Currents* education essay opened with the assertion that "the elementary and secondary educational systems in the St. Louis metropolitan area are marked by diversity." Nearly three decades later, this characteristic is compellingly true, but askew, particularly as measured by the economic status of students. One of every five K-12 students in metropolitan St. Louis[1] lives in a household with poverty-level income. But while there are children from households with poverty-level income in every school district in the metropolitan St. Louis area, those households are not evenly distributed across the metropolitan landscape. Rather, they are tightly clustered. Over the past thirty years, poverty among school-age children has increased in numbers and expanded in geography yet remains highly concentrated, exerting an ever more significant impact on educational outcomes.

A stark indicator of the uneven distribution can be seen by examining the census data for children living in poverty by school district. While the percentage of persons under age 18 in poverty ranges from 1.2 percent to 58.2 percent across metropolitan St. Louis school districts, as shown in Table 1 there are 72 districts with a child poverty rate of less than 20 percent, exactly half that number with a poverty rate of 20 to 39 percent and 7 districts with 40 percent or more of their children living in households with poverty-level income. Appendix A provides details on which districts are in each of the categories.

Table 1. Number of St. Louis Area School Districts by Percent of Children in Poverty-Level Income Households

1%–9%	10%–19%	20%–29%	30–39%	40—49%	50% or more
39	33	23	13	5	2

Source: U.S. census data

The challenge for educators and for the region is that students from poverty-level households consistently have lower levels of academic achievement, and the academic gap between these students and students of higher income households is widening.

The Context

There are 126 public school districts in the metropolitan St. Louis area providing education to approximately 396,000 students.[2] In addition, there are 418 private schools providing education to approximately 85,650 students.[3] Data on academic achievement and household income of private school students are not available, limiting this essay to an examination of the academic impact of household poverty-level income to students in the public school systems.

Data sources vary regarding the extent of poverty in St. Louis area schools. U.S. census data for 2012 report 20.6 percent of metropolitan St. Louis persons less than 18 years of age live in a household with poverty-level income. Census data also show that in the majority of school districts (82 percent), the percentage of poverty-level income households with persons under age 18 is higher than the percentage of all households in the district that have poverty-level income, meaning households with children are more likely to have poverty-level incomes than those without children. Alternatively, school district data on the number of children qualifying for the U.S. Department of Agriculture's (USDA) free/reduced price lunch program report 43.4 percent of children in the St. Louis region eligible under the USDA income guidelines.[4] While there are students eligible for the free/reduced lunch program in every school district in the metropolitan St. Louis area, of the more than 170,000 students that qualify, more than 50 percent are concentrated in just 14 of the 124 public school districts for which data are reported; in fact 4 districts account for more than 25 percent of the eligible students.

Poverty and Academic Performance

Because the data available from the Illinois and Missouri state education offices are not uniform, this essay first will examine the impact of poverty-level household income on academic performance (the "poverty gap")[5] at the district level using data from the Missouri Department of Elementary and Secondary Education and then at the student level using data from the Illinois State Board of Education.

District-Level Impact

Table 2 records for 56 school districts in the Missouri portion of the metropolitan St. Louis area the 2010 census data, grouped in quintiles, for the percentage of all persons with a poverty-level income and the corresponding percentage of accreditation points as measured by the school district's Annual Performance Report (APR).[6] The APR is a composite of scores for each of the Missouri School Improvement Program 5 (MSIP 5) accreditation performance standards.

Table 2. Level of Poverty and District Accreditation

Quintile	Average 2010 % poor in district	Average 2012 % APR points
1st	4.95%	94.12
2nd	8.05%	92.49
3rd	11.0%	88.85
4th	15.44%	81.75
5th	23.43%	69.43

Source: U.S. Census and Missouri Department of Elementary and Secondary Education

The performance standards are academic achievement, subgroup achievement, high school readiness (K-8 districts) or college and career readiness (K-12 districts), attendance rate, and graduation rate (K-12 districts). School districts that earn 70 percent or more of the APR points are accredited, districts with 50 to 69 percent are provisionally accredited, and districts that earn less than 50 percent are unaccredited.

The data in Table 2 show that as the poverty level increases, academic performance declines. While the decline in academic performance from the first to the second quintile is less than 2 percent, the decline from the second to the third quintile increases to approximately 4 percent, then 8 percent from the third to the fourth, and 12 percent from the fourth to the fifth. In the first quintile, districts with an average of less than 5 percent of their residents in poverty-level income households achieved on average over 94 percent of the possible accreditation points. In the fifth quintile, on average over 23 percent of the school district population lived in poverty in 2010 but those districts averaged 69 percent of the annual accreditation points, representing a 26 percent decline in academic performance from the districts with the least poverty to the districts with the most poverty.

The most dramatic impact occurs when poverty levels reach 20 percent. Although there is persistent decline across the quintiles, the decline in percentage of APR points earned from the 1st to the 4th quintile is 12.37 points, from 94.12 percent of APR points earned to 81.75 percent earned. The decline from the 4th to the 5th quintile is an equivalent 12.32 points. Urban affairs professor George Galster reports that neighborhood research shows a tipping point of negative impacts when the concentration of poverty reaches 20 percent (Galster, 2012). These data for academic performance in St. Louis area school districts with high concentrations of poverty are consistent with this research. As shown in Table 1 there are 41 school districts with community poverty levels over 20 percent. While much attention has been given to the threshold criteria of whether or not a district is accredited, the evidence is clear that there is a more extensive academic achievement gap that should be of regional concern.

Student-Level Impact

The challenge of lower academic achievement of students from poverty-level income households is not just a significant factor in districts with a high concentration of poverty. As the data in Table 3 for the Illinois public school districts in the St. Louis area show, there is a large gap between economically disadvantaged students and all other students as measured by reading and math tests in each of the five quintiles.

Table 3. Reading and Math Skills of All District Students Compared to Economically Distressed Students

Quintile	Reading		Math		2010 % poor in district
	All	ED	All	ED	
1st	70.68	54.36	68.38	52.01	3.99
2nd	64.90	53.12	63.28	48.59	7.54
3rd	61.25	50.08	59.17	48.14	11.00
4th	52.08	42.56	51.59	42.99	15.20
5th	50.98	44.16	53.80	47.28	22.85

Source: 2013 Illinois School District Report Card

These data tell two stories. The first is that learning for economically disadvantaged students is consistently behind that of the rest of their classmates. In the case of the 1st quintile, the lowest level of poverty districts, economically disadvantaged students score over 23 percent lower on both reading and math tests. In the 2nd through the 4th quintile reading scores, economically disadvantaged students score just over 18 percent lower while the difference in math scores ranges from 23 percent lower in the 2nd quintile to 16 percent lower in the 4th quintile. In the 5th quintile, where the poverty rate in the school districts averages over 20 percent, the economically disadvantaged students are respectively 13 and 12 percent behind their non-economically disadvantaged classmates in reading and math.

The second story told by the data is that, similar to the data in Table 2, as poverty increases, academic achievement declines for both economically disadvantaged students as well as the rest of the students in their classrooms. As poverty increases from approximately 4 percent in the first quintile to nearly 23 percent in the fifth quintile, reading scores for all students drop 20 points and math scores over 14 points. Inversely, for the economically disadvantaged students, their performance marginally increases as the poverty density decreases.

Why Is This Important?

There are at least two reasons why the disparity in educational outcomes between children of poverty-level income households and their peers who live in households of greater means should be considered a critical issue for both education professionals and the St. Louis community.

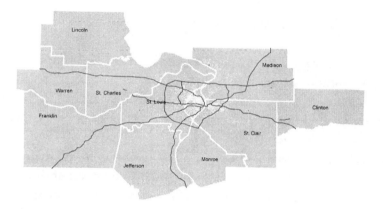

Map 1 Poverty 1980

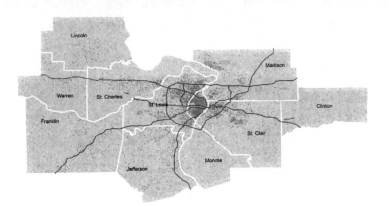

Map 2 Poverty 2010

The first reason is that the problem is getting worse. Despite economic growth and fifty years of the War on Poverty, poverty rates particularly among households with children have increased. This economic immobility is what Jared Bernstein of the Center on Budget and Policy Priorities calls "sticky poverty."[7] As shown in Maps 1 and 2, over the thirty year period 1980–2010 there was not only an absolute increase in poor persons but also the continuing trend of poor persons living in areas of concentrated poverty.

The 2000 census recorded 258,189 persons in poverty in metropolitan St. Louis. The 2008–2012 American Community Survey data document a 34 percent increase, to 346,019. In 2000, 40.4 percent of poor persons lived in census tracts with poverty rates of 20 percent or more and by 2008-2012, 47.3 percent lived in tracts of 20 percent or more poor persons, increasing concentrated poverty from 106 to 146 census tracts.[8]

Over the past decade poverty has become more suburban in the metropolitan St. Louis area, thereby affecting a larger number of school districts. In 2000, 68 percent of poor persons lived in the suburbs rather than the central city. By 2013, the suburban percentage increased to 77 percent.[9,10]

The fact that the number of children living in poverty in the metropolitan St. Louis area is increasing is only half the problem. Perhaps even more compelling is that the gap in educational outcomes is widening over time. As Sean Reardon, Stanford University endowed professor of poverty and inequality in education, states, the income differential between poverty households and non-poverty households is not the dominant factor in the increase in the academic achievement gap between the two groups. Research has shown an increasing level of academic performance for middle-income households, likely due to greater parental investment in academic supports for their children, while academic performance for poverty-level households stagnates (Reardon, 2011).

The second reason education of the poor is a relevant and critical issue is that the challenge of concentrated poverty is at best complex and at worst intractable. A recent study by the Federal Reserve Bank concludes ". . .a wide range of economic, demographic, and social forces have played a part in contributing to high-poverty communities. These include economic restructuring and change, suburbanization, racial and economic segregation, demographic shifts (including immigration and trends in family formation), and the consequences of certain federal policies and programs (Federal Reserve Bank, 2008)."[11] Poverty is not a one-dimensional phenomenon. Child psychologist Bruce Ferguson and his colleagues identify a number of poverty-related factors that impact school performance: how pervasive poverty is in a given population, how far below poverty level the household income is, how long the household is in poverty, how old the child is when the household experiences poverty, and the community context the household experiences when in poverty (Ferguson et al., 2007).

The education community in the St. Louis area has not effectively deployed the financial resources available to address the issue. Despite the expenditure of over $100,000,000 per year in Title I funds ($33,320,975 to Illinois metro districts and $70,602,355 to Missouri metro districts in 2013), there has been little progress in improving the academic outcomes of students from poverty-level income households.[12] The Title I allocations fund in part the work of over thirty alternative schools, school-based programs, after-school programs, mentoring programs, and family support programs. The public school systems, the nonprofit organizations, and the foundations in the St. Louis area need a strategic assessment of the financial and organization resources engaged to address education of students from poverty-level households in order to develop a more effective plan for their use.

At the same time, a characteristic of public education in both Illinois and Missouri is the low level of funding provided by the state government. The 2011 fiscal year data from the National Center for Educational Statistics show Illinois 47th at 32.2 percent and Missouri 49th at 29.6 percent among the 50 states.[13] Illinois has been on a multiyear process of reducing expenditures to work toward a balanced budget. In 2005, Missouri changed from an equity to an adequacy strategy.[14] An analysis has shown that the school districts in the seven Missouri counties in the St. Louis area are underfunded by $181,630,443.[15] Providing additional financial resources to school districts is not a sufficient response to the challenge, but it is a necessary part of the solution.

Strategic Responses

Given the complexity of the problem and the scale of the challenge, an effective strategy will require many components. While these are not the only challenges that need to be addressed, recent literature has identified one critical issue in the classroom and one outside the classroom. First, because poverty has real and significant developmental and physiological consequences, in order to be effective teachers must know and account for these consequences in how they manage the classroom. Second, teachers cannot be solely responsible for changing the outcomes for poor students. School districts must establish a system of supports outside of the classroom that are as critical as effective teaching.

Former teacher Eric Jensen has identified seven differences between students from poverty-level income households and their classmates from households with higher incomes (Jensen, 2013). As detailed in Table 4, for each category of difference Jensen indicates the effect on classroom performance. For example, because students from poor households are less likely to receive proper medical treatment (among a number of health differences) and consume food of lower nutritional value, there are differences in brain development compared to students who do receive better medical care and better nutrition. These differences affect students' ability to concentrate in class, their reasoning capacity, and their memory. Another difference is that students from lower-income households most often are exposed to a much smaller vocabulary during their preschool years, so that when they are in the classroom they're exposed to many words they do not know or understand, which affects their ability to comprehend learning materials.

Table 4. Differences between Low-Income and Non-Low-Income Students That Affect Classroom Engagement

Difference	Affect
Health and Nutrition	attention, reasoning, learning, memory
Vocabulary	smaller vocabulary—less likely to know words the teacher uses or are in reading material
Effort	depressive symptoms—learned helplessness
Hope and the Growth Mind-Set	thinking failure or low performance likely
Cognition	high levels of distractibility, difficulty monitoring the quality of their work, difficulty generating new solutions to problems
Relationships	chaotic home life, absent adult role models
Distress	chronic activation of immune system, impairs working memory

Table 4 identifies all the categories of differences and the classroom effect on students from poverty-level households. Jensen argues that unless teachers acknowledge these differences and accommodate them in their pedagogy, the teachers will continue to have differences in learning outcomes between poor and nonpoor students.

While nonschool supports have been promoted for many years, in 2005 the Harvard Family Research Project combined two principles in an effort to make them more effective (Weiss and Coffman, 2005). Not only are school and nonschool contexts equally critical for student learning, but also the learning opportunities and contexts should complement one another. Defined as "complementary learning," the Harvard Family Research Project maintains that the key to implementation of these principles is creating "an integrated, accessible set of community-wide resources that support learning and development."[16] The nonschool supports must be linked and delivered at appropriate scale in order to be effective. While they do not reference Jensen's categories of differences between poor and nonpoor students, the aim of providing the services as they recommend would be to affect the range of physiological and developmental differences Jensen identifies.

> ". . . schooling, while necessary, is not sufficient for high academic achievement." (Little, 2005)

What might complementary learning look like in metropolitan St. Louis? A starting place could be an assessment of the current use of Title 1 funds and an exploration of the potential for improved integration across districts of the school and nonschool services provided. The fact that school districts in metropolitan St. Louis receive $100 million in Title I funds creates a resource pool that could be used more effectively. There is both great need for and great potential in making such an effort.

Endnotes

1. This essay uses the February 2013 U.S. Office of Management and Budget delineation of the St. Louis metropolitan area that includes eight Illinois counties and seven Missouri counties. http://www.whitehouse.gov/sites/default/files/omb/bulletins/2013/b-13-01.pdf

2. This figure includes all districts in the fifteen counties in Illinois and Missouri, both K-8 and K-12 districts. K-8 districts operate only elementary schools.

3. Sources: public schools—the Illinois State Board of Education and the Missouri Department of Elementary and Secondary Education; private schools—Private School Review, http://www.privateschoolreview.com/

4. Students with a household income 130% of poverty-level income qualify for free meals, and students with a household income 185% of poverty-level income qualify for reduced-price meals. http://www.gpo.gov/fdsys/pkg/FR-2012-03-23/pdf/2012-7036.pdf

5. Jon Marcus, "The Poverty Gap," Harvard Education Letter, Volume 28, Number 4 (July-August 2012). http://hepg.org/hel-home/issues/28_4/helarticle/the-poverty-gap_539

6. Poverty data were not available for the Orchard Farms R-V and Richwoods R-VII districts.

7. J. Bernstein (2012) http://jaredbernsteinblog.com/shuffling-off-to-st-louis%E2%80%A6/

8. http://www.brookings.edu/research/interactives/2014/concentrated-poverty#/M41180

9. http://www.brookings.edu/research/reports/2014/09/19-census-metros-progress-poverty-kneebone-holmes

10. http://www.frbsf.org/community-development/files/cp_fullreport.pdf D Erickson, C. Reid, L. Nelson, A. O'Shaughnessy, and A. Berube, editors (2008) "The Enduring Challenge of Concentrated Poverty in America: Case Studies from Communities Across the U.S.," pg. 170.

11. Title I, Part A (Title I) of the Elementary and Secondary Education Act, as amended (ESEA) provides financial assistance to local educational agencies (LEAs) and schools with high numbers or high percentages of children from low-income families. http://www2.ed.gov/programs/titleiparta/index.html

12. http://nces.ed.gov/pubs2013/2013342.pdf. S.Q. Cornman. (July 2013). Revenues and Expenditures for Public Elementary and Secondary Education: School Year 2010–11 (Fiscal Year 2011).

13. http://www.msbafuturebuilders.org/documents/research/Missouri%20K-12%20Foundation%20Formula.pdf. Future Builders Foundation, N.D., The Missouri K-12 Foundation Formula

14. http://www.mobudget.org/files/A_Shaky_Foundation.pdf Missouri Budget Project, N.D., A Shaky Foundation: Missouri Underfunding the School Formula.

15. H.B. Weiss, J. Coffman, M. Post, S. Bouffard, and P. Little. "Beyond the Classroom: Complementary Learning to Improve Achievement Outcomes," The Evaluation Exchange, Vol. XI, No. 1 (2005), pg. 1.

Bibliography

Ferguson, H.B., Bovaird, S., and Mueller, M.P. "The Impact of poverty on educational outcomes for children," *Paediatrics and Child Health*, Vol. 12, No. 8, (2007):701-706.

Jensen, Eric. "How Poverty Affects Classroom Engagement," *Educational Leadership*, Vol. 70, No. 8 (2013): 24-30.

Lacour, M., and L.D. Tissington. "The Effects of Poverty on Academic Achievement," *Educational Research and Reviews*, Vol. 6, No. 7 (2011): 522–527.

Little, Priscilla. "Supplementary Education: The Hidden Curriculim of High Academic Achievement," *The Evaluation Exchange*, Vol. XI, No. 1 (2005): 7.

Reardon, Sean F. "The Widening Achievement Gap between the Rich and the Poor: New Evidence and Possible Explanations," in Greg J. Duncan and Richard J. Murane, editors, *Whither Opportunity? Rising Inequality, Schools, and Children's Life Chances* (New York, NY: Russell Sage Foundation, 2011): 91–116.

Weiss, H.B., J. Coffman, M. Post, S. Bouffard, and F. Little. "Beyond the Classroom: Complementary Learning to Improve Achievement Outcomes," *The Evaluation Exchange*, Vol. XI, No. 1 (2005): 2–6, 17.

Appendix A

Poverty Level by District

> 50%	40%–49%	30%–39%	20%–29%	10%–19%	1%–9%
Cahokia CUSD 187	Normandy	High Mount SD 116	Valley Park	Calhoun CUSD 40	Signal Hill SD 181
Madison CUSD 12	East Alton SD 13	Kingston K-14	Ferguson-Florissant R-II	Dupo CUSD 196	Bunker Hill CUSD 8
	Riverview Gardens	Jennings	Gillespie CUSD 7	Meramec Valley R-III	Windsor C-1
	St. Louis City	Wright City R-II of Warren Co	Granite City CUSD 9	North Mac CUSD 34	Carlinville CUSD 1
		Mulberry Grove CUSD 1	Willow Grove SD 46	Troy R-III	Webster Groves
		Central SD 104	Belleville SD 118	Winfield R-IV	Wood River–Hartford ESD 15
		Lonedell R-XIV	Marissa CUSD 40	Grant CCSD 110	Carlyle CUSD 1
		North Wamac SD 186	Collinsville CUSD 10	Hazelwood	Edwardsville CUSD 7
		Elsberry R II	Northwestern CUSD 2	Breese ESD 12	Wesclin CUSD 3
		Lebanon CUSD 9	Sunrise R-IX	Maplewood–Richmond Heights	New Athens CUSD 60
		Potosi R-III	Ritenour	Pattonville R-III	Crystal City 47
		Bethalto CUSD 8	Belle Valley SD 119	Roxana CUSD 1	Triad CUSD 2
			Warren Co. R-III	Grandview R-II	Mehlville R-IX
			Alton CUSD 11	Fox C-6	Jersey CUSD 100
			Venice CUSD 3	Festus R-VI	Wentzville R-IV
			Desoto 73	Northwest R-1	Valmeyer CUSD 3
			Dunklin R-V	New Haven	Wolf Branch SD 113
			Sullivan	Union R-XI	Silex R-I
			Hancock Place	Southwestern CUSD 9	Bayless
			University City	Washington	Parkway C-2
			Staunton CUSD 6	Spring Bluff R-XV	Aviston SD 21
			St. Clair R-XIII	Mount Olive CUSD 5	Germantown SD 60
			St. Charles R-VI	Strain-Japan R-XVI	Damiansville SD 62
				Freeburg CCSD 70	O'Fallon CCSD 90
				Harmony Emge SD 175	Clayton
				Whiteside SD 115	Kirkwood R-VII
				Bond County CUSD 2	Francis Howell R-III
				Pontiac-W Holliday SD 105	Ft. Zumwalt R-II
				Hillsboro R-III	Rockwood R-VI
				Valley R-VI	Albers SD 63
				Affton 101	St. Rose SD 14-15
				Jefferson Co. R-VII	Waterloo CUSD 5
				Lindbergh Schools	Highland CUSD 5
					Columbia CUSD 4
					Ladue
					Millstadt CCSD 160
					Bartelso SD 57
					Smithton CCSD 130
					Shiloh Village SD 85

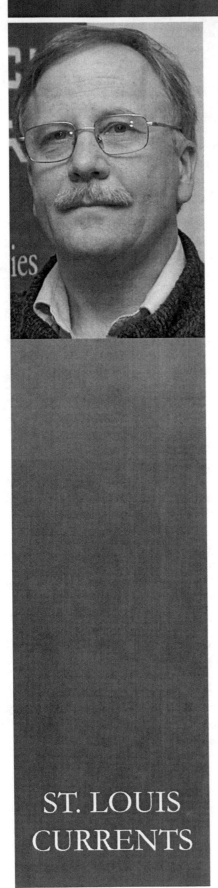

About the Author

Mark Tranel, Ph.D., is director of the Public Policy Research Center (PPRC) at the University of Missouri–St. Louis, where he has worked for over twenty years, serving as its director since 2003. He has been the principal investigator or project manager on over seventy research projects covering a wide range of disciplines, and has conducted a number of applied research projects in the areas of business development and demographic studies of the St. Louis metropolitan area. Dr. Tranel has conducted evaluations of early childhood education programs, public housing redevelopment projects, collaboration among educational institutions, impediments to fair housing, health promotion among noncustodial fathers, state funding of transportation, and services provided to families at risk of the children being placed in foster care, among others. He teaches Evaluation Research Methods in the UMSL Public Policy Administration Program and is the editor of the third volume in the St. Louis Metromorphosis Series, *St. Louis Plans*. He serves on the board of directors of a number of nonprofit organizations and on the Special Administrative Board of the Riverview Gardens School District.

ST. LOUIS
CURRENTS

Urban Green Space

Forest Park is one of the country's fine urban parks, and is certainly the jewel in St. Louis's crown. It is only one of many open and accessible green spaces that add to the quality of life in the region.

John Wagner's essay provides a thoughtful look at the region's open spaces and how they enhance life in the twenty-first century. The region's systems of parks and trails not only give meaningful areas for recreation, they also provide environmental benefit and economic impact.

The resulting "civic environmentalism" from the region's shared green space is an important mechanism for guiding the region's development and building a better place in which everyone can live.

The Region's Parks and Their Impact

John Loren Wagner, Ph.D.

As urban areas become larger and more spread out, communities throughout our region and nation have developed a renewed interest in understanding the relationship between cities and the open spaces within them. Eighty percent of people in the United States now live in metropolitan areas,[1] and many of these city residents experience open spaces and nature through their community's park system.

City parks in the United States run the gamut in size. The fifty largest cities alone (excluding their suburbs) contain more than 600,000 acres of open space, with parks ranging in size from the jewel-like 1.7-acre Post Office Square in Boston to the vast 24,000-acre Franklin Mountain State Park in El Paso, Texas[2]. St. Louis mirrors this range, with the 1.50-acre Pontiac Square Park in Soulard to the nearly 1,300-acre Forest Park on the city's western border.[3]

The St. Louis metropolitan region has a vast array of parks and open spaces beyond the city of St. Louis. The St. Louis County Department of Parks and Recreation provides a broad range of leisure activities beyond those traditionally associated with urban and suburban parks. Across the Missouri River, the St. Charles County Parks and Recreation Department was created by a vote of the county's residents in 1997[4], demonstrating significant interest in the community to foster these amenities for the benefit of St. Charles County residents. In western Illinois, known as the Metro East portion of the region, the municipalities of Madison and St. Clair Counties offer a variety of parks and trails for the benefit of their residents. These parks, along with national, state, and municipal parks, provide the residents of the St. Louis region with a variety of opportunities to enjoy the natural, ecological, civic, and financial benefits their parks have to offer.

Although the idea of nature in our urban areas is not new, recent research has reinforced previous theories with evidence of benefits that demonstrate the major role parks play in urban regeneration initiatives that contribute to healthier, more connected, and socially vibrant communities. Collectively, urban parks provide playfields, teach ecology, offer exercise trails, mitigate flood waters, host concerts and plays, protect wildlife, supply space for gardens, and give a respite from city life, among many other activities.[5] Parks also support the ecological health of urban environment as they cool the surroundings, help reduce pollution, and assist with stormwater management.[6] A growing body of research shows that contact with the natural world improves our physical and psychological health.[7]

Economic and social benefits are also provided by urban parks. Property values tend to increase in neighborhoods surrounding parks. Parks also support economic revitalization and recovery efforts as cities showcase these green spaces to attract and retain businesses, residents, and tourism.[8]

Among the most important benefits of city parks, and perhaps the most difficult to quantify, is the role they serve in community development. Parks generate valuable contributions to larger urban policy objectives, including job opportunities, youth development, public health, and community building. These contributions help strengthen the fabric of the neighborhoods and the communities in which parks are located.[9] Urban parks make inner-city neighborhoods more livable. They offer recreational opportunities for children, youth, and families. They also provide places within urban neighborhoods where people from all socioeconomic levels can experience a sense of community.

The significant role of public parks in the St. Louis region cannot be underestimated. From the natural and recreational amenities to their role in bringing people together, orchestrating face-to-face interaction and strengthening community, parks serve a vital function within each community.

Parks in the St. Louis Region

The city of St. Louis Department of Parks, Recreation, and Forestry has 111 parks under its jurisdiction, comprising 3,250 acres.[10] The crown jewel of the city's park system, and one of the most popular destinations in the region, is Forest Park. Opened to the public on June 24, 1876, Forest Park is one of the largest urban parks in the United States. At 1,293 acres, it is approximately 500 acres larger than Central Park in New York. It hosted the Louisiana Purchase Exposition (World's Fair) in 1904, which attracted more than twenty million visitors from around the world.[11] Like many urban parks in the United States, the end of the twentieth found dwindling resources for urban parks, leading to a sharp decline in the condition of Forest Park. With community support, the park changed course. As embodied in the 1995 master plan for Forest Park, and with continuing support of the city and the region, Forest Park has been revitalized and today attracts more than twelve million visitors a year.[12] It is home to the region's major cultural institutions – the Zoo, Art Museum, History Museum, Science Center, and the Muny Opera—and also provides opportunities for golf, tennis, baseball, bicycling, boating, fishing, handball, ice skating, and rollerblading, along with opportunities to experience nature. Forest Park is a unique institution and recognized as an important gathering place for residents across the region.

With its opening in 1838, Lafayette Park is not only St. Louis's oldest park, but one of the first parks west of the Mississippi. This nearly thirty-acre park was named to honor Marquis de Lafayette, a French statesman who served as a volunteer under General George Washington in the Continental Army during the American Revolution.[13] Lafayette Park serves as the anchor of the popular Lafayette Square neighborhood.

About three miles south of Forest Park, residents can visit the 289-acre Tower Grove Park, which opened on October 20, 1868, eight years before Forest Park was dedicated. While the land was conveyed to the city of St. Louis by Henry Shaw, Tower Grove Park is governed by a special board of commissioners appointed by the Missouri Supreme Court and supported by the Friends of Tower Grove Park, a not-for-profit organization established in 1988 to support the park's restoration. Today, Tower Grove Park is a National Historic Landmark and includes more than 7,500 trees comprised of 325 tree species.[14]

In 1874, the Missouri legislature established land for three parks in what was then St. Louis County: O'Fallon Park in northern St. Louis County, Forest Park in the center, and Carondelet Park in the south.[15] Of the three, Forest Park opened first in 1876. The 127-acre O'Fallon Park followed next, opening in 1908. Finally, Carondelet Park opened in 1929, and is currently ranked as the city's third–largest park with 180 acres. Each of these parks provides recreational opportunities and access to nature for St. Louis's residents.

CityGarden is one of St. Louis's newest parks and is truly urban in nature. Situated downtown, this 2.9-acre park located on Market Street between 8th and 10th Streets, provides trees, green space, fountains, wading pools, sculptures, and artwork for the enjoyment of those residents, workers, and visitors traversing the heart of the city. CityGarden is a part of the larger Gateway Mall project, originally conceived in St. Louis's comprehensive plan of 1907. This plan and the mall project embraced City Beautiful principles, which allowed for a linear open green space, one block wide, from the Gateway Arch at Memorial Drive to Union Station at 20th Street.

The St. Louis County Parks and Recreation Department was founded in 1950 and manages 70 parks on 12,700 acres of land situated in the 524 square-miles that comprise St. Louis County, Missouri.[16] Nearly twelve million people use a St. Louis County Park annually for passive recreation including biking, walking, using playgrounds, playing tennis, and cross-country skiing, as well as basketball, swimming, ice skating, soccer, archery, shelter rentals, and concerts.[17]

St. Louis County parks have developed over the years through a variety of means. The department acquired Sylvan Springs Park and the first part of Jefferson Barracks Park as surplus federal lands. West Tyson Park and Lone Elk Park were later acquired from a former federal munitions depot. The department also benefited from the personal generosity of county residents. Buder Park was given in 1954 by the estate of Gustav A. Buder Sr. in memory of his wife, Lydia. John Allen Love donated Love Park in 1959 and Janet Bissell Dimond bequeathed the Bissell House to the Parks and Recreation Department in 1961. Also, in 1968 Laumeier Sculpture Park was a bequest of Matilda Laumeier, and Greensfelder Park came from the Regional Planning and Conservation Foundation. Leicester Busch Faust and his wife, Mary, gave one hundred acres for Faust Park in 1968 to forever preserve the original estate of Missouri's second governor, Frederick Bates. The couple then doubled the size of Faust Park to two hundred acres in 1996 with a second bequest. The bond issue of 1969 provided $25 million for the purchase of Queeny Park, which serves as the home of the Greensfelder Recreation Complex and Dog Museum.[18]

The St. Louis County Parks and Recreation Department is unique among park agencies throughout the region and the country. While most of its parks provide traditional urban or suburban park amenities, several are quite distinct in their use, offering a unique experience to park visitors.

Lone Elk Park is a wildlife management area, with bison, wild turkey, waterfowl, elk, and deer. The park is heavily fenced in order to keep the wildlife inside the park. Dogs are not allowed in the park, even if riding in a car. Laumeier Sculpture Park is an outdoor sculpture park and open air museum located on 105-acres of land, and attracts more than 300,000 visitors annually.[19] The Museum of Transportation is perhaps the most unique of the department's seventy parks. Founded in 1944 by a group of historically minded citizens who had acquired the mule-drawn streetcar Bellefontaine, the 129-acre museum houses what has been recognized as one of the largest and best collections of transportation vehicles in the world. In 1948, the Transport Museum Association (TMA) incorporated as a nonprofit educational organization to better serve the financial and volunteer needs of the museum. On September 1, 1979, the St. Louis County Department of Parks and Recreation formally assumed operation of the museum, accepting it as a gift from the original founders.[20]

Looking east across the Mississippi River to Illinois, Madison and St. Clair Counties provide an abundance of recreational opportunities for their residents. The thirty-seven municipalities and the Madison County Government offer a variety of open space opportunities with sixty-five parks and a system of trails managed by Madison County Transit.[21] St. Clair County features forty-seven parks throughout the county's thirty-two municipalities.[22]

National and State Parks

While the governance structure and some amenities are different in state and national parks, these areas still provide environmental and social benefits to the region and residents who visit these parks. There are two national parks in the St. Louis region: the Ulysses S. Grant National Historic Site in south St. Louis County and the Jefferson National Expansion Memorial, better known as the Gateway Arch.[23] Both parks offer cultural and historical amenities rather than the natural amenities provided by many of the region's other parks and conservation areas.

The iconic Arch is just as wide as it is tall—630 feet, or 63 stories. Completed in 1967, the Arch is part of a larger memorial situated on 91 acres in downtown St. Louis adjacent to the Mississippi River. Other elements include the Old Courthouse and Luther Ely Smith Square,[24] the park-like setting between the Arch and the Old Courthouse. The Jefferson National Expansion Memorial was designated a National Historic Landmark in 1987.

State parks are also prominent throughout the St. Louis region. There are nineteen Missouri state parks in the St. Louis region,[25] as well as numerous areas managed by the Missouri Department of Conservation. Powder Valley Nature Center in Kirkwood in the heart of St. Louis County provides hikers and nature lovers with 112 acres of oak hickory forest to explore. Further west in St. Louis County, the Dr. Edmund A. Babler Memorial State Park contains 888 acres of wooded green space easily accessible from the surrounding suburban landscape. The Columbia Bottom Conservation Area in north St. Louis County encompasses land adjacent to the confluence of the Missouri and Mississippi Rivers. The Missouri Conservation Department purchased these 4,318 acres in 1997 to create an urban conservation area that includes a view of the confluence of the Missouri and Mississippi Rivers, more than 6.5 miles of river frontage, about 800 acres of bottomland forest, and a 110-acre island.[26]

There are twenty-eight state parks in Illinois's west central Region, which encompasses the Metro East part of the St. Louis region. Most prominent among these parks is Horseshoe Lake in Madison County, which offers a wide variety of recreational and hiking opportunities on 2,960 acres of land.[27]

There are countless other parks managed by individual municipalities throughout the region, and it is these parks, located closer to residents' homes in their own city or neighborhood, that likely provide the greatest social and economic benefits. Further, when considered collectively, these local parks may also provide significant environmental benefits as well.

Environmental/Ecological Benefits of Parks

There are numerous environmental and ecological benefits provided by urban parks, including pollution abatement, stormwater management, and cooling of the urban heat island.[28] Parks generate these benefits through the care and maintenance of its trees.

It has been estimated that if a city's tree canopy is increased by five percent in urban areas, temperatures will fall between 2 and 4 degrees Fahrenheit, as the tree foliage helps reduce the ambient air temperature.[29] Trees in the parks also sequester ("lock up") carbon dioxide (CO_2) in their roots, trunks, stems, and leaves as they grow, and in wood products after they are harvested. This improves air quality in the process.[30] But not all trees sequester CO_2 at the same rate as they age, an important aspect to consider in park management.

Figure 1 illustrates the pounds of CO_2 sequestered per tree annually as it matures.[31] "DBH"—the "diameter at breast height"—is an indicator of the age of a tree. For example, a 6-inch DBH tree is a much younger tree than a 27-inch DBH tree. The graphic shows a wide-ranging ability of individual species to sequester CO_2 as they mature. The northern red oak ranked far ahead of the other species listed.[32] The American elm actually started out by sequestering more CO_2 than the northern red oak at 6-inch DBH, but quickly levels out and does not sequester much more CO_2 in its mature stage.

Figure 1. Pounds of CO_2 Sequestered Per Tree Annually by Species (Wagner, 2013)

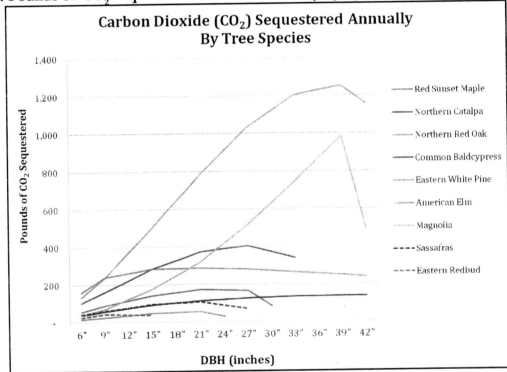

If sequestering CO_2 was all park managers were interested in accomplishing with a tree planting campaign, we would see many more oak trees planted throughout our urban parks. While these numbers can be useful in knowing how much CO_2 is being sequestered, other issues need to be considered as well. For example, the eastern white pine, while ranking low in CO_2 sequestration (one of the lowest of the nine shown in Figure 1) due to the fact that it has needles instead of

Biodiversity

Traditional landscape designs in parks have historically promoted the wide-scale replacement of native plant species in favor of exotic species that originated and evolved elsewhere, resulting in the establishment of invasive plants and animals in many parks and surrounding regions. The bias toward landscaping with introduced ornamentals has been so complete that suburban and urban ecosystems throughout the United States are now dominated by plant species that originated in Southeast Asia, Europe, and South America.[37]

The lack of native plants affects the park's animal population as they depend on plants for food and shelter. Reversing this trend can be promoted by planting the appropriate species of native trees. Figure 4 emphasizes the importance of tree species biodiversity and its relation to providing habitat for and attracting wildlife. This graph, derived from Tallamy and Shropshire's research (2008), shows the number of species in the listed genera that serve as host trees for species of Lepidoptera—butterfly and moth larvae—which are in turn important pollinators and food sources for birds and other animals.[38]

Figure 4. Tree Species by Genera That Are Host to Lepidoptera Species. (Tallamy and Shropshire, 2008)

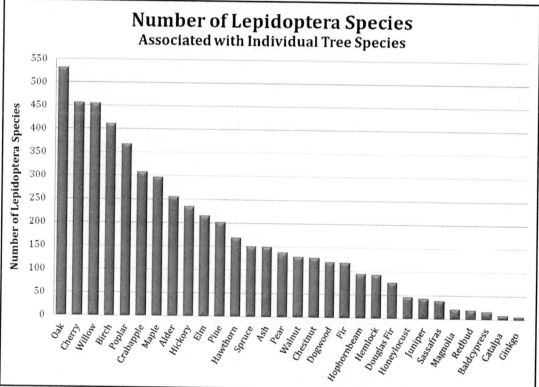

Wakeman (2009) points out that lepidopteran larvae (caterpillars) are extremely valuable sources of food for many terrestrial birds, particularly warblers and neotropical migrants. Tallamy and Shropshire's work (2008) categorizes native and alien plant genera in terms of their ability to support insect herbivores and, by inference, overall biodiversity. They ranked all native plant genera by the number of Lepidoptera species recorded using them as host plants. Ensuring that tree species in these genera and others are kept healthy would support and attract an increasing diversity of wildlife to urban and suburban parks.

Large Urban Parks

Large urban parks, such as Forest Park and Powder Valley Nature Center, function differently than the smaller neighborhood or "pocket" parks. In addition to their social and cultural impacts, large parks are also valued for their greater ecological function. They store and process stormwater more effectively, cool air temperature in the surrounding area more efficiently, and provide habitat for a wider array of plant and animal populations.[39] Large amounts of land are necessary to produce the effects of nature and to design a natural system that is ecologically sustainable—that is, big enough to be its own ecosystem.[40]

Larger parks also provide habitat for a wider array of plant and animal populations. This aspect is particularly important in maintaining or increasing biodiversity in urban areas, where the effects can extend beyond the boundary of the park. An example of this would be the case of bird populations that nest in the park and pollinate plants beyond the park's boundaries.[41] Similarly, an animal that has a large range or one that occupies a large amount of space in the course of its daily activities would logically benefit from living in a larger park. Animals of this type might not even be able to exist in a smaller park.

Wagner's (2013) study of Forest Park as a "sustainable park" emphasizes the importance of using native plant species and providing the infrastructure to allow maximum environmental benefits. The landscape of a sustainable park is much different than the landscape of the earlier "pleasure ground" parks such as Central Park in New York City, or even Forest Park when it was first created.

The large urban parks of the late 1800s were the result of massive rock excavation and earth moving, after which most of the plantings consisted of exotic (nonnative) species. A contemporary sustainable park would be composed primarily of species native to the area that are more drought resistant and less expensive to maintain, enhancing the overall sustainability of the park. Visitors to the earlier pleasure ground parks mistakenly thought that these areas existed naturally, that they were simply there because the land was not developed with the surrounding area. These early parks were, in fact, created using a vast amount of resources. As Peter Harnick (2010, p. 3) points out, these parks were "about as natural as Disneyland."

Large parks remain fundamental to the present-day landscape, not only because they address the stormwater and pollution "filtration" functions for densely built urban centers, but also because they are distinct, memorable places. They have the ability to absorb the identity of a region or neighborhood as much as they project one, becoming socially and culturally recognizable places that are unique and irreproducible.[42] Large parks are more difficult to finance and maintain, particularly if they are maintained by municipal governments, although state and national parks are not immune to budget cuts. Large parks are characterized by greater ecological complexity, along with more diverse and dispersed programs, which combine to put significant management pressure on their public sponsors. At the same time, large parks serve more diverse constituencies reflective of the communities surrounding them. While a smaller park might be situated within a coherent and often homogeneous neighborhood, larger parks are typically adjacent to several different communities and embedded within a larger region, so are required to serve more diverse socioeconomic groups.[43]

Social and Economic Benefits of Parks

Parks provide public spaces for residents to assemble and experience a sense of nature in the urban environment. The role of urban parks is evolving to include "community development tool" to its already substantial list of benefits. Urban parks offer a variety of ways to *physically* connect with nature and other people from the local community. In large, densely populated cities, public parks are among the community's most highly valued assets, for the opportunities they afford for organized or spontaneous contact with other community members in a natural setting.

Urban parks also provide economic benefits in the form of increased property values for both residential and commercial sites, as well as enhanced revenues in surrounding neighborhoods. The City Parks Alliance notes that proximity to an urban park can boost residential property values by as much as 15 percent.

McCormack et al (2010) highlight the importance of social environments for park use. Specifically, the sociodemographic characteristics of surrounding neighborhoods, as well as the presence of community groups as park users and in park governance, can influence how people perceive a park. Low, Taplin, and Scheld (2005) note that involving community members in park planning and ongoing management activities may result in parks that more effectively balance the needs of specific population groups. In addition, involving community members in the planning process also provides a sense of place and guardianship over the park, contributing to greater use of the park's facilities and to higher levels of physical activity and better health across populations.

Wagner's (2013) study of Forest Park found that the 1995 Forest Park master plan that guides management of the park today was the result of numerous, often intense, public meetings about the park's use and future. Many who use the park today feel that this strong sense of ownership by the community throughout the planning process contributed to the success of the plan and the growing popularity of Forest Park today.

Civic Environmentalism

There is another benefit of urban parks, or more generally of nature and environmental awareness, that has been examined more frequently in the literature—the concept of *civic environmentalism*. More than thirty years of United States environmental policies were built on a "command and control" centralized model. These policies have produced a mixed record of environmental improvement.[44] While the air and water may be cleaner than they were several years ago, the level of biodiversity has decreased with a lagging interest in nature and the environment in general. There are numerous reasons for this lack of curiosity with nature, not the least of which is the digitalized, television-focused, computer-generated age in which we live. Shutkin (2000, p.122) adds ". . . with its emphasis on legal and technical solutions, mainstream-professional environmentalism has failed to encourage active political and civic participation." The result is a civilization that tolerates environmental degradation.

This lack of interest in civic affairs was highlighted by Robert Putnam (2000) in his book *Bowling Alone*, which documents how society is becoming increasingly disconnected from family, friends, and neighbors. Shutkin (2000) views civic environmentalism as having the capacity not only to achieve goals of environmental improvement, but to also reverse the trends discussed by Putnam. Indicators of civic health in a community, like the strength of social networks and associations, rates of employment and poverty, and the degree of participation in political and civic affairs, can serve as a useful proxy for more traditional environmental indicators, much as the level of pollutants indicates environmental health and stability. They are a benchmark by which environmental progress can be measured. Shutkin (2000) proposes a systems approach to civic affairs and nature, a "holistic approach," that appreciates how environmental problems and their solutions are directly linked to social, political, and economic issues. Not coincidentally, this "systems approach" is analogous to the concept of "ecology" as applied to contemporary management of natural resources.

Light (2002) believes that our relationship to nature is shaped locally in our everyday life, not in an occasional outing to a distant wilderness preserve or state or national park. Encouraging a direct participatory relationship between urban residents and the natural environment in neighborhood parks is one way of eliciting a sense of environmental stewardship. Light (2006) also asserts that communities that have a participatory relationship with the land around them are less likely to allow it to be harmed, in contrast with "top-down" regulations or mandates from a higher authority that may be ignored or opposed locally.

One way to encourage civic environmentalism in a community is to provide opportunities for residents to participate directly in restoration projects or other park activities, providing a foundation for something like "ecological citizenship."[45] These hands-on activities, what Light (2002) refers to as "the problem of dirty hands," have a way of encouraging the development of ecological citizenship. He also indicates that good restorations favor projects that produce good outcomes for nature and the park, and also good outcomes by forming stronger bonds between citizens.

Volunteers have proven to be invaluable to Forest Park and the St. Louis County Department of Parks and Recreation. Volunteer hours from 2006 to 2011 for Forest Park Forever, the nonprofit friends association formed to support the park, are shown in Figure 5, while volunteer hours for St. Louis County Parks are illustrated in Figure 6. Over the five-year time period for both organizations, the number of volunteer hours rose steadily each year, with a five-year increase of 41.4% for Forest Park Forever and 37.7% for St. Louis County Parks. While not all of the volunteer hours concerned environmental restoration and may not have advanced "ecological citizenship" as perceived by Light (2002), the volunteers' satisfaction for having donated their time and efforts most likely contributed to stronger ties to their colleagues and community.

Figure 5. Forest Park Forever Volunteer Hours, 2006 to 2011 (Wagner, 2013)

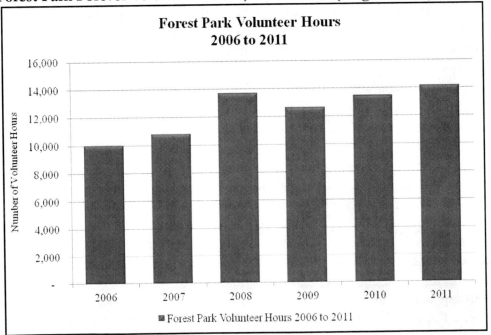

Figure 6. St. Louis County Department of Parks and Recreation Volunteer Hours, 2008 to 2013 (St. Louis County Parks and Recreation Annual Report, 2013)

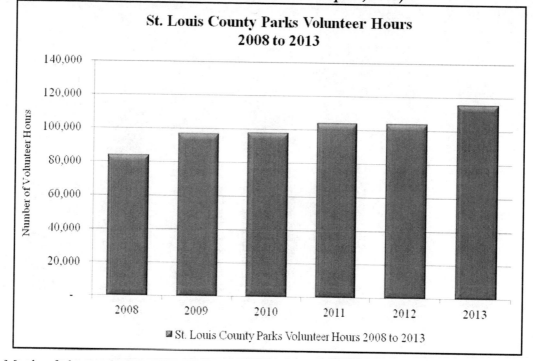

Much of the work done by volunteers in Forest Park and within the St. Louis County Parks system is work that would otherwise have been done by paid employees, so a significant financial value can be attributed to their work. As noted in Figures 8 and 9 for Forest Park Forever and St. Louis County, respectively, the volunteers' efforts added considerably to the budgets of these two organizations, more so with each passing year, even when adjusted for inflation.

While not specifically addressing volunteerism, Carl Leopold (2004), son of renowned environmentalist Aldo Leopold, offered this perspective about restoration activities: ". . . we see the mutually beneficial relationship that can come from restoration, which not only serves to increase the ecological quality of a site, but also generates environmental thinking on the part of the participant. Ecological restoration may be a prime way to educate people in developing an ethical attitude toward the land." (p. 152)

Figure 7. Financial Value of Forest Park Forever Volunteer Hours, 2006 to 2011 (Wagner, 2013)

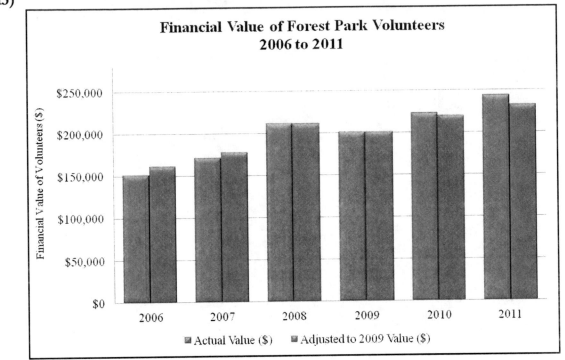

Figure 8. St. Louis County Department of Parks and Recreation Volunteer Hours, 2008 to 2013 (St. Louis County Parks and Recreation Annual Report, 2013)

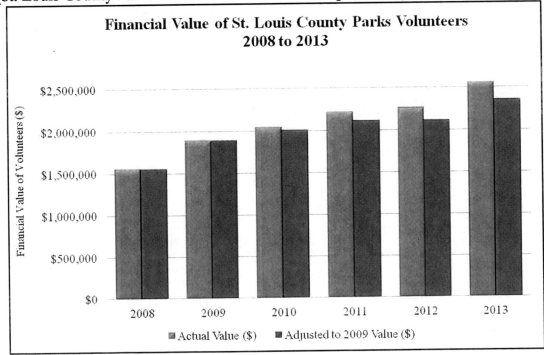

Nature-Human Relationship

The psychological and physiological benefits of parks and the nature they provide are equally as important as other benefits, although somewhat less understood. Just as Frederick Law Olmsted theorized in the 1870s when discussing Central Park, urban parks today provide restoration from mental fatigue caused by modern urban life.[46] There is increasing evidence that trees and vegetation provide benefits that are even more profound than the aesthetic and environmental benefits usually associated with the natural environment. For example, Dwyer, Schroeder, and Gobster (1994) argue that humans have very deep emotional, symbolic, and spiritual ties to trees. Also, Frumkin (2001) notes that contact with the natural environment may be directly beneficial to health. Positive physiological reactions, including lowered heartbeat and blood pressure, as well as calming effects have been recorded in people in response to urban scenes that contain trees, forests, and vegetation.[47] The benefits extend to psychological health as well. Environmental psychologist Rachel Kaplan (1983) has written, "Nature matters to people. Big trees and small trees, glistening water, chirping birds, budding bushes, colorful flowers—these are important ingredients in a good life." Howard Frumkin (2001) agrees, adding: "But perhaps these are more than aesthetic preferences. Perhaps humans find tranquility in certain natural environments—a soothing, restorative, and even a healing sense. If so, contact with nature might be an important component of well-being." (p. 234)

Mirroring the ecological importance of biodiversity, Miller (2005) adds that the loss of biodiversity, especially in urban areas, leads to the "extinction of experience," as yet another factor that contributes to the estrangement of people from nature.

There may also be certain innate ethical sensibilities that could be explored by contact with nature, particularly in parks that we have access to every day. Important theoretical foundations were laid in 1984 by Harvard biologist Edward O. Wilson (1984) when he hypothesized the existence of "biophilia," the innately emotional affiliation of human beings to other living organisms. The idea of biophilia suggests that humans have a "deep biological need for affiliating with life and nature" (Kellert, 1995, p. 26), the result of centuries of co-evolution and symbiotic interaction with nature and other life. As Stephen Kellert (1995) notes in his book *The Value of Life*, tapping into this need may take some work:

"Unlike the "hardwired" instincts of breathing or feeding, which occur almost automatically, the biophilic values must be cultivated to achieve their full expression. They depend on repeated exposure and social reinforcement before emerging as meaningful dimensions of human emotional and intellectual life. Once learned and supported, however, they become key elements of human personality and culture." (p. 26)

I can think of no better place to cultivate our own biophilic requirements than by visiting a nearby park in St. Louis.

Endnotes

1. Peter Harnik, 2006.
2. Peter Harnik, 2003.
3. Parks, Recreation, and Forestry, City of St. Louis.
4. Parks and Recreation, St. Charles County.
5. Peter Harnik,, 2003.
6. R.H. Piatt,, 1994 and P.M Sherer., 2006.
7. , P.M. Sherer., 2006.
8. Ibid.
9. C. Walker, 2004.
10. Parks, Recreation, and Forestry, City of St. Louis.
11. C. Loughlin & C. Anderson, 1986.
12. Parks, Recreation, and Forestry, City of St. Louis.
13. Ibid.
14. Tower Grove Park.
15. C. Loughlin.& C. Anderson1986.
16. Parks and Recreation: Annual Report 2013, St. Louis County.
17. Parks and Recreation: Annual Report 2013, St. Louis County.
18. Parks and Recreation, Saint Louis County, Missouri.
19. Laumeier Sculpture Park.
20. Transport Museum Association.
21. Madison County.
22. St. Clair County.
23. National Parks Conservation Association.
24. Luther Ely Smith was a St. Louis lawyer and civic booster. He is credited with bringing the competition of the Arch's design and is called by the National Park Service as the "father of the Jefferson National Expansion Memorial.
25. Missouri State Parks: St. Louis Region.
26. Missouri Department of Conservation.
27. Horseshoe Lake State Park (Madison County).
28. C.T. Ryan 2006; P.M. Sherer2006.
29. A. Garvin, 2008.
30. R.V. Pouyat et al., 2006 and D.J. Nowak and D.E. Crane, 2002.
31. Wagner, 2013.
32. Ibid. The application of the i-Tree model valued all oak species as having the same ability to sequester CO_2.
33. Technically the needles on all evergreen trees – pine, spruce and fir – are considered its leaves.
34. D.J. Nowak et al., 2006, Spirn, 1984, Alberti, 2008 and Garvin, 2008. In 1987, the U.S. Environmental Protection Agency (EPA) replaced the earlier Total Suspended Particulate (TSP) air quality standard with a PM-10 standard. The new standard focuses on smaller particles that are likely responsible for adverse health effects because of their ability to reach the lower regions of the respiratory tract. The PM-10 standard includes particles with a diameter of 10 micrometers or less (0.0004 inches or one-seventh the width of a human hair).
35. Wagner, 2013.
36. Wagner, 2013.
37. D.W. Tallamy and K.J. Shropshire, 2008.
38. A. Wakeman, 2009.
39. J. Corner, 2007.
40. J. Czerniak, 2007.
41. J. Corner, 2007.
42. A. Berrizbeitia, 2007.
43. J. Beardsley,2007.
44. C.T. Rubin, 2002.
45. A. Light, 2006.
46. T. Beatley & K. Manning,1997; R.L. Ryan, 2006. The rationale for this is not the same as it was in Olmsted's time. His goal was to provide a setting for proper socialization, part of which was relief from the urban scene. Nature asa relief from the urban setting today does not carry such connotations.
47. R.S. Ulrich, 1981.

Bibliography

Beardsley, John. "Conflict and Erosion: the Contemporary Public Life of Large Parks." *Large Parks* (2007): 198–213.

Beatley, Timothy. *The Ecology of Place: Planning for Environment, Economy, and Community.* Island Press, 1997.

Berrizbeitia, Anita. "Re-Placing Process." *Large Parks.* Princeton Architectural Press, New York (2007): 175–197.

Carr, Stephen, ed. *Public Space.* Cambridge University Press, 1992.

Corner, James. "Forward." *Large Parks.* Princeton Architectural Press, New York (2007): 19–34

Czerniak, Julia. "Speculating on Size." *Large Parks.* Princeton Architectural Press, New York (2007): 11–14

Frumkin, Howard. "Beyond Toxicity: Human Health and the Natural Environment." *American Journal of Preventive Medicine* 20(3) (2001): 234–240.

Garvin, Alexander. "Greening Cities: A Public Realm Approach." *Growing Greener Cities: Urban Sustainability in the Twenty-First Century.* University of Pennsylvania Press (2008): 60–83.

Harnik, Peter. "The Excellent City Park System: What Makes It Great and How to Get There." *The Human Metropolis: People and Nature in the 21st-Century City. University of Massachusetts Press* (2006): 47-60.

Harnik, Peter. *The Excellent City Park System: What Makes It Great and How to Get There.* Trust for Public Land, 2003.

"Horseshoe Lake—State Park (Madison County)." Illinois Department of Natural Resources. 2015. <http://dnr.state.il.us/lands/landmgt/parks/r4/horsesp.htm>

Kaplan, Rachel. "The Role of Nature in the Urban Context." *Behavior and the Natural Environment.* Springer US, 1983. 127–161.

Kellert, Stephen R. *The Value of Life: Biological Diversity and Human Society.* Island Press, 1997.

"Laumeier Sculpture Park." 2015. <http://www.laumeiersculpturepark.org>

Leopold, A. Carl. "Living with the Land Ethic." *BioScience* 54(2) (2004): 149–154.

Light, Andrew. "Ecological Citizenship: The Democratic Promise of Citizenship." *The Human Metropolis: People and Nature in the 21st Century City.* University of Massachusetts Press (2007): 169–182.

Light, Andrew. "Restoring Ecological Citizenship." *Democracy and the Claims of Nature* (2002): 153–172.

Loughlin, Caroline, and Catherine B. Anderson. *Forest Park.* University of Missouri Press, 1986.

Low, Setha, Dana Taplin, and Suzanne Scheld. *Rethinking Urban Parks: Public Space and Cultural Diversity.* University of Texas Press, 2009.

Madison County Website. *Parks and Recreation.* 2015. <http://www.madisoncountywebsite.com/Madison_County_Illinois_local_parks_recreat on_outdoors_amusement_wildlife _IL.html>.

McCormack, Gavin R., et al. "Characteristics of Urban Parks Associated with Park Use and Physical Activity: a Review of Qualitative Research." *Health & Place* 16(4) (2010): 712–726.

Miller, James R. "Biodiversity Conservation and the Extinction of Experience." *Trends in Ecology & Evolution* 20(8) (2005): 430-434.

Missouri Department of Conservation. 2015. < http://mdc4.mdc.mo.gov>

Missouri State Parks: St. Louis Region. *Missouri Department of Natural Resources.* 2015. <http://mostateparks.com/page/57758/st-louis-region>

National Parks Conservation Association. 2015. <http://www.npca.org/>

Nowak, David J., and Daniel E. Crane. "Carbon Storage and Sequestration by Urban Trees in the USA." *Environmental Pollution* 116(3) (2002): 381–389.

Parks, Recreation, and Forestry. The City of St. Louis, Missouri. 2015. <https://stlouis-mo.gov/government/ departments/parks/>

Parks and Recreation: Annual Report 2013. St. Louis County. 2013. <https://www.stlouisco.com/Portals/8/docs/Document Library/parks/PDFs/Publications/AR2013.pdf>

Parks and Recreation. Saint Louis County Missouri. St. Louis County Government, 2015. <http://www.stlouisco.com/parksandrecreation>

Park and Recreation. St. Charles County. CivicPlus, 2015. <http://parks.sccmo.org/parks/>

Parks and Recreation. St. Clair County Website. 2005. <http://www.stclaircountywebsite.com/StClair_County_Illinois_local_parks_recreation_ outdoors_amusement_lakes_nature_pre-serve_IL.html>

Piatt, R. H. " The Ecological City: Introduction and Overview." *The Ecological City: Preserving and Restoring Urban Biodiversity* (1994): 1–17

Pouyat, Richard V., Ian D. Yesilonis, and David J. Nowak. "Carbon Storage by Urban Soils in the United States." *Journal of Environmental Quality* 35(4) (2006): 1566–1575.

Rubin, Charles T. "Civic Environmentalism." *Democracy and the Claims of Nature: Critical Perspectives for a New Century* (2002): 335–351.

Ryan, Robert L. "The Role of Place Attachment in Sustaining Urban Parks." *The Human Metropolis: People and Nature in the 21st-Century City*. University of Massachusetts Press (2006): 61–74

Schroeder, H.W., and P.H. Gobster. 1994. "The Ecological City: Introduction and Overview." *The Ecological City: Preserving and Restoring Urban Biodiversity* (1994): 137–150

Sherer, P. M. "The Benefits of Parks: Why America Needs More City Parks and Open Space," The Trust for Public Land." *White Paper* (2006).

Shutkin, William A. *The Land That Could Be: Environmentalism and Democracy in the Twenty-First Century.* MIT Press, 2001.

Tallamy, Douglas W., and Kimberley J. Shropshire. "Ranking Lepidopteran Use of Native Versus Introduced Plants." *Conservation Biology* 23(4) (2009): 941–947.

Tower Grove Park. 2015. <http://www.towergrovepark.org/>

Transport Mueseum Association. 2015. <http://transportmuseumassociation.org/>

Ulrich, Roger S. "Natural Versus Urban Scenes Some Psychophysiological Effects." *Environment and Behavior* 13(5) (1981): 523–556.

Wagner, John L. "(Unpublished Doctoral Dissertation) Saint Louis University." "Evolution of a Sustainable Park: Forest Park, St. Louis, Missouri." St. Louis, 2004.

Wakeman, Ann. "Prairie Gardening with Propagated Plants." *Missouri Prairie Journal* 30(9) (2009): 6–13.

Walker, Chris. "The Public Value of Urban Parks: Beyond Recreation, a Broader View of Urban Parks." *The Urban Institute* (2004).

Wilson, Edward O. *Biophilia.* Harvard University Press, 1984.

About the Author

John Loren Wagner, Ph.D., is currently the Project Manager for Economic Development at the Bi-State Development Agency (Metro) in St. Louis and staffs the agency's Bi-State Development Research Institute. He has also worked in the St. Louis region as a City Planner in both the public and private sector, for the City of Chesterfield and at an area law firm. Dr. Wagner also spent four years as the Community Policy Director at FOCUS St. Louis.

With a particular interest in the environment, Dr. Wagner earned his doctorate of Public Policy in 2013. His dissertation explored the sustainability of Forest Park, a 1,300-acre urban park in the heart of metropolitan St. Louis. John is also an alumnus of the Land Ethic Leaders Program at the Aldo Leopold Foundation and is also a contributor to the Center for Humans and Nature, writing in 2013 on how nature is critical to a 21st century urban ethic. Dr. Wagner currently serves as the Board Chair of the St. Louis Metropolitan Research Exchange.

ST. LOUIS CURRENTS

The Global Environment at the Local Level

A century of industrial output has dramatically changed the region's environment. St. Louis reflects the consequences of its industrial legacy in many ways including site pollution, air quality, and even climate change.

John Posey examines the data on climate change in St. Louis. First, there is a deep analysis of the problem. Greenhouse gas emissions are measurable in St. Louis and their effects must be addressed. Second, there are ways to mitigate the changing environment. Stormwater management and wetland restoration are only two ideas explored.

The region need not be fatalistic about its future. There are strong coalitions and substantial projects at work regionally, and Posey gives cause for optimism about the region's future.

St. Louis in the Anthropocene: Responding to Global Environmental Change

John Posey, Ph.D.

Introduction

St. Louis is getting warmer and wetter. Recent decades have seen increases in average temperatures, and in extreme heat days. Average annual precipitation in the region is also increasing, as is the frequency of intense precipitation events. These trends present challenges to urban systems, including transportation, stormwater and public health. The changing local climate occurs in a broader context of global environmental change. The combination of climate change and destruction of habitat is causing a loss of biodiversity that may be unprecedented in human history.

The goal of this essay is twofold. First, it describes how climate change is affecting the St. Louis region, as well as projections for the future. Second, it discusses ways in which organizations in the St. Louis region are responding to challenges associated with global environmental change.

These efforts may be classified in three broad categories, although boundaries blur. Some, like the city of Creve Coeur, are actively working to reduce emissions that lead to climate change, an approach known as *greenhouse gas mitigation*. Others are engaged in reducing vulnerability to climate impacts. Although these efforts are generally not pursued with the explicit goal of reducing vulnerability to climate change, they still represent effective ways to make the region more resilient. This approach is known as *adaptation*. An example is the ambitious rainscaping project currently being pursued by the Metropolitan St.Louis Sewer District (MSD). A final approach is the *conservation and restoration* of habitats in the region. An example of a group pursuing this approach is the River des Peres Watershed Coalition.

Global environmental change is one of the defining features of the historical era in which we live.

Many St. Louis organizations are attempting to rise to the challenge, in a variety of ways. Although St. Louis residents may have little control over global greenhouse gas concentrations, many individuals and organizations are trying to do their part to protect the environment, and to cope with local consequences of global change.

Welcome to the Anthropocene

Stratigraphers, scientists who study layers in the earth's crust, are not normally known for shocking announcements. But in 2008, the Stratigraphy Commission of the Geological Society of London issued an opinion with startling implications: the Holocene epoch, which began at the end of the last ice age, has ended. A new geological epoch, the Anthropocene, has begun.

In dry scientific language, the commission laid out its finding that human-caused changes in sediment, biota, and geochemistry are sufficiently significant and well-established to warrant a new epoch in the geological time scale. Regarding changes in plant and animal species, the commission found:

The combination of extinctions, global species migrations and the widespread replacement of natural vegetation with agricultural monocultures is producing a distinctive contemporary biostratigraphic signal. These effects are permanent, as future evolution will take place from surviving (and frequently anthropogenically relocated) stocks.[1]

One of the most significant drivers of environmental change is greenhouse gas emissions. In preindustrial times, the concentration of atmospheric carbon dioxide (CO_2) was 280 parts per million. In 2013, the concentration passed 400 parts per million.[2] It has been well understood for over a century that greenhouse gases make life on earth possible by trapping infrared radiation. In the 1890s, Svante Arrhenius, the first Swede to win the Nobel Prize in physics, calculated that a doubling of CO_2 in the atmosphere would result in a temperature increase of several degrees, a hypothesis that has been supported by recent experience.[3] In addition to changing average temperatures and shifting precipitation patterns, greenhouse gases also alter the carbon cycle, resulting in ocean acidification and other ecological stresses. The recently released National Climate Assessment found that "never before have such rapid, global-scale changes occurred during the history of human civilization."[4]

Land use change also creates stress on human systems and ecosystems. This includes the clearing of native forest and grassland resulting in habitat destruction and fragmentation, as well as the destruction of wetlands and floodplains through development and channelization. Land use change interacts with climate change. For example, the combination of land use and climate change has led to changes in flooding frequency and severity, as well as to habitat loss.[5]

Local and Global Environmental Change

Trends

Since 1980, average annual temperature has been increasing by more than a twentieth of a degree (F) per year. Table 1 shows average temperatures by decade. Before 1990, only one decade, the dustbowl era 1930s, experienced a decade with average temperatures in excess of 57° F. Both the 1990s and the first decade of the twenty-first century surpassed this threshold, and thus far, average temperatures in the current decade are even warmer.[6]

Figure 1 provides another view of trends in annual average temperatures. Over the last 120 years, there have been warm decades and cool decades. The 1930s was an unusually warm period, and the decade from the mid-1960s through the mid-1970s was unusually cool. For the entire period of 1893–2013, the trend line is flat. Since 1980, however, there has been a significant upward trend. The number of years exceeding the long term average has been twice as common in the last 30 years as in the previous 91. The last 30 years are warmer than previous decades even if we compare the last three decades with the period 1893–1960 to exclude the cooler period of the 1960s and 1970s. There have also been fewer cool years in recent decades, with only one year since 1980 showing an average temperature less than 55□. In the period of 1893–1980, and even in the 1893–1960 periods, cooler temperatures were more common.

downscaled projections found unanimous agreement among models and downscaling methods that temperatures would be projected to rise more than 2° under the A2 scenario.[13] Seventeen of the 18 outputs projected temperatures rising more that 3°, with most in the 4° to 5° range. Under the B1 scenario, temperature increases were somewhat lower, although 9 out of 10 statistically downscaled results projected increases greater than 3°.[14] Projected increases in summer temperatures were greater with each of the 8 dynamically downscaled results and 8 of the 10 statistically downscaled outputs, projecting increases greater than 3.5° under the A2 scenario.

There is also broad agreement among downscaled projections that rising global greenhouse gas concentrations would be associated with increases in average annual precipitation in the St. Louis region. Under the A2 scenario, 6 out of 8 dynamically downscaled results and 9 out of 10 statistically downscaled results projected an increase in precipitation under the A2 scenario. For the B1 scenario, 8 out of 10 models projected increased precipitation. In addition, all but two of the 18 downscaled outputs projected increases in days with more than an inch of precipitation under the A2 scenario. Statistically downscaled results for the B1 scenario projected changes in the same direction as the A2 scenario, albeit lower in magnitude.

Impacts

Several different types of climate impacts on urban systems and populations have been identified. Hotter temperatures, especially in summer, can have several types of health impacts.[15] First, hotter summer temperatures are associated with heat-related illness. Second, warmer temperatures can change the geographic distribution of infectious diseases. Third, hotter summers reduce air quality, with potential impacts on individuals with respiratory conditions such as asthma.

Changes in temperature and precipitation also affect agriculture.[16] While some plants benefit from longer growing seasons, as well as from additional CO_2 in the atmosphere, the benefits are offset by heat stress and changing precipitation patterns. The 2014 National Climate Assessment concludes that, on balance, the impacts on agriculture are negative.

Warmer temperatures also affect energy use, requiring less heat in the winters, and more air conditioning in summers.[17] Warmer temperatures can also impact the transportation system by causing material stress on pavement and bridge expansion joints.[18]

In the St. Louis region, some of the most readily observed impacts are associated with stormwater management. Increases in winter and spring precipitation suggest a rising risk of riverine flooding, which heightens the urgency of repairing the region's urban levees.[19,20] An increase in days with more than an inch of precipitation suggests a rising risk of flash floods.[21]

There has been a clear increase in flooding on the Mississippi River at St. Louis.[22] In the thirty years between 1984 and 2013, flood stage was exceeded 54 times. In the previous thirty years, 1954–1983, there were only 23 recorded crests above flood stage. From 1924–1953, there were 24 crests that exceeded flood stage. It should be noted that much of the increase in riverine flood frequency is attributable to land use change rather than climate change.[23] Levee systems built over the last century have destroyed about half of the Mississippi River's floodplain, constricting the river flow and leading to higher river stages. However, research indicates that both climate change and land use change are responsible for a significant fraction of change in streamflow on the Mississippi River.[24]

Trends in flash flooding are not as well documented. There is no entity that systematically collects information on homes or cars that are damaged in flash flooding. Available news reports, however, indicate that flash flooding leads to significant damage. From April 2013 to April 2014, there were at least four storms leading to flash flooding in the St. Louis metropolitan area. These storms forced evacuations or damaged cars in Jefferson County, West Alton, University City, the city of St. Louis, East St. Louis, and eastern St. Clair County.[25,26,27,28,29]

Other evidence comes from the Missouri Department of Transportation's (MODOT) Twitter feed.[30] MODOT's Intelligent Transportation System monitors conditions throughout the region using cameras and monitors linked to a traffic management system via fiber optics. The Traffic Management Center sends Twitter alerts when roadways are closed due to flooding. According to the MODOT Twitter feed, there were 18 road closures due to flooding between April 2013 and April 2014. This count may underestimate the actual number of streets affected, as MODOT does not monitor local streets in subdivisions. While there is no available data on long-term trends in road closings, MODOT data indicates that flash floods disrupt transportation networks on a regular basis.

MSD data on sewer overflows also provide a means to estimate the magnitude of problems caused by flash flooding. In 2013 there were 15 days on which precipitation, as measured at Lambert International Airport, exceeded an inch. Each of these days was associated with multiple sewer overflows. Together, these 15 rain events coincided with more than 750 separate overflows of combined sewer systems.[31,32] Combined sewer overflows are a major water pollution concern. It is not known how many of these storms created a buildup of water on streets or damage to the built environment.

In other parts of the country, the most pressing challenges associated with climate change include, depending on the location, sea level rise, wildfire, or agricultural impacts. For an urban region in the middle of a continent, stormwater management issues are among the most frequent climate-related challenges. As precipitation in general, and extreme precipitation events in particular, are projected to increase in coming decades, stormwater management issues can reasonably be expected to assume greater urgency.

Climate change in St. Louis takes place in the context of global environmental change.

Since the dramatic increase in speciation known as the Cambrian Explosion, there have been five major extinction events, the most recent of which was the asteroid-induced mass extinction that killed the dinosaurs sixty-five million years ago. Recently observed extinctions have led prominent scientists to ask whether the earth is now experiencing a "sixth extinction."[33,34] It should be noted that it is very difficult to estimate both the current number of species, as well as extinction rates.[35] It is also the case that a focus on extinctions can lead to understating a serious loss of biodiversity; a remnant of a few hundred individual members of a species can survive for long periods, even after becoming locally extinct in numerous ecosystems. For these reasons, it is not clear that "sixth extinction" rhetoric is the most useful way to characterize the ongoing loss of global biodiversity.

Still, there is evidence across a broad range of indicators that significant degradations of biodiversity are occurring.[36] Indicators include extinction risk, habitat loss, invasive species, overexploitation, and climate change impacts. A critical question is how many species can be preserved in the face of ongoing pressures on biodiversity.

Responding to environmental change

Mitigation

At least seventeen local governments in the region have signed the Mayors' Agreement on Climate Protection.[37] This agreement, drafted by the U.S. Conference of Mayors, includes a pledge to advocate for federal and state action to limit greenhouse gas emissions, as well as commitments to conduct a greenhouse gas inventory detailing sources of emissions, and to develop a municipal climate action plan. The agreement also commits signers to seeking ways to reduce energy use in municipal buildings and fleets, to promote alternative modes of transportation, and to support urban forestry.

The city of Creve Coeur has been a regional leader in the effort to reduce greenhouse gas emissions. Creve Coeur adopted a climate protection plan in 2010.[38] The plan included a greenhouse gas inventory, as well as a commitment to reduce community-wide emissions by 20% by 2015. Among the action items in the plan are public education and awareness campaigns, and directives to seek energy conservation opportunities in municipal facilities. Since adopting the plan, the city has taken several steps.[39] These include installing decorative LED lighting on Olive Boulevard, which reduced electricity use by 70%; installing a new energy efficient boiler and water heater in the government center; and installing energy efficient lighting fixtures at municipal facilities. In addition, installation of radiant heating at public works facilities reduced winter gas bills by 75%.

Nongovernmental actors also promote conservation and the use of alternative energy. Ameren, the region's leading electrical utility, offers programs to encourage the use of more energy efficient appliances. Ameren has also expanded its use of renewable energy, including construction of a 5.7 megawatt solar energy center with 19,000 panels, expected to begin electrical production by the end of 2014.[40] Utilities in Missouri have an incentive to increase use of alternative fuels thanks to Proposition C, enacted by voters in 2008, which mandates that 15% of electricity come from renewables by the year 2021. In addition, the Missouri Gateway chapter of the U.S. Green Business Council promotes the use of Leadership in Energy and Environmental Design (LEED) standards in new construction.

On June 18, 2014, the U.S. Environmental Protection Agency (EPA) released a proposed rule that would require states to reduce the carbon intensity of electrical power plants.[41] In Missouri, the proposed rule would reduce carbon intensity by 21%; for Illinois, the reduction amounts to 33%. At this writing, the rule has not been promulgated, and is still subject to change. States would be allowed to determine what methods to use in achieving the new standard. If, as expected, the new rule goes into effect, mitigation activities in the region may be expected to expand dramatically.

Adaptation

Greenhouse gas emissions are a global problem. While citizens of every region have a role to play in reducing emissions, mitigation efforts in the St. Louis region will not, by themselves, dramatically change global atmospheric greenhouse gas levels. However, through its choice of adaptation measures, regional actors have a significant level of control over the level of vulnerability to climate change impacts.

Considerable uncertainty exists about future climatic conditions. The uncertainty results both from the impossibility of predicting future emissions, and from the impossibility of perfectly capturing future conditions using models. While there can be a fairly high level of confidence regarding the direction of change, particularly with respect to global temperatures, the magnitude of the change is less clear.

There is a temptation to use a "predict and plan" method of adjusting to future climatic conditions. This approach would create a best estimate of future conditions, and plan for that contingency. Given the level of uncertainty, however, the most rational choice may be one that performs adequately across a range of possible scenarios. The phrase "no regrets option" refers to activities that yield net benefits even in the most minimal climate change scenario. One approach to climate adaptation is to look for options that are justified by current levels of climate vulnerability, and that would pay greater benefits as the climate continues to change.[42]

Many organizations in the St. Louis region are taking steps to make the region less vulnerable to challenges associated with climate change, particularly the increased frequency of heavy precipitation events. These activities are undertaken in response to current conditions, not in anticipation of future conditions. Such measures still constitute effective climate adaptation. Activities such as rainscaping make the region more resilient to current challenges, and can be expected to become even more important as the climate changes. Activities of four organizations are discussed below: the Metropolitan St. Louis Sewer District (MSD), Heartlands Conservancy, Forest ReLeaf, and the city of St. Louis.

MSD is currently implementing a plan known as Project Clear. The plan was developed under a court order to eliminate overflows in sewers that carry both stormwater and raw sewage. As part of the implementation plan, MSD is undertaking a comprehensive redesign of the stormwater management system serving the city of St. Louis and most of St. Louis County. In total, the cost is expected to be $4.7 billion over twenty-three years.[43]

While much of Project Clear addresses structural infrastructure issues, a significant amount is also being devoted to measures aimed at reducing the quantity of stormwater entering streams and sewers. MSD is currently investing $100 million in rainscaping in an area that covers most of the city of St. Louis, plus a few adjacent suburbs. The project uses vacant or abandoned land to create attractive public spaces that also help avoid excessive runoff by capturing stormwater in the ground close to where it falls.

A rain garden is a depressed area that is designed to absorb rainwater runoff. The MSD rainscaping effort is creating rain gardens with amended soils and native plants to maximize runoff absorption. The rain gardens range in size from a single lot to an entire block. After construction of each rain garden, MSD is committed to maintaining the property, as well as to testing and monitoring.

The rainscaping does not preclude future redevelopment of the parcels used for raingardens. Development agreements are recorded with each parcel used specifying the area of impervious surfaces allowed in future development. The agreements specify that the roof drain not be connected to the sewer, and requires MSD review and permitting. All future owners will be bound by these conditions. By using green roofs, porous pavements, and rain barrels, future development can comply with these conditions while preserving the parcel as a stormwater management asset for the community.

Urban forestry plays an important role in enhancing the resilience of communities. Street trees provide benefits in stormwater management and road maintenance. They also act as a carbon sink, and counteract the tendency of urban areas to retain heat, a phenomenon known as the urban heat island effect. A study of urban forestry benefits in Kansas City found that street trees retain 600 million gallons of stormwater each year, and can reduce the urban heat island effect by 10 to 15 degrees. Trees shading asphalt save the city up to 60% of road maintenance costs over thirty years. Trees also improve urban air quality.[44]

Forest ReLeaf of Missouri is an organization that has promoted urban forestry in the St. Louis region since 1993. Over the last twenty years, the organization has distributed more than 120,000 trees at low or no cost.[45] Through Project Communitree, Forest ReLeaf distributes free trees and shrubs for planting on public spaces or properties owned by nonprofit organizations. Project ReLeaf distributes larger five- to twelve-foot foot trees at reduced cost. A third program, Priority

ReLeaf distributes free trees to low-income communities in the city of St. Louis and St. Louis County. For all programs, technical assistance is provided to ensure that trees are properly planted and cared for. Forest ReLeaf has conducted urban tree canopy assessments for portions of the city of St. Louis and St. Louis County, and identified goals for expanding the area covered by the canopy. Street trees result in improved quality of life and measurable infrastructure cost savings in the present, and help to create communities that are more resilient in the face of a changing climate.

The use of permeable pavement also offers opportunities to reduce stormwater runoff. During a heavy rainstorm, runoff from streets and parking lots can overwhelm sewer systems, carry pollution into streams, and promote erosion. The Missouri Botanical Garden has built a parking lot that uses rain gardens, bioswales, and permeable pavement to maximize the amount of stormwater that is retained in the ground during a heavy storm.[46] The city of St. Louis has also undertaken a pilot project to assess the effectiveness of using permeable pavement in alleys.[47]

In the alley pilot project, three alleys were converted from impervious to permeable pavement. A location off of Eads Avenue was converted from asphalt to permeable concrete. Locations off of Cardinal Avenue and Geyer Avenue were converted from brick to permeable asphalt and permeable pavers, respectively. Sewer flow monitoring was used to measure stormwater volumes before and after construction of permeable pavements. The locations using permeable concrete and permeable pavers were found to reduce stormwater by more than a third. The Cardinal Avenue location, which used permeable asphalt, reduced runoff 13% compared to the older brick pavers.

The three examples cited here show illustrative programs in the areas of rainscaping, urban forestry, and permeable pavement. Many other organizations and governments in the region are also promoting and implementing green infrastructure solutions, although the capacity of local governments to adapt to changing conditions varies widely.[48] In each case, present problems rather than future climatic conditions have inspired the action. But these actions will make the region more resilient as the number of intense storms increases. Perhaps the reality of a changing climate will help to build support for these ongoing projects.

Conservation and Restoration

Responses to climate change are usually categorized as either adaptation or mitigation. But a third type of response is also crucial. Given the ongoing extinction crisis and the continued loss of habitat, the conservation and restoration of ecosystems constitutes a vital response to global environmental change. While mitigation seeks to limit the damage caused by fossil fuels, and adaptation aims to make individuals and communities less vulnerable to unavoidable changes, conservation and restoration seek to begin repairing some of the damage done by anthropogenic environmental change.

Actions taken in St. Louis cannot by themselves repair most of the damage done globally. St. Louisans, for example, have little influence over oceanic pH levels, the destruction of the Amazon, or the melting of polar ice caps. Still, St. Louisans have a key role to play in protecting the habitat that survives in the region, and enhancing biodiversity in the region.

Conservation and restoration overlap with adaptation and mitigation. A prairie restoration project, for example, will have benefits both as a carbon sink and as a stormwater management tool. What distinguishes conservation and restoration as an approach is that it seeks to repair, or heal, some of the damage done to natural systems. Following is a brief description of a few efforts that have been underway in the St. Louis region in recent years.

Riverlands Migratory Bird Sanctuary: One of the most significant restoration projects in the region in recent years has been the Riverlands Migratory Bird Sanctuary, a partnership of the Audubon Society and the U.S. Army Corps of Engineers. The sanctuary consists of 3,700 acres immediately adjacent to the Melvin Price Lock and Dam in West Alton, Missouri.[49] It is considered one of the most important migratory flyways in North America, serving as a migration corridor for millions of birds, including iconic species such as the trumpeter swan and the bald eagle. Included in the 3,700 acres is a 1,200-acre wetland and prairie restoration project. In consultation with the Missouri Department of Conservation, native grasses were planted in wet and semi-wet regimes. Prescribed burning is used to maintain the area. Another unique aspect of the sanctuary is a floating habitat, which uses two pontoon dredge barges to act as an artificial sandbar habitat.

Confluence Area: Ducks Unlimited is a national organization devoted to preserving habitat for migratory waterfowl. Working with several local partners, including the Great Rivers Habitat Alliance, Ducks Unlimited has named the confluence of the Mississippi River and the Missouri River a conservation priority area. The confluence area drains water from half of the continental United States, and provides habitat for more than 250 bird species. Currently, Ducks Unlimited holds 26 easements on properties in the floodplain area, which collectively total over 8,000 acres.[50] These easements, either purchased from owners or donated by owners, limit future development on the properties, in order to preserve its ecological value. Ducks Unlimited and its partners have also secured nine separate grants under the North America Wetlands Conservation Act (NAWCA). These grants have allowed the restoration of an additional 23,000 acres in the confluence area, most of which are on public lands.

Metro East: Heartlands Conservancy has been a leader in protecting ecological resources in the Metro East portion of the St. Louis region. The organization acts as a land trust, which either acquires land or owns easements that have been donated or purchased from land owners. The organization has played a role in protecting over 5,000 acres in southwestern Illinois.[51] A recent success story is the preservation of the Arlington Wetland in Pontoon Beach, Illinois. The 83-acre wetland wraps around an oxbow remnant of the Mississippi River, and provides important wildlife habitat in addition to stormwater storage and recreational opportunities. Heartlands Conservancy also worked closely with a partner, the Clifftop Alliance, to protect the Mill Creek Natural Area in Randolph County. This 115-acre project boasts geology and biota that are unique to the region.

LaBarque Creek: Located in northwest Jefferson County, the LaBarque Creek watershed holds one of the most pristine aquatic systems in the St. Louis region.[52] The 13-square-mile watershed supports over 40 species of fish and contains rare terrestrial habitat, including sandstone glades.[53] Friends of LaBarque Creek is an organization of local residents dedicated to preserving the unspoiled character of the watershed. Working with numerous local partners, including the Open Space Council, the Nature Conservancy, and the Missouri Department of Conservation, the organization promotes the acquisition of land and easements. There are over 3,000 acres of publicly owned land held by either the Missouri Department of Conservation or the Missouri Department of Natural Resources.

River des Peres: If LaBarque Creek is one of the most pristine streams in the St. Louis region, the River des Peres is one of the most degraded. The nine-mile river is a tributary of the Mississippi River, and flows through portions of the city of St. Louis and St. Louis County. In the 1930s, as part of a Works Progress Administration (WPA) flood control project, the river was channelized, with much of its upper section redirected underground into pipes. In addition to causing ecological degradation, the straightening of the river created faster streamflow, which contributes to erosion. MSD controls the banks of the river.

The River des Peres Watershed Coalition is a small organization dedicated to protecting and restoring the river.[54] Working with several partners, including the Deer Creek Watershed Alliance, the Green Center in University City, and MSD, the organization sponsors educational events and clean-ups, and recruits volunteers to attack invasive species and plant native grasses. The long-term goal is to restore the river to once again be a natural and cultural resource for the region.

MDC Stewardship Grants: The Missouri Department of Conservation supports small-scale ecological restoration in the region and throughout the state through its Stewardship Grants program.[55] There are several recent examples of projects supported by the program in the St. Louis region. A grant supported restoration in Calvary Cemetery, which contains the last remaining prairie remnant in the metro area. Intensive restoration, including a prescribed burn in 2008, has been in process since 2007. The Bethany-Peace United Church of Christ in Bellefontaine Neighbors received grant funds for chemical and seed for a half-acre prairie restoration project accomplished with church and community volunteers. MDC grants have also supported restoration in natural areas of Forest Park in St. Louis.

Conclusion

As noted earlier, there are far too many ongoing projects in the St. Louis region to catalog in a short essay. These efforts are, however, illustrative of projects, both large and small, with which citizens of the region are responding to the challenges of global and local environmental change.

The scope of the environmental challenges facing this generation can lead to two opposite fallacies. The first is fatalism, assuming that the challenges are too great for any individual to meaningfully impact. The second fallacy is complacency, the assumption that other people are worrying the issue, and that we'll muddle through somehow. Despite these attitudinal impediments to action, the examples cited in this essay show that there are a wide variety of ways in which St. Louisans are engaging with the challenges associated with environmental change.

As described in this essay, St. Louisans are responding to environmental change in a multitude of ways. Some focus on reducing the greenhouse gas emissions that constitute one of the fundamental drivers of global environmental change. Some focus on addressing local manifestations of climate change in ways that reduce the vulnerability of individuals and communities. Others focus on actively repairing the damage that has been done to ecosystems.

St. Louisans have some control over how much environmental change affects society and ecosystems locally. Ultimately, though, the drivers of environmental change will be determined by policy choices at the national and even international level. There are, however, reasons to persist in addressing environmental challenges at the local level, despite what George Monbiot calls "the greatest failure of collective leadership since the first world war."[56] Anyone who lived through the end of the Cold War or the peaceful revolution in South Africa must concede that social change can occur very rapidly, when conditions are ripe. It is possible that leaders and publics may suddenly be moved to act to address the wholesale alteration of the atmosphere and its attendant effects on ecosystems and society. If this optimistic view turns out to be correct, then any actions taken to preserve biodiversity and minimize human vulnerability will have been worthwhile. Even with a less optimistic view of potential change, local actions can at least postpone the loss of habitats and the most severe societal consequences of planetary transformation, an objective that is also worthy.

Endnotes

1. J. Zalasiewicz et al. "Are We Now Living in the Anthropocene?" *GSA Today* 18 (2008):4–8.

2. N. Jones, "Troubling Milestone for CO_2," *Nature Geoscience* 6 (2013): 589.

3. J. Walsh et al. "Appendix 4: Frequently Asked Questions," *Climate Change Impacts in the United States: The Third National Climate Assessment*, Ed. J. M. Mellillo, T .C. Richmond, and G .W. Yohe (U.S. Global Change Research Program 2014): 790–820.

4. Walsh et al., p. 796.

5. S. Wang, Z. Zhang, T. McVicar, J. Guo, Y. Tang, A. Yao, "Isolating the Impacts of Climate Change and Land Use Change on Decadal Streamflow Variation: Assessing Three Complementary Approaches," *Journal of Hydrology* 507 (2013):63–74.

6. National Climatic Data Center, Climate Data Online: Daily Summaries. www.ncdc.noaa.gov/cdo-web/search. Accessed May 1, 2013.

7. For annual temperature, annual precipitation, and days with more than an inch of rain, differences between the 1893-1979 period and the 1980–2013 period are significant at p<.01. For days with temperatures over 95°, the difference is significant at p<.05. For variables representing counts (i.e., days over 95° and days with more than an inch of rain), the natural logarithm of values was used in a t test.

8. R. Pielke, T. Stohlgren, L. Schell, W. Parton, N. Doesken, K. Redmond, J. Moeny, T. McKee, T. Kittel, "Problems in Evaluation Regional and Local Trends in Temperature: An Example from Eastern Colorado, USA," *International Journal of Climatology* 22 (2002): 421–434.

9. K. Kunkel, L. Stevens, S. Stevens, L. Sun, E. Janssen, D. Wuebbles, S. Hilberg, M. Timlin, L. Stoecker, N. Westcott, J. Dobson. Regional Climate Trends and Scenarios for the U.S. National Climate Assessment: NOAA Technical Report NESDIS 142-3. U.S. Department of Commerce, National Oceanic and Atmospheric Administration, 2013.

10. J. Ramirez-Villegas, A. Challinor, P. Thornton, A. Jarvis, "Implications of Regional Improvement in Global Climate Models for Agricultural Impact Research," *Environmental Research Letters* 8 (2013): doi:10.1088/1748-9326/8/2/024018

11. J. Walsh, et al. "Our Changing Climate," *Climate Change Impacts in the United States: The Third National Climate Assessment*, Ed. J. M. Mellillo, T. C. Richmond, and G. W. Yoye (U.S. Global Change Research Program 2014): 19–67.

12. A. Stoner, K. Hayhoe, X. Yang, D. Wuebbles. "An Asynchronous Regional Regression Model for Statistical Downscaling of Daily Climate Variables," *International Journal of Climatology* 33 (2013): 2473–2494.

13. J. Posey. "Climate Change in St. Louis: Impacts and Adaptation Options," *International Journal of Climate Change: Impacts and Responses* 5 (2013): 49–67.

14. Dynamically downscaled projections were not available for the B1 scenario.

15. G. Luber, et al., "Human Health," *Climate Change Impacts in the United States: The Third National Climate Assessment*, Ed. J. M. Mellillo, T. C. Richmond, and G. W. Yoye (U.S. Global Change Research Program 2014): 220–256.

16. J. Hatfield, G. Takle, R. Grotjahn, P. Holden, R. Izaurralde, T. Mader, E. Marshall, D. Liverman, "Agriculture," *Climate Change Impacts in the United States: The Third National Climate Assessment*, Ed. J.M. Mellillo, T.C. Richmond, and G.W. Yoye, (U.S. Global Change Research Program 2014): 150–174.

17. J. Dell, S. Tierney, G. Franco, R. Newell, R. Richels, J. Weyant, T. Wilbanks, "Energy Supply and Use," *Climate Change Impacts in the United States: The Third National Climate Assessment*, Ed. J. M. Mellillo, T. C. Richmond, and G. W. Yoye (U.S. Global Change Research Program 2014): 113–129.

18. H. Schwartz, M. Meyer, C. Burbank, M. Kuby, C. Oster, J. Posey, E. Russo, A. Rypinski, "Transportation," *Climate Change Impacts in the United States: The Third National Climate Assessment*, Ed. J. M. Mellillo, T. C. Richmond, and G. W. Yoye, (U.S. Global Change Research Program 2014): 130–149.

19. J. Posey, "Midwestern Levees," *Climate Change in the Midwest: A Synthesis Report for the National Climate Assessment*, Ed. J. Winkler, J. Andresen, J. Hatfield, D. Bidwell, D. Brown (Island Press, Washington, D.C., 2014): 238–243.

20. J. Posey, W. Rogers, "The Impact of Special Flood Hazard Area Designation on Residential Property Values," *Public Works Management and Policy* 15 (2010):81–90.

21. J. Posey, "Climate Impacts on Transportation in the Midwest," *Climate Change in the Midwest: A Synthesis Report for the National Climate Assessment*, Ed. J. Winkler, J. Andresen, J. Hatfield, D. Bidwell, D. Brown (Island Press, Washington, DC 2014): 212–223.

22. National Weather Service, "Historical Crests for Mississippi River at St. Louis," http://water.weather.gov/ahps2/crests.php?wfo=lsx&gage=eadm7. Accessed June 19, 2014.

23. R. Criss, "Flood Enhancement through Flood Control," *Geology* 29 (2001): 875–878.

24. X. Xu, B. Scanlon, K. Schilling, A. Sun, "Relative Importance of Climate and Land Surface Changes on Hydrologic Changes in the U.S. Midwest since the 1930s: Implications for Biofuel Production," *Journal of Hydrology* 497 (2013):110–120.

25. T. Kaplan, "Festus Residents Evacuated as Flood Waters Rise," KSDK television broadcast, April 18, 2013.

26. KTVI, "St. Louis Area Hit Hard by Flash Flooding," television broadcast, June 17, 2013.

27. B. Piper, "West Alton Residents Ordered to Evacuate Due to Flooding," television broadcast, June 3, 2013.

28. KTVI, "Flood Clean-Up Begins in East St. Louis," television broadcast, April 19, 2013.

29. KTVI, "Flood at Scott Air Force Base Caught on Video," http://fox2now.com/2013/04/19/video-of-flood-at-scott-air-force-base/, posted to website on April 19, 2013, accessed June 20, 2014.

30. Missouri Department of Transportation, "MODOT STL Traffic," https://twitter.com/StLouisTraffic, accessed June 20, 2014.

31. Metropolitan St. Louis Sewer District Semi-Annual Report, Reporting Period January 1, 2013, to June 30, 2013.

32. Metropolitan St. Louis Sewer District Semi-Annual Report, Reporting Period July 1, 2013, to December 31, 2013.

33. A. Barnosky et. al., "Has the Earth's Sixth Mass Extinction Already Arrived? *Nature* 471 (2011): 51–57.

34. D. Wake, V. Van Vredenburg, "Are We in the Midst of the Sixth Mass Extinction? A View from the World of Amphibians," *Proceedings of the National Academy of Sciences of the United States of America* 105 Supplement 1 (2008): 11466–11473.

35. N. Stork, "Re-Assessing Current Extinction Rates," *Biodiversity and Conservation* 19 (2010):357–371.

36. S. Butchart, "Global Biodiversity: Indicators of Recent Declines," *Science* 328 (2010): 1164–1168.

37. U.S. Conference of Mayors, "List of Participating Mayors," http://www.usmayors.org/climateprotection/list.asp, accessed June 20, 2014.

38. City of Creve Coeur, Missouri, "A Climate Action Plan to Save Energy and Reduce Greenhouse Gas Emissions 20% by 2015," http://www.creve-coeur.org/DocumentCenter/Home/View/924, accessed June 20, 2014.

39. City of Creve Coeur, Missouri, "Climate Action Task Force," http://www.creve-coeur.org/index.aspx?NID=727, accessed June 20, 2014.

40. Ameren, "Ameren Supports Renewable Energy," https://www.ameren.com/Environment/Pages/Renewables.aspx, accessed June 20, 2014.

41. U.S. Environmental Protection Agency, "Carbon Pollution Emission Guidelines for Existing Stationary Sources: Electric Utility Generating Units: A Proposed Rule," *Federal Register* (June 18, 2014): 34829–34958.

42. H. Schwartz, "Adapting to Climate Change: Another Challenge for the Transportation Community," *Adapting Transportation to the Impacts of Climate Change: State of the Practice 2011*, Transportation Research Board of the National Academies, Transportation Research Circular Number E-C152 (2011): 2–9.

43. Brian Hoelscher, "Project Clear: Using Rainscaping to Meet Regulatory Requirements," presentation at Earth Day Symposium, St. Louis, Missouri, April 1, 2014.

44. B. Graham, H. Miller, "Street Trees Pay Us Back," *Missouri Conservationist* 71 (2010): 10–15.

45. D. Coble, "Project CommuniTree: Engaging Citizenry: Local Approaches to Sustainable Living," presentation at Earth Day Symposium, St. Louis, Missouri, April 2, 2014.

46. D. Frank, "Unpaving Paradise: Retrofitting Our Existing Parking Lot to Improve Water Quality," presentation at Earth Day Symposium, St. Louis, Missouri, April 2, 2014.

47. J. Zhou, "St. Louis Green Alleys Study: Permeable Pavement for Volume Reduction in Combined Sewers," presentation at Earth Day Symposium, St. Louis, Missouri, April 1, 2014.

48. J. Posey, "The Determinants of Vulnerability and Adaptive Capacity at the Municipal Level: Evidence from Floodplain Management Programs in the United States," *Global Environmental Change* 19 (2009): 482–493.

49. U.S. Army Corps of Engineers, "Riverlands Migratory Bird Sanctuary," http://www.mvs.usace.army.mil/Missions/Recreation/RiversProjectOffice/RiverlandsMigratoryBirdSanctuary.aspx, accessed June 20, 2014.

50. Ducks Unlimited, Missouri State Conservation Report 2014, http://www.ducks.org/resources/media/Conservation/Reports/State%20Conservation%20Reports/master/missouri.pdf, accessed June 20, 2014.

51. Heartlands Conservancy, "Places We've Protected," https://www.heartlandsconservancy.org/what-we-do/conservation-of-open-space/places-weve-protected/, accessed June 20, 2014.

52. U.S. Department of the Interior, Fish and Wildlife Service, "LaBarque Creek: Land Stewardship Initiative," http://www.fws.gov/midwest/federalaid/documents/05MOWAP06DmjsPart%202.pdf, accessed June 20, 2014.

53. Missouri Department of Conservation, LaBarque Creek Watershed Conservation Plan, http://www.jeffcomo.org/uploads/Stormwater/Manuals/LaBarque%20Creek%20Watershed%20Conservation%20Plan%209-03-09%20kjm.pdf, accessed June 20, 2014.

54. River des Peres Watershed Coalition, www.riverdesperes.org, accessed June 20, 2014.

55. E. Shank, "Community Conservation," presentation at Earth Day Symposium, St. Louis, Missouri, April 1, 2014.

56. G. Montbiot, "End of an Era," *London Guardian*, June 25, 2012.

Bibliography

Ameren, "Ameren Supports Renewable Energy," https://www.ameren.com/Environment/Pages/Renewables.aspx, accessed June 20, 2014.

Barnosky, A., et. al., "Has the Earth's Sixth Mass Extinction Already Arrived? *Nature* 471 (2011): 51–57.

Butchart, S., "Global Biodiversity: Indicators of Recent Declines," *Science* 328 (2010): 1164–1168.

City of Creve Coeur, Missouri, "A Climate Action Plan to Save Energy and Reduce Greenhouse Gas Emissions 20% by 2015," http://www.creve-coeur.org/DocumentCenter/Home/View/924, accessed June 20, 2014.

City of Creve Coeur, Missouri, "Climate Action Task Force," http://www.creve-coeur.org/index.aspx?NID=727, accessed June 20, 2014.

Coble, D., "Project CommuniTree: Engaging Citizenry: Local Approaches to Sustainable Living," presentation at Earth Day Symposium, St. Louis, Missouri, April 2, 2014.

Criss, R., "Flood Enhancement through Flood Control," *Geology* 29 (2001): 875–878.

Dell, J., Tierney, S., Franco, G., Newell, R., Richels, R., Weyant, J., Wilbanks, T., "Energy Supply and Use," *Climate Change Impacts in the United States: The Third National Climate Assessment*, Ed. J. M. Mellillo, T. C. Richmond, and G. W. Yohe (U.S. Global Change Research Program 2014): 113–129.

Ducks Unlimited, Missouri State Conservation Report 2014, http://www.ducks.org/resources/media/Conservation/Reports/State%20Conservation%20Reports/maste r/missouri.pdf, accessed June 20, 2014.

Frank, D., "Unpaving Paradise: Retrofitting Our Existing Parking Lot to Improve Water Quality," presentation at Earth Day Symposium, St. Louis, Missouri, April 2, 2014.

Graham, B., Miller, H., "Street Trees Pay Us Back," *Missouri Conservationist* 71 (2010): 10–15.

Hatfield, J., Takle, G., Grotjahn, R., Holden, P., Izaurralde, R., Mader, T., Marshall, E., Liverman, D., "Agriculture," *Climate Change Impacts in the United States: The Third National Climate Assessment*, Ed. J. M. Mellillo, T. C. Richmond, and G. W. Yoye (U.S. Global Change Research Program 2014): 150–174.

Heartlands Conservancy, "Places We've Protected," https://www.heartlandsconservancy.org/what-we- do/conservation-of-open-space/places-weve-protected/, accessed June 20, 2014.

Hoelscher, Brian, "Project Clear: Using Rainscaping to Meet Regulatory Requirements," presentation at Earth Day Symposium, St. Louis, Missouri, April 1, 2014.

Jones, N., "Troubling Milestone for CO_2," *Nature Geoscience* 6 (2013): 589.

Jacoby, H., et al., "Mitigation," *Climate Change Impacts in the United States: The Third National Climate Assessment*, Ed. J. M. Mellillo, T. C. Richmond, and G. W. Yoye (U.S. Global Change Research Program 2014): 648-669.

Kaplan, T., "Festus Residents Evacuated as Flood Waters Rise," KSDK television broadcast, April 18, 2013.

KTVI, "St. Louis Area Hit Hard by Flash Flooding," television broadcast, June 17, 2013.

KTVI, "Flood Clean-Up Begins in East St. Louis," television broadcast, April 19, 2013.

KTVI, "Flood at Scott Air Force Base Caught on Video," http://fox2now.com/2013/04/19/video-of-flood-at-scott- air-force-base/, posted to website April 19, 2013, accessed June 20, 2014.

Luber, G., et al., "Human Health," *Climate Change Impacts in the United States: The Third National Climate Assessment*, Ed. J. M. Mellillo, T. C. Richmond, and G. W. Yoye (U.S. Global Change Research Program 2014): 220–256.

Metropolitan St. Louis Sewer District Semi-Annual Report, Reporting Period January 1, 2013, to June 30, 2013.

Metropolitan St. Louis Sewer District Semi-Annual Report, Reporting Period July 1, 2013, to December 31, 2013.

Missouri Department of Conservation, LaBarque Creek Watershed Conservation Plan, http://www.jeffcomo.org/uploads/Stormwater/Manuals/LaBarque%20Creek%20Watershed%20Conserva tion%20Plan%209-03-09%20kjm.pdf, accessed June 20, 2014.

Missouri Department of Transportation, "MODOT STL Traffic," https://twitter.com/StLouisTraffic, accessed June 20, 2014.

Montbiot, G., "End of an Era," *London Guardian*, June 25, 2012.

National Climatic Data Center, Climate Data Online: Daily Summaries. www.ncdc.noaa.gov/cdo-web/search. Accessed May 1, 2013.

National Weather Service, "Historical Crests for Mississippi River at St. Louis," http://water.weather.gov/ahps2/crests.php?wfo=lsx&gage=eadm7. Accessed June 19, 2014.

Piper, B., "West Alton Residents Ordered to Evacuate Due to Flooding," television broadcast, June 3, 2013.

Posey, J. "Climate Change in St. Louis: Impacts and Adaptation Options," *International Journal of Climate Change: Impacts and Responses* 5 (2013): 49–67.

Posey, J., "Climate Impacts on Transportation in the Midwest," *Climate Change in the Midwest: A Synthesis Report for the National Climate Assessment*, Ed J. Winkler, J. Andersen, J. Hatfield, D. Bidwell, D. Brown (Island Press, Washington, D.C. 2014): 212–223.

Posey, J., "The Determinants of Vulnerability and Adaptive Capacity at the Municipal Level: Evidence from Floodplain Management Programs in the United States," *Global Environmental Change* 19 (2009): 482–493.

Posey, J., "Midwestern Levees," *Climate Change in the Midwest: A Synthesis Report for the National Climate Assessment*, Ed J. Winkler, J. Andersen, J. Hatfield, D. Bidwell, D. Brown (Island Press, Washington, DC 2014): 238–243.

Posey, J., Rogers, W., "The Impact of Special Flood Hazard Area Designation on Residential Property Values," *Public Works Management and Policy* 15 (2010):81–90.

Ramirez-Villegas, J., Challinor, A., Thornton, P., Jarvis, A., "Implications of Regional Improvement in Global Climate Models for Agricultural Impact Research," *Environmental Research Letters* 8 (2013): doi:10.1088/1748- 9326/8/2/024018

River des Peres Watershed Coalition, www.riverdesperes.org, accessed June 20, 2014.

Schwartz, H., "Adapting to Climate Change: Another Challenge for the Transportation Community," *Adapting Transportation to the Impacts of Climate Change: State of the Practice 2011*, Transportation Research Board of the National Academies, Transportation Research Circular Number E-C152 (2011): 2–9.

Schwartz, H., Meyer, M., Burbank, C., Kuby, M., Oster, C., Posey, J., Russo, E., Rypinski, A., "Transportation," *Climate Change Impacts in the United States: The Third National Climate Assessment*, Ed. J. M. Mellillo, T. C. Richmond, and G. W. Yoye (U.S. Global Change Research Program 2014): 130–149.

Shank, E., "Community Conservation," presentation at Earth Day Symposium, St. Louis, Missouri, April 1, 2014.

Stoner, A., Hayhoe, K., Yang, X., Wuebbles, D. "An Asynchronous Regional Regression Model for Statistical Downscaling of Daily Climate Variables," *International Journal of Climatology* 33 (2013): 2473–2494.

Stork, N., "Re-Assessing Current Extinction Rates," *Biodiversity and Conservation* 19 (2010):357–371.

U.S. Army Corps of Engineers, "Riverlands Migratory Bird Sanctuary," http://www.mvs.usace.army.mil/Missions/Recreation/RiversProjectOffice/RiverlandsMigratoryBirdSanctu ary.aspx, accessed June 20, 2014.

U.S. Conference of Mayors, "List of Participating Mayors," http://www.usmayors.org/climateprotection/list.asp, accessed June 20, 2014.

U.S. Department of the Interior, Fish and Wildlife Service, "LaBarque Creek: Land Stewardship Initiative," http://www.fws.gov/midwest/federalaid/documents/05MOWAP06DmjsPart%202.pdf, accessed June 20, 2014.

U.S. Environmental Protection Agency, "Carbon Pollution Emission Guidelines for Existing Stationary Sources: Electric Utility Generating Units: A Proposed Rule," *Federal Register* (June 18, 2014): 34829–34958.

Wake, D., Van Vredenburg, V., "Are We in the Midst of the Sixth Mass Extinction? A View from the World of Amphibians," Proceedings of the National Academy of Sciences of the United States of America 105 Supplement 1 (2008): 11466–11473.

Walsh, J., et al. "Appendix 4: Frequently Asked Questions," *Climate Change Impacts in the United States: The Third National Climate Assessment*, Ed. J. M. Mellillo, T. C. Richmond, and G. W. Yoye (U.S. Global Change Research Program 2014): 790–820.

Walsh, J., et al. "Our Changing Climate," *Climate Change Impacts in the United States: The Third National Climate Assessment*, Ed. J. M. Mellillo, T. C. Richmond, and G.W. Yoye (U.S. Global Change Research Program 2014): 19–67.

Wang, S., Zhang, Z., McVicar, T., Guo, J., Tang, Y., Yao, A. "Isolating the Impacts of Climate Change and Land Use Change on Decadal Streamflow Variation: Assessing Three Complementary Approaches," *Journal of Hydrology* 507 (2013):63–74.

Xu, X., Scanlon, B., Schilling, K., Sun, A., "Relative Importance of Climate and Land Surface Changes on Hydrologic Changes in the U.S. Midwest since the 1930s: Implications for Biofuel Production," *Journal of Hydrology* 497 (2013):110–120.

Zalasiewicz, J., et al. "Are We Now Living in the Anthropocene?" *GSA Today* 18 (2008):4–8.

Zhou, J., "St. Louis Green Alleys Study: Permeable Pavement for Volume Reduction in Combined Sewers," presentation at Earth Day Symposium, St. Louis, Missouri, April 1, 2014.

About the Author

John Posey, Ph.D., is the director of research for the East-West Gateway Council of Governments, the metropolitan planning organization for the St. Louis metropolitan area, and an urban planner who has worked in state and local government since 1992. Dr. Posey participated in the third National Climate Assessment as an appointed federal advisory committee member and as a lead author of the transportation chapter. He was also an invited expert reviewer for the fifth Assessment Report of the Intergovernmental Panel on Climate Change. He holds a Ph.D. from the Bloustein School of Planning and Public Policy at Rutgers University. His civic activities include membership on the board of directors of the River des Peres Watershed Coalition.

ST. LOUIS
CURRENTS

ST. LOUIS
CURRENTS

Understanding Sales Tax

Sales taxes are an increasingly common revenue stream in the metropolitan area. St. Louis County's system for allocating part of its local sales tax among county government and the ninety municipalities is complex and controversial.

On the one hand, this provides a reliable revenue stream to cities that do not have the capacity or potential for large shopping districts. The shopping centers held by a few cities would not be as successful if every small municipality opened competing venues.

On the other hand, point-of-sale cities put forth considerable effort to develop retail sites, and pooling the revenues deprives them of reaping the full benefit of their investment.

The matter likely will be decided in court or the state legislature one day. Jim Brasfield offers an important look at the sales tax pool, the winners and losers of this arrangement, and the choices the region has in moving forward.

Dividing Sales Tax: Conflict and Consensus

Jim Brasfield, Ph.D.

Introduction

You are wandering through Macy's, and a jacket catches your fancy. The weekend special price is $100, which is within your budget. The purchase impulse draws you to the cash register. After the bar code scan, the figure on the screen shows $108.63. The extra $8.63 is the sales tax. Unlike VAT tax in Europe, this sales tax is not built into the price of the item, but added at the point of sale.

Even at $108, the jacket is a fine buy. But what happens to the $8.63? About half of it goes to the general revenue fund or special funds of the state of Missouri, and the rest is divided among various local governmental entities. The money flows through a maze of pathways to arrive at the designated jurisdictions. This chapter examines the political disputes and policy machinations that have culminated in the current distribution system within St. Louis County. The primary focus will be on a specific one-and-a-quarter-cent piece of the $8.63. This .0125 cents will ultimately be shared by the local government in which the store is located, as well as St. Louis County government and more than fifty other municipalities in the county.

How much does this one and a quarter cent matter to the local community? The average citizen does not think much about it. But the mayors and city managers earnestly care about this flow of money because it represents the largest segment of tax revenues to pay for public safety officers, street workers, and city parks maintenance.

State laws determine the flow of the money and the share received by various local governments. They have been the subject of debate and political controversy for over forty years. Many political scientists argue that policy is path dependent. Once a policy has been established, it shapes future policy decisions and renders radical change less likely. This pattern seems evident in the evolution of sales tax distribution policy.

We will examine the history of the disputes surrounding the distribution of sales tax, and trace the policy path that has taken us to the current system. The chapter concludes with possible policy changes for the rest of the decade and beyond. This effort will be both descriptive and analytic. Neither the current system, nor a modification, will be characterized as good or bad.

Some economists criticize the sales tax as regressive, because those with lower incomes spend more of their available money on necessities that are often subject to a sales tax. However, voters in St. Louis County have tended to support the sales tax as a means of raising revenue for local government. Thus, we ignore the regressive question, and assume local sales tax will continue to be a critical source of revenue for municipalities.

History—The Sales Tax Wars

The state sales tax was a Depression-era financial innovation adopted by state governments desperate for revenue beginning with Mississippi. Missouri was one of twenty-six states that enacted a sales tax during the 1930s. In the 1960s and 1970s many states expanded the sales tax to include an optional local sales tax. The Missouri legislature joined this trend in 1969 by allowing municipalities to adopt a one-cent local option sales tax. Over thirty states have authorized this form of local revenue.

Many municipalities in St. Louis County, especially those with commercial areas, quickly adopted the tax. In the early 1970s, as now, some municipalities generated much larger sales tax revenue than others. Cities with regional shopping centers or other significant retail businesses collected more sales tax per capita than those with less retail. Municipal officials in cities with lower per capita sales tax revenue concluded the system was unfair, and sought legislative remedies. High sales tax cities responded by arguing that service costs associated with retail sales justified the higher revenue stream. Forty years later the basic equity argument has never been resolved.

As early as 1973, legislation was introduced in the state legislature to replace the municipal sales tax in St. Louis County with a countywide sales tax distributed on the basis of population among the municipalities and county government, but this was strongly opposed by many cities. The following brief history of the continuing dispute over sales tax distribution will be divided into three eras: 1977–1982, 1983–1993, and 1994–present.

The Grand Compromise—1977–1982

In 1977 the Missouri legislature passed legislation based on a compromise that provided for a countywide one-cent sales tax to replace the local option tax in St. Louis County. Voters approved the countywide tax in a referendum that year. However, the legislation allowed municipalities that had previously enacted the local option tax to either retain all the tax collected within their boundaries, or to become part of the sales tax pool along with unincorporated St. Louis County. Sales tax collected in the pool area was divided on a per capita basis. Subsequently, about one third of the municipalities opted to be point-of-sale (or A) cities, and the remaining two thirds were in the Pool (B) cities along with the unincorporated county. Generally speaking, the largest and the smallest cities were in the pool. Medium-sized cities with significant retail centers had the greatest incentive to remain point of sale. The law allowed cities to re-examine their choice after each census, but if an A city opted to join the pool, it could never again return to point-of-sale status. Over the past forty years only a few cities have switched when the opportunity was available.

The compromise provided a revenue infusion for both low per capita sales tax cities and St. Louis County government. Many pool cities still believed the arrangement was unfair, but the issue did not return to the political agenda until 1983.

Annexation and Incorporation—1983–1993

The Missouri Supreme Court's Graeler decision of the early 1960's effectively froze municipal boundaries in St Louis County by allowing county government to exercise a veto over any annexation or incorporation proposal. In the 1970s most of the rapidly growing neighborhoods of the country were in the unincorporated areas. This led to a growth in the pool revenue, which benefited B cities and the county. When the city of Town and Country attempted to annex adjoining land, the county sought to block the effort based on the *Graeler* decision. In its 1983 *Town and Country* decision, the Missouri Supreme Court reversed *Graeler*, and allowed the city of Town and Country to proceed with the annexation. Local officials interpreted this decision as opening the door for additional annexations and incorporations.

Mayors of cities on the boundary of an unincorporated area began to study maps with special attention to nearby shopping centers. A municipality could significantly increase its revenue by annexing a neighboring incorporated area with a retail center. A land rush appeared imminent as rival cities eyed major retail centers. However, the county and pool cites saw this as a zero-sum game. Any annexations or incorporations that included major shopping areas would sharply decrease pool revenue.

After a period of short, but heated, debate between the A cities and the B cities/county government, a compromise was reached that froze the pool area. Even if a point-of-sale city expanded its boundaries by annexation, the newly annexed area would remain in the pool. Also, any newly incorporated city would remain in the pool. This compromise was enacted into law by the state legislature in 1983.

The county government still perceived a threat to its revenue flow and service provision system as a result of the *Town and Country* decision, and proposed a board of freeholders be formed to reorganize local government in St. Louis County. The Missouri Constitution allowed for the establishment of a city-county board of freeholders to consider various forms of municipal reorganization. County Executive Gene McNary and St. Louis mayor Vince Schoemehl created a Board of freeholders in 1987. They proposed incorporation of the entire county with municipal consolidation to reduce the number of cities to less than forty, and leave no part of the county unincorporated.

Under the freeholder plan 75 percent of the one-cent sales tax would be distributed among municipalities on a per capita basis. The plan was never brought to a vote. There was a legal challenge, and the U.S. Supreme Court found the process unconstitutional because non–property owners were excluded by definition from freeholder board membership. The freeholder plan was not revived, and in 1991 a new county executive, Buzz Westfall, was elected.

In the decade after the 1983 legislation froze the pool, the anticipated wave of annexations/ incorporations did not occur. Annexations were limited and the incentive to annex commercial areas without a residential component was weak. However, there were two significant incorporations in West County—Maryland Heights and Chesterfield.

By the late 1980s there was growing dissatisfaction among pool cities with their share of the total one-cent sales tax. There were extensive discussions and various study groups examining sales tax distribution. The last study group produced a 1988 Municipal League–backed attempt to pass an additional countywide quarter-cent sales tax that would have mostly been distributed to the sales tax pool and low per capita point-of-sale cities. It failed at the ballot box.

The 1990 census represented ominous fiscal news for many pool cities. Older cities almost universally suffered population declines, thus causing a revenue loss from the pool. The county as a whole grew only slightly in the 1980s, but inner suburbs tended to lose population and outer suburbs gained. The unincorporated county, as a pool participant, gained at the expense of older suburban municipalities.

Post Reform—1994 to present

In 1991 newly elected county executive Buzz Westfall had no interest in pursuing a municipal consolidation agenda, but he did seek to restart the sales tax distribution discussion. The County Planning Department in late 1992 produced a plan that would:

- Freeze the per capita receipts for point-of-sale cities at two times the countywide average for the base year.
- Distribute the surplus above two times the county average to the pool.
- Phase in the plan over three years.
- Allow municipalities to enact up to a quarter-cent sales tax to help offset the loss.

- The use tax, which was about to be distributed to local governments, would go to the pool (2/3) and to county government (1/3), with the county arguing this would help offset other revenue losses due to annexation.

Eventually this freeze would have resulted in most point-of-sale cities having per capita sales tax receipts no larger than those received by pool cities. Many would eventually be advantaged by going into the pool subsequent to either the 2000 or 2010 census. Again, after each census an A city has the option of becoming a B city, but can never opt to return to point-of-sale status once they have switched.

The Westfall plan was strongly supported by B cities, and introduced in the state legislature. It sparked an intense debate within the local government community. Point-of-sale cities organized to oppose the plan, and offered an alternative that featured:

- All cities and the unincorporated area to become point of sale.
- Cities above the countywide average contribute a percentage of the one-cent tax revenues to a shared fund based on a sliding scale.
- Cities authorized to pass a quarter-cent optional sales tax with a percentage of this contributed to a municipal fund that brings all cities up to a per capita minimum that was close to the projected per capita average for cities under the Westfall plan.
- Use tax revenue goes 2/3 to the fund and 1/3 to county.
- County unincorporated will be considered point of sale and county will keep all of the one cent raised—county not eligible to seek quarter-cent tax.

As the legislature began consideration of the Westfall plan, an intense negotiation with A cities ensued. This culminated in a compromise plan, which was ultimately adopted by the legislature in 1993. The main features of the compromise plan were:[1]

- Point-of-sale cities above the countywide average to share one-cent sales tax on the basis of a progressive sliding scale with three-year phase beginning in 1994 (1993 base year); sharing would range from 7.5% to 25% for most cities.
- In 2000 there is a minimum level of sharing of 7.5% for cities over the countywide average and 12.5% for cities over 1.25 times the county average.
- All areas of St. Louis County to retain current pool or point of sale status.
- All point-of-sale cities above countywide average participate in redistribution.
- Optional quarter-cent sales tax available to all cities with different sliding scale sharing.
- Use tax distributed one-third to county and two-thirds to all cities with sales tax receipts below the countywide average (this is mostly pool cities).
- County retains a portion of sales tax lost due to future annexation and incorporation.

Point-of-sale and pool cities, as well as the county, supported the compromise legislation. Sharing was phased over the three years. Many cities began to enact the quarter-cent sales tax, especially point-of-sale cities. They concluded this would replace the revenue lost under the sharing plan.

The table below illustrates the 2013 distribution of the one-cent sales tax.

Table 1. One-Cent Sales Tax Collected and Retained 2013 by Category

	2010 Pop	% Pop	Tax Generated	% Total	Net Tax Received	% of Total Received	Received as % of Generated
A cities	281,728	28%	$76,893,009	49%	$58,404,945	38%	76%
B cities	334,664	34%	$39,874,489	25%	$42,598,680	28%	107%
B areas (annex area A city)	61,561	6%	$9,465,566	6%	$7,835,971	5%	83%
County	321,001	32%	$31,370,368	20%	$43,640,990	29%	139%
Total	998,954		$157,603,432		$152,480,586		

Point-of-sale cities generated nearly half the total sales tax, and the B areas (those areas annexed by A cities since 1983) accounted for another 6%. The unincorporated county and B cities generated 45% of the tax. Since the unincorporated county, B areas, and B cities all constitute the pool, a total of 51% is generated in pool territory. After TIF reduction and the sharing applications, A cities retained 38% of total tax received, and the county and B cities received 29% and 28%, respectively.

The final column shows the tax ultimately received as a percent of tax generated. A cities received 75% of the tax they generated, B cities 107%, and the county 139%. However, since there are large geographic differences in the tax generated, these aggregate totals do not reflect the reasons for the dissatisfaction with the status quo among some cities.

Some retail construction has used tax increment financing (TIF). The $6.2 million in TIF withdrawals in 2013 were made before the application of the sharing formula. These represented twenty-seven jurisdictions, but only four exceeded $300,000, and these accounted for 65% of all TIF withdrawals. Major TIF projects seem less likely in the future, and this will probably be a declining element in the sales tax distribution.

Table 2. Top Nine Sales Tax Generators—2013

Municipality	Type	2010 Pop	Gross Amount	% of Total
ST. LOUIS COUNTY (unincorporated)	B	321,001	31,370,368	19.9%
CHESTERFIELD	B	47,484	12,521,117	7.9%
MARYLAND HEIGHTS	B	27,472	7,611,654	4.8%
FLORISSANT	B	52,158	6,327,657	4.0%
BRIDGETON	A	11,516	5,852,053	3.7%
BRENTWOOD	A	8,055	5,725,742	3.6%
DES PERES	A	7,853	5,301,719	3.4%
FENTON	A	3,626	4,853,061	3.1%
RICHMOND HEIGHTS	A	8,603	4,785,523	3.0%
TOTALS		500, 515	88,201,220	56%

Table 2 illustrates that 56% of all sales tax is generated in nine jurisdictions. If we exclude the county unincorporated areas, the eight top generating cities represent 17% of the population and account for a third of the sales tax. Three of them are B cities, but Chesterfield and Maryland Heights are prohibited from switching under the 1983 law.

The 1993 reform compromise also opened the way for additional legislatively authorized optional sales taxes. The long dispute over distribution of the one cent had made it difficult to consider other local option sales taxes for St. Louis County. A half-cent capital improvement sales tax (with sharing in St. Louis County) was enacted in 1995. Another half cent for parks and stormwater was also authorized by the state legislature without a sharing provision.

The sales tax battles of the past forty years can be described as a "multi-person game" with three major sets of participants in the conflict/negotiations that have characterized the various stages of the debate. The major players are A cities (especially high-generation As), B cities, and the county government. Within the A city coalition there are some whose tax generation places them only slightly above the pool average. They have not been as vehement in their defense of the point-of-sale principle as high per capita cities, but have rarely broken ranks.

Some B cities generate a relatively high amount of sales tax, but because of their large population have a point-of-sale per capita yield smaller than the pool average distribution. Other B cities are small, landlocked, and have little opportunity to generate significant additional sales. The newest type of B city is the A city wannabes. These cities, if given a choice, would probably select A city status, but cannot because of the 1983 legislation that froze the pool. They are not firm members of the B city coalition.

The county unincorporated area is the top sales tax generator, but also has the largest population. As a pool participant, the county has been an active member of the pool coalition. Under current law the county has no option to become point of sale, and receives a larger pool distribution than it generates. The county also has a more diverse flow of revenue than most municipalities. Since county officials have both A and B city residents as constituents, they have not usually sought a narrow advantage. County executive Westfall was instrumental in putting sales tax distribution on the legislative agenda in 1993, but in the ensuing twenty years county government has defended the status quo, rather than pursuing additional changes.

Policy revision begins when events or key individuals place an issue on the political agenda. Once on the active agenda, policy modification requires an idea for how to modify current policy that appears feasible and acceptable to a potential majority coalition in the legislature. In each of the examples of legislative action the first step was achievement of a broad coalition among the St. Louis County players before the legislature acted. Examples of triggering events have been the *Town and Country* decision, which potentially threatened the viability of the pool, and population declines, which caused B cities to face reduced revenue from the pool. The 1993 reform effort was triggered by B city worries about population decline, and the willingness of the county executive to place this high on his legislative priority in 1993.

Neither the Westfall original plan nor the A city response represented wholly new ideas. The one-cent sales tax was a fixed pie with modest annual total growth. For an A city there was the prospect that aggressive pursuit of new retail development could generate substantial sales tax increments. In the pool area retail expansion was also occurring, but the payoff for individual pool cities was modest. Both the Westfall and A city proposals assumed sharing of revenue by high-yield cities. Both also assumed that a new quarter-cent sales tax would be authorized to help A cities recover at least some of the revenue lost to sharing. Use of an additional quarter-cent sales tax to enhance the pool was an idea that had been widely discussed and was the subject of a ballot measure a few years earlier. Compromise was relatively easy because the differences were not conceptual or philosophical, but centered on how much of the point-of-sale city annual sales tax revenue would be shared. The negotiations became an exercise in how to split the difference between the opposing plans.

Despite the persistence of the basic conflict over forty years, sales tax distribution has only episodically been on the active policy agenda. In the last few years some high per capita A cities have pressed the legislature to modify the 1993 law by reducing their percent of sharing. A few high sales tax generating B cities are ineligible to shift to A city status, and they have sought to revisit the 1983 legislation freezing the pool. Sales tax distribution is a visible and continuous issue, but not the only agenda item for St. Louis County municipalities. Legislative success on other issues requires cooperation across the A and B city divide. Plus all are members of the St Louis County Municipal League, which has sought to find consensus rather than conflict on this issue. This has mitigated the intensity of the conflict.

The 1993 legislation produced almost two decades of peace in the "sales tax wars" that had been fought episodically since the mid 1970s. In the past it was the pool cities and the county putting sales tax distribution on the agenda by pushing for legislation that approaches the goal of per capita distribution. In the last few years sales tax distribution has again appeared on the agenda of the state legislature. This time fairness is cited as the reason for change by some high per capita generating point-of-sale cities, as well as recently incorporated cities, which would retain greater sales tax revenue if they were allowed to become point of sale.

Unlike many other parts of the country, municipalities in St. Louis County do not rely heavily on property tax. Even for pool cities, sales tax represents a significant share of total revenue. Any changes in the distribution formula risk significant revenue losses for some. Thus, most of the participants have sought incremental changes developed as part of a consensus among local elected officials.

The Future

There have been three major legislative actions on St. Louis County sales tax distribution enacted over the past forty years. In the last few years some officials have attempted to place the issue back on the legislative agenda. Based on recent discussions within the Municipal League and the expressed concerns of various municipal officials, it is possible to identify several current complaints about the existing system:

- Some high tax generating cities wish to change the system to allow them to retain larger share of taxes collected.
- A number of cites with the optional quarter-cent sales tax (a part of which is shared with the pool) have argued that only jurisdictions that have enacted the quarter-cent tax should be participants in the sharing.
- The formula for sharing the one-cent and the quarter-cent tax are mathematically complicated. Some contend the system would be better understood and more predictable if the formula was less complicated.
- A number of municipal officials contend that county government receives too large a portion of the shared taxes. There are distinct elements to this contention:
  - The special annexation adjustment is no longer needed because the 1993 concern that major annexations would occur thus impacting the service bureaucracy proved to be unfounded.

– The county government receives significant sharing proceeds from the quarter-cent tax enacted by thirty-seven cities, but is not authorized to seek voter approval to collect the quarter cent in unincorporated county.

Should we expect sales tax distribution to be back on the policy agenda in the near future? Chesterfield generated the most sales tax of any city in 2013, yet they are permanently in the pool because the city was incorporated after 1983. In 1993 Fenton already had very high per capita sales tax revenue. They subsequently annexed land that became a major retail center. Both cities have pressed for revision of the 1993 law to allow them to keep a larger share of the one-cent tax. In 2012 a Municipal League committee recommended changes in sales tax distribution, and this was one of the items considered by a special committee of the state legislature.

After a sharp decline in aggregate sales tax collection during the recent recession, the county-wide yield has begun to grow, although it is not likely to return to the level of 2007 until later in the decade. The chart assumes a one percent a year growth until 2020.

Chart 1. Total One-Cent Sales Tax Collection 1994–2020

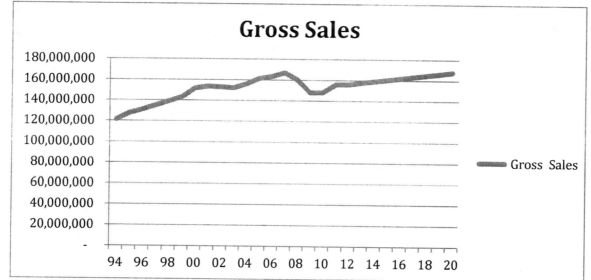

Five Possible Adjustments

Five policy adjustments are described below. The first two represent radical change from the status quo and are thus characterized as outliers. The other three are incremental changes that have been widely discussed in recent years.

Outliers

I. All Point of Sale

In the rest of the state of Missouri, as well as most other areas of the country, all revenue generated by local option sales taxes are retained in the community in which they are collected. The current arrangement in St. Louis County is the product of three major pieces of legislation creating a unique system for the county. Under this adjustment each municipality, and St. Louis County for the unincorporated areas, retains the sales taxes collected in its jursidiction. The total sales tax collected (both one cent and quarter cent) would be retained by the taxing jurisdiction.

A variant of this option is to retain some sharing provision (either in the one cent or quarter cent or both) that would supplement the point-of-sale yield for very low per capita sales tax revenue cities. The county and most pool cities would experience significant revenue loss. The winners would be a handful of high sales tax generating cities. It seems very unlikely that the county and pool cities would support this change.

II. All Share Per Capita

In the mid-1970s many municipal leaders argued that the local option sales tax should be collected countywide and distributed to municipalities and county government on a per capita basis. This was opposed by high generating cities, and the 1977 legislation reflected a compromise in which the tax was deemed a county tax to be distributed on a per capita basis, but allowed those cities with an existing tax to opt to retain the tax. This option would change the 1977 legislation to require all cities to receive the tax on a per capita basis.

If all sales tax was distributed per capita in 2013, the distribution would have been $152 rather than the current pool distribution of $127. Several A cities would have been better off in 2013 with a $152 per capita yield, but most probably prefer to remain point of sale with the prospect of greater revenue in the future. This adjustment is more likely to gain broad support than the all point-of-sale option, but still seems doubtful as a policy change.

Under this adjustment, cities might be allowed to retain the quarter-cent tax, if they have enacted it. Or, it could also be shared among all jurisdictions.

Incremental Adjustments

If sales tax distribution reaches the active policy agenda in the near future, incremental adjustments to the 1993 law are more likely than radical change. Discussions in the last few years have centered around three issues:

- Use of the quarter-cent tax
- The impact of the 1983 legislation freezing the pool area
- The county yield from the pool and special adjustments

Three possible incremental adjustments are described below. They are not mutually exclusive, and variations/combinations are feasible.

III. Universal Quarter Cent

This adjustment envisions no change in the basic distribution formula for the one-cent tax. The only modification is the presumption that all cities currently authorized to enact the quarter-cent would do so, and St. Louis County would be legislatively authorized to seek voter approval for the tax in the unincorporated areas. The quarter-cent tax was an essential piece of the 1993 legislation because the enactment of it (even with partial sharing) was perceived as allowing most A cities to recover the revenue that was to be shared. By expanding the total sales tax collected, A cities could engage in substantial sharing of revenue without significant net loss. Thus, they would have a powerful incentive to enact the tax. In the subsequent twenty years, 37 municipalities have enacted the tax of which 27 are A cities. They generate about eighteen million dollars, which is a little less than half of the potential for the tax, if it was approved in all jurisdictions. St. Louis County was not authorized to enact the tax, but as a pool area it shares in the proceeds from the tax.

There have been proposals to amend the quarter-cent sharing to only include those that have enacted the tax, or to limit sharing to other cities only and not St. Louis County. A legislative formulation might be to authorize St. Louis County to enact with voter approval a quarter-cent sales tax in the unincorporated areas, and to stipulate that after a three-year waiting period sharing would only take place among those jurisdictions that enacted the tax. If some municipalities or the county did not wish to enact the tax, they would no longer participate in the quarter-cent sharing after three years.

IV. Reversal of the 1983 Freezing of the Pool

The 1983 legislation permanently froze the point-of-sale areas. Any annexed areas or new cities would be in the pool without a point-of-sale option. This limit on newly incorporatated/ annexed areas is an element of current dissatisfaction among those cities. As noted in Table 2 above, the two highest generating cities are not eligible for A city status. Several A cities have annexed areas that generate significant sales tax. Without some other adjustment, a change in this provision would result in a significant decline in pool revenue.

Table 3. Impact on the Pool of Reversing the 1983 Freeze

	Pop	Sales Tax Generated	Pool Allocation	Difference (Loss to Pool)
Chesterfield	47,484	12,521,117	5,141,800	7,379,316
Green Park	2,622	1,074,868	283,923	790,946
Maryland Heights	27,427	7,611,654	2,974,082	4,636,851
Wildwood*	35,517	1,761,134	3,845,954	
A cities that annexed post 1983	61,561	9,465,566	6,666,126	2,799,440
	174,611	32,434,340	18,912,606	15,606,554

* Wildwood would likely remain a B city.

Thus a reversal of the 1983 legislation freezing the pool would likely need other adjustments in the sharing arrangements to compensate the pool for all or most of the estimated $15,600,000 lost revenue. This represents a high approximation because it does not include the amount shared if these cities and annexed areas became point of sale. Thus the actual pool loss might be closer to $12,000,000. These compensatory sharing provisions would probably involve modifications to both the sharing of the one-cent and the quarter-cent tax.

County Adjustments

Some of the dissatisfaction with the current system reflects an argument that St. Louis County emerged from the 1993 legislation with more revenue than necessary. The argument focuses on two elements:

- The county receives an annexation adjustment to reflect loss of territory to annexations or incorporations. The presumption is that the county government bureaucracies cannot necessarily be reduced as a result of population loss, but loss of population means loss of revenue from the pool. This presumed significant new annexations and incorporations would occur in the 1990s. This change has not occurred at the level anticipated.
- The county receives a share of the quarter-cent sales tax collected in municipalities, but is not legislatively authorized to enact the tax.

This adjustment presumes two changes to the 1993 law. The annexation adjustment would be phased out over three years. In 2013 the county received an additional $2,126,439 as a result of the annexation adjustment, with 70% coming from A cities and their annexed areas. Modification of this provision of the 1993 law would not provide significant additional revenue to finance other major changes.

The county would be authorized to enact with voter approval a quarter-cent sales tax, and would share it on the same basis as municipalities. If the county enacted a quarter-cent tax, it would produce over $7,000,000 gross revenue before any sharing provisions.

Adjustment Evaluation

None of the three adjustments are mutually exclusive. All or parts of them might be enacted into law. Elimination of the annexation adjustment is a modest simplification of the current formulas, but change in the other elements of the formula would potentially create unanticipated changes in the existing revenue stream. Unless there is a desire to change the basic structure of the distribution, formula simplification may not be as important as greater transparency. From the beginning of the sharing system, St. Louis County government has been responsible for the implementation of the sharing system. An annual report that provides more details about the calculation that determines each city's share may reduce the complaints about the complexity of the formula.

Conclusion

Each of the major changes in sales tax distribution were the result of a conflict over perceived inequities followed by negotiation that led to a consensus compromise. There is no reason to presume the future will be different. The major participants (B cities, A cities, and the county) each have a stake in the viability of the system for everyone. The state legislature has in the past only changed policy based on a local agreement.

In 1993 Buzz Westfall was one of the most powerful Democrats in the state. There was a Democratic governor and legislative majority, but the sales tax reform legislation was the product of a consensus negotiated by the local stakeholders. The legislature has the constitutional authority to modify current law without a local consensus. They could next year eliminate the 1983 freezing of the pool or make all jurisdictions point of sale, but this seems unlikely.

Exogenous conditions or a fresh perception of inequity are the most likely triggers for a new round of negotiations. Will the gross sales tax yield in St. Louis County decline absolutely as a result of retail expansion in St. Charles and the trend to more Internet sales? Will the 2020 census again find population declines among pool cities that reduce their annual tax yield? Will the movement to have the city of St. Louis reenter St. Louis County succeed, and introduce a whole new perspective into the discussion? Will there be a new round of annexations/incorporations/consolidations that significantly modifies both the role of the county and the perception of fairness of the current system of tax distribution?

If one gazes into a crystal ball to envision what the distribution of sales tax in St. Louis County will be in 2020 and beyond, the most likely scenario is "no change." All cities face pressure to provide adequate wage increases for employees. Personnel costs are the most significant item in local budgets. Each municipality would like a system that enhances their revenue. Without additional revenue, any change in the current system would entail significant loss for some participants.

The 1993 reform legislation shifted about 20% of the tax collected in point-of-sale cities to the pool. The quarter cent added significant additional money for both A and B cities, including those that did not enact the tax. The authorization of the quarter cent offered A cities the opportunity to recover all or most of the revenue to be lost in the new sharing plan. An additional benefit of the tax reform is that the truce paved the way for other local sales taxes, most notably the capital improvement tax and the park/stormwater tax. With voter approval, this has enabled cities to generate additional revenue for essential local services.

Path-dependent policy changes are likely to be incremental and build on past decisions. Authorization of the quarter-cent tax was a key component of the 1993 law. Some jurisdictions adopted it, and others did not. The county was not authorized to collect it. A future modification of the existing system will probably employ the additional use of the quarter cent as part of any change in the current distribution system, because it offers a way to shift existing redistribution without significant loss.

Any change is likely to be the result of a negotiated agreement among the various stakeholders in St. Louis County, who then seek legislative endorsement of the local consensus.

Endnotes

1. The formula for the distribution of the one-cent tax is: $25.5*\log_{10}(.035*(\text{City's per capita sales tax} - \text{adjusted prior year county average per capita sales tax}))$

   The formula for the distribution of the quarter cent tax is: $11.627*\log_{10}(.015*(\text{City's per capita sales tax} - \text{adjusted prior year county average per capita sales tax}))$

About the Author

James Brasfield, Ph.D., is professor of management at the George Herbert Walker School of Business & Technology, Webster University. He has been on the faculty of Webster University since 1976 and was the chair of the Department of Management for nineteen years. He has a Ph.D. in Political Science from Case Western Reserve University (1973) and MA in political science from St. Louis University. Dr. Brasfield was mayor of the city of Crestwood from 1996 to 2002 and on the Crestwood Board of Aldermen from 1978 to 2006. Jim has been president of the St. Louis County Municipal League, and chairman of the board of the Greater St. Louis Health System Agency. He was president of the Webster University Faculty Senate from 2001 to 2007. Currently he is a member of the Municipal Parks Grant Commission and the board of directors of Voyce. He is past president of the Organized Section on Health Politics and Policy of the American Political Science Association, and is currently book review editor of the *Journal of Health Politics, Policy and Law*. His book *Health Policy: The Decade Ahead* was published by Lynne Rienner Publishers in 2011.

ST. LOUIS
CURRENTS

Economic Reinvention

As we learned from Jeffrey Smith's earlier essay, the St. Louis region has been an historical hub of economic activity for the entire country. It has been a formidable economic engine almost from its very beginning.

Today, the St. Louis region's economy has proven to be a rather well-balanced and stable system—though in some measures far from where leaders would like it to be. Still, the region has historic strengths on which to build, and is producing some creative ideas for the future.

The Great Recession took its toll on St. Louis's economy as it did across the country, but it was the down cycle of the economy that showed what St. Louis has done right and where St. Louis still needs to improve. Bob Lewis and Ruth Sergenian provide their expert commentary on the region's economy and what lies ahead.

The St. Louis Regional Economy: Recession, Recovery, and Reinvention

Robert M. Lewis, A.I.C.P., C.Ec.D. and Ruth Sergenian, M.U.P.

Introduction

The St. Louis Metropolitan Statistical Area (MSA) functions as a single global economy. Even with divisions by two great rivers, two state lines, hundreds of local government boundaries, and myriad administrative jurisdictions, the region is woven together by the daily interactions of businesses and the talented people who work for them. The 15-county metropolitan area[1] has 2.8 million residents, more than 1.4 million workers, and over 77,000 business establishments. It has a larger economy than the state of Kansas, and the Missouri side of the region accounts for 43 percent of the state's economy.[2]

Built originally on commerce, the region's economy began as a trading center in 1764, grew into a manufacturing powerhouse well into the twentieth century, and has undergone dramatic restructuring over the past two decades. St. Louis is now one of the nation's most diverse metropolitan economics with the services-providing sectors predominating. About 73 percent of gross metropolitan product (GMP) and 87 percent of nonfarm employment are in the services-providing sectors,[3] virtually identical to the American economy.[4] The $146 billion[5] St. Louis regional economy is balanced, dynamic, broad-based, highly resilient,[6] and growing.

This balance, however, can hide both unique challenges, as well as the special concentrations of talent and experience that form the foundation for the region's ability to adapt as economic circumstances change. While highly diversified, St. Louis presently has four economic clusters that are strategic targets for growth: Financial and Information Services, the Health Economy, Multimodal Logistics and Advanced Manufacturing, and Biosciences. These aren't new to St. Louis; they have always been part of the region's economic diversity and, in many ways, are outgrowths of the region's history as a center of commerce and industry. But they have become leading clusters in the changing world economy.

Moreover, balance is not reflected state to state. Metro West (the Missouri counties) captures about 83 percent of all private sector jobs in the metro area while Metro East captures 17 percent.[7] This is in notable contrast to population distribution, where Metro West has 75 percent and Metro East 25 percent. A great many more Metro East residents commute to Metro West for jobs than vice versa, thus giving Metro East a larger population profile than economic profile within the region.[8]

The U.S. Great Recession and Sluggish Recovery

From December 2007 to June 2009, the United States experienced the longest and worst economic recession since the Great Depression. Over the course of the "Great Recession," the nation lost 7.7 million jobs. The depth of the job losses and the length of time to full recovery were and, in some ways, remain more severe than any of the previous three recessions.

Nationally, employers began to add jobs again in 2010, but the economic recovery that followed the Great Recession has proceeded at a markedly slow pace with unevenness across industries and different parts of the country. It took five years after the official end of the recession (i.e., mid-214) for the nation as a whole to recover finally all the jobs lost during the recession (see Figure 1).

However, the nation's recovery has been uneven, and twenty-two states had still not regained their pre-recession job count peaks by the end of 2014, including both Illinois and Missouri. Each sector responded differently to the recession. The U.S. health care and energy sectors actually grew substantially, while jobs in real estate and construction continued to shrink after 2010, even as the overall job counts reached recovery. In general, industry sectors that typically provide mid-level wages lost jobs, as detailed later. Further, even though the economy overall is back to its pre-recession job level, it hasn't added sufficient jobs needed to keep pace with growth in the working-age population.[9]

Figure 1. U.S. Indexed Job Losses in Four National Recessions, 1981–2007[10]

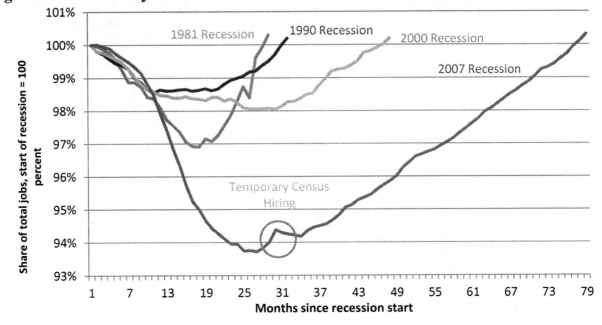

The St. Louis Great Recession and Job Recovery

From 1969 to 2013, the region's wage and salary employment grew at an annual average rate of 0.7 percent, half the nation's annual growth rate of 1.4 percent (see Figure 2). A key pattern is that the most recent job recovery curve in metro St. Louis compared to the nation is not dissimilar to the last recession nor to job growth between the mid-1980s and the year 2000.

To the good, the greater St. Louis employment changes during the Great Recession followed the national trends closely, thus avoiding some of the dramatic losses in other metro areas. According to an analysis by the Brookings Institution, St. Louis's employment losses and unemployment levels during the recession ranked the region 41th among the 100 largest metros—roughly middle of the pack. The region's recovery, however, has been sluggish comparatively. Lagging job creation by the fourth quarter of 2014 pushed the region's rank for employment recovery down to 88th of the largest 100 metros, and the unemployment rate was 47th.[11]

Figure 2. Annual Rate of Change in Wage and Salary Employment, St. Louis MSA and U.S., 1969–2015[12]

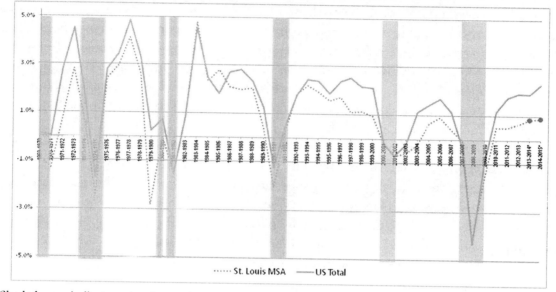

Note: Shaded areas indicate national recessions.

In response to the Great Recession, companies in St. Louis, as well as around the nation, quickly sought to avoid the worst risks by modifying business plans, changing product and service lines, reducing labor costs, modifying organizational structures, or—when all else failed—closing their doors. Even the strongest firms were cautious, often putting investment and hiring plans on hold even if they foresaw growth potential for themselves.

The St. Louis Regional Chamber identified nearly 26,000 job layoffs between 2007 and 2009 that were either announced in Worker Adjustment and Retraining Notification (WARN) notices or the media. Examples of larger layoffs of 250 or more workers include:

- Auto industry: DaimlerChrysler, Federal Mogul, Integram, General Motors, and Lear
- Steel industry: Amsted Rail, Granite City Steel; and U.S. Steel Corp.
- Other manufacturing: Anheuser-Busch InBev, MEMC, and Spartech
- Bioscience: KV Pharmaceuticals, Monsanto, and Pfizer
- Financial services and insurance: U.S. Fidelis and Wachovia
- Retail trade: Macy's
- Services: Metro Transit, St. Louis Board of Education, Hyatt Hotels, Aramark, Go Fig Inc., Verizon Wireless, and Western Union
- Mining: Monterey Coal Company Mine No. 1

While some of the layoffs were temporary, others were permanent losses that were not regained as the region entered economic recovery. For instance, DaimlerChrysler closed its two Fenton plants in St. Louis County and Macy's closed its downtown St. Louis store.

The Great Recession formally ended in June 2009 after which announcements of St. Louis business expansions returned with several local companies reporting plans to add 200 or more employees. From the financial services sector, Scottrade Inc., U.S. Bank, Stifel Financial, and Edward Jones reported creating new jobs. Other St. Louis employers that announced plans to add jobs once the recovery was underway included Unisys, Convergys, Express Scripts, and even General Motors, despite the major disruptions in the auto industry during the recession.

As regional employment started to recover in 2009, subsequent data show job creation unfortunately paused in 2012 before beginning to pick up the pace again in 2013 through the first quarter of 2015. This put St. Louis behind schedule to recover on pace with the nation. The pause was led by several sectors that mostly depend upon local demand to drive expansion. For example, construction employment contracted as the local residential and commercial real estate markets were not ready to begin expanding. Employment in retail trade was flat, in part reflecting cautious consumers and sluggish housing construction. Local companies in the professional and business services industry were also conservative, delaying demand for legal, accounting, marketing, building, and administrative support services in 2012.

By March 2015, the region had regained 58 percent of the jobs lost between peak employment and the recession's lowest level of employment (trough). The education and health care sectors, fortunately, were counter cyclical, adding jobs throughout the recession. Financial activities and professional and business services industries have returned to their pre-recession employment peaks. About 88 percent of the trade transportation and utilities sector's jobs and about one-quarter of the manufacturing jobs have been regained. Employment in the information and government sectors has continued to drop even as the overall economy recovers slowly (see Figure 3).[13]

Figure 3. St. Louis MSA Employment by Industry Sector, Great Recession and Recovery

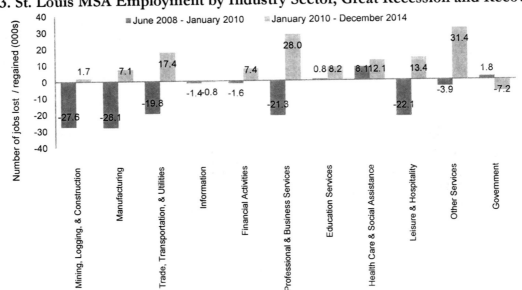

While the region's job creation trails, a shift-share analysis showed that, from 2010 through 2013, three St. Louis sectors—education and health services, manufacturing, and financial activities—had positive competitive changes, indicating certain local advantages in promoting further employment growth.[14] A shift-share analysis identifies the portion of job growth in metro St. Louis that is attributable to national job growth. If a local sector's growth rate is the same as the national rate, then the region probably cannot claim to be any different than the national economy, but where there is faster growth than the nation, the added portion can be attributable to specialized local strengths.

A forecast of regional employment is difficult because of the bumpy recovery; few trends were easy to predict with confidence. In early 2015, IHS Global forecasts that the region will return to its pre-recession employment peak in 2016 or 2107,[15] nine or ten years after the start of the recession and up to three years behind the nation!

Regional Economic Output

The St. Louis gross metropolitan product (GMP) was $145 billion in current dollars in 2013. GMP measures the value of all the goods and services produced within a metro area each year. From 2001 to 2008, the region's GMP expanded at an annual rate of 1.1 percent. From 2009 to 2013, the pace of the region's expansion slowed to an annual average of 0.7 percent, while at the same time the nation's economy expanded by an annual average rate of 2 percent. In early 2015, Moody's Analytics forecast the region's GMP will continue to be weak through 2014 and then increase at an accelerating pace through 2016.

For the four years leading up to the Great Recession, the region's goods-producing sectors, which include manufacturing and construction, declined in value, while growth in services-providing sectors drove the region's increase in GMP (see Figure 4). Some of the goods-producing weakness can be attributed to the closure of the Ford and Chrysler auto plants between 2006 and 2009. Following the recession, the goods-producing industries resumed making net positive contributions to the region's economic growth.

Figure 4. Annual Change in Real Gross Metropolitan Product, St. Louis MSA, 2001–2013[16]

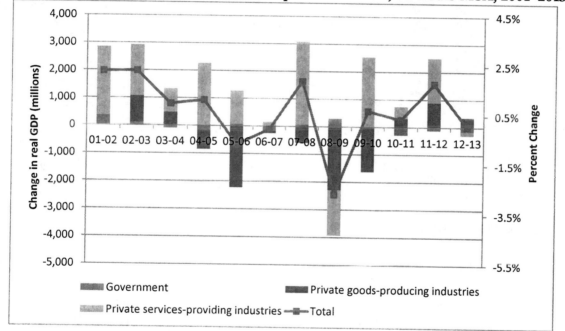

People, People, People

The old adage that business site selection is driven primarily by "location, location, location" is changing. Location is no longer defined solely by access to transportation and natural resources. In fact, the top "location concern," identified by recent surveys of corporate executives and site selection consultants, is the availability of a skilled labor pool, followed by highway accessibility, and then labor costs.[17] Site selection is now also about "people, people, people."

The St. Louis region's labor force participation rates have remained somewhat higher than the national rate, while at the same time the unemployment rate tracks very closely with the nation. Nationally, the unemployment rate reached a high of 10.6 percent in January 2010 and St. Louis hit a high of 10.4 percent in July 2009. The decline in unemployment has been slow, however, both nationally and in St. Louis. Some of the drop in the unemployment rate, moreover, has been driven by a shrinking labor force as people give up on finding work in a sluggish economy, choosing to return to school or retire.[18]

The region's unemployment rate was 6.3 percent in 2014. The region's labor force increased during 2014, while the region's unemployment rate continued it's steady decline—a sign of expanding confidence by the region's workers (see Figure 5). This pattern continued in the first quarter of 2015. Forecasts project the region's unemployment rate falling to 5.0 percent in 2016. [19]

Figure 5. Annual Labor Force and Unemployment Rates, St. Louis MSA, 2005–2014[20]

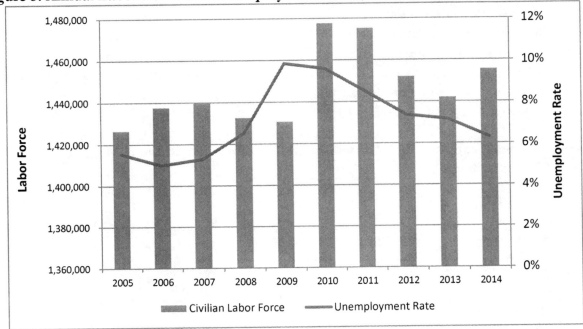

The Need for Higher Skills

The region's employment losses and gains by occupational category (rather than economic sector) during the Great Recession and subsequent recovery shed some light on structural changes that were slowing the recovery. Researchers looking at the national economy found that, "while technological advances and globalization have created new jobs for workers at the high end of the skill spectrum and spared the service job workers at the low end, these forces have displaced many jobs involving routine tasks—traditionally the sphere of the middle skill worker."[21]

Metro St. Louis fared similarly. The region's employment decreased by a net of nearly 38,000 between 2007 and 2014. Using wages as a proxy for skill levels and sorting occupations by skill level shows that, over the recession and ongoing recovery, St. Louis area occupations at the highest and lowest skills (and wages) increased while declines were concentrated in the middle[22] (see Figure 6). As the recovery began, companies were making capital investments in computerized machinery and equipment to take over routine tasks done typically by these occupations in order to make their companies more productive even while using fewer employees.

Figure 6. Change in Employment by Skill Group, St. Louis MSA, 2007–2014

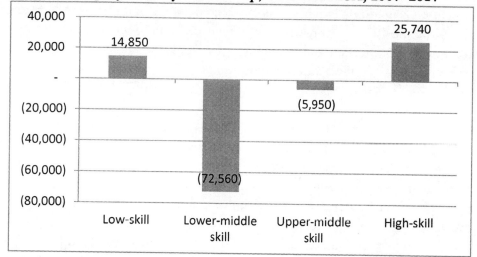

Construction occupations, part of the upper-middle skill group, posted one of the largest losses with a decline of 18,900 jobs between 2007 and 2014. Fortunately, construction will rebound as the regional recovery does. In contrast, two lower middle-skill occupational categories that experienced significant losses are less likely to rebound in the coming years: office and administrative support occupations fell by 24,500 and production (manufacturing) occupations lost 21,600.

The lowest skilled occupations, on the other hand, including examples like food preparation and personal care services, generally must be performed in-person and on-site. They are also very hard to computerize or otherwise convert to machines (though there is known research on programming robots to assist people with certain disabilities!). There may also be wage suppression effects as middle-skilled people are forced to take lower-skilled jobs, thus increasing the supply of such workers.

The occupational categories that experienced the most regional growth also require more skills, experience, and formal training—and they pay more. Examples include management occupations, with the recent addition of nearly 20,000 jobs, followed by health-care practitioners and technical occupations, which added over 10,900 jobs in the 2007–2014 period. Computer and mathematical occupations and business and financial operations added 6,100 and 6,600 jobs, respectively.

One of the hallmarks of the St. Louis regional economy is that its educational attainment levels actually exceed national averages and those of many peer metros. More than 586,000 residents of metro St. Louis have a bachelor's degree or higher, or 30 percent of adults over age 25, just above the national average of 29.1 percent. Only 13 of the largest 20 metro areas have bachelor's degree attainment higher than St. Louis, despite St. Louis ranking 19th in population and 21st in economic scale.

In 2011, the St. Louis region's business community began to not only formally recognize the importance of college completion and other forms of post-secondary training for economic health of individuals and for the community as a whole, but to commence innovative programs to increase educational attainment.[23] Local colleges and universities, public-private partnerships, civic and nonprofit programs, government and higher education programs, and business-led initiatives have all been working to improve college completion. Connecting these groups together and coordinating efforts got underway in 2013 as the region seeks to increase the share of adults with bachelor's degrees or higher.

The region's labor force already has valuable concentrations of life scientists, engineers, computer analysts, professional managers, and other highly specialized occupations needed for the twenty-first-century economy. The Brookings Institution found that 22 percent of the region's workers are in STEM occupations (science, technology, engineering, and/or mathematics), ranking the region 18th out of the 100 largest metros. Brookings finds that metro areas with higher STEM knowledge have stronger economies and the impact of STEM knowledge is reflected in wages. The average wage for STEM jobs in the St. Louis metro is $66,000, compared to $37,600 for non-STEM jobs.[24]

Capturing More of the Nation's Population Growth

The region's challenge to maintain and expand a competitive talent pool is exacerbated by slow population growth. While the St. Louis MSA population increased by only 4.2 percent between 2000 and 2010, the nation's population increased by 9.7 percent.

Natural increase (births minus deaths) is the source of the region's net growth. While about 50,000 new residents migrate into St. Louis each year, a larger number migrate out. Following decades of slowing negative net migration, the pace of out-migration picked up during the Great Recession. Moody's forecast for the St. Louis economy unfortunately observed that, "in the long run, lackluster population growth will ensure that the metro area modestly underperforms the U.S."[25]

Interestingly, although net migration is negative, there has been a small but steady net influx of foreign-born immigrants in the region. About 5,000 foreign-born residents have moved into the region annually since 2010.[26] Moreover, Brookings's analysis of immigration around the nation finds that St. Louis has a highly skilled foreign-born population.[27] Community leaders identified the importance of the foreign-born population and found that, although less than 5 percent of the 2.8 million St Louis residents are foreign-born, this group offers a significant opportunity for growth in both numbers and skills. The St. Louis Mosaic Project[28] was launched in 2012 in response to the potential economic benefits of increasing its foreign-born population. The Mosaic Project engages business leaders to hire international talent and government leaders to work to reduce barriers to foreign workers and their families. The initiative has developed programs to connect immigrants and international students to services, information, and networking opportunities that reinforce the St. Louis community's culture of inclusion and welcoming.

Reinvention and Growth

The region's forward-looking economic development agenda has long been driven by an asset-based approach to economic development focusing on clusters of export industries, the distinctive composition of a competent talent pool, and the unique geographic and infrastructure assets of the region. The St. Louis Regional Chamber and economic partners around the bi-state region have used the cluster approach to guide economic development since 2000, periodically refining analysis to reflect changes in the regional, national, and global economies.

A key measure to identify strengths is the location quotient, which is a measure of concentration. When measured for jobs, it represents the ratio of an industry's share of employment in a given area to that industry's share of employment in the overall U.S. economy. When a local industry's employment concentration is greater than the nation, local firms in that industry typically produce more goods or services than the local market demands and, therefore, are exporters that bring "new money" into the region. This type of concentration specialization drives wealth creation within the region.

One of the good news stories about St. Louis is that the composition of the region's overall employment base is very similar to the U.S. as a whole. Major economic sectors tend to have location quotients hovering around 1.0, indicating relative parity with the U.S. economy. But digging deeper into the region's major sectors, location quotient analysis reveals particular specialization within four key industry clusters—Financial and Information Services, Health Science and Services, Multimodal Logistics and Advanced Manufacturing, and Bioscience.

These clusters are in different phases of development and require different intervention techniques to foster growth. While the Financial and Information Services and Health Sciences and Services clusters are and have been growing, the Multimodal and Logistics and Advanced Manufacturing cluster is large and well established. The Biosciences cluster is newer and smaller in scale, but presents an important opportunity for astounding growth.

Financial and Information Services

The region's Financial and Information Services cluster has a location quotient of about 1.0, indicating a similar concentration of employment in the regional economy as in the national economy. But throughout the recession and recovery, an exceptional mix of regional investment companies led to these sectors' quick recovery from the Great Recession, and then some. The cluster regionally employs 82,300 in 6,300 companies and is aligning to become an increasingly competitive force in the national market.

Employment in this overall cluster outperformed the economy as a whole, as shown in Figure 8. The securities brokerage niche, a component within the securities, commodity contracts, and investment industry, is a notable strength, having added 2,500 jobs since 2009 with a total of more than 8,200 through 2013, and its employment location quotient rose dramatically from 1.98 in 2009 to 3.09 in 2013. This growth occurred even as securities brokerage jobs declined nationally. The *Wall Street Journal* reported that the presence of a qualified talent base along with an affordable business environment has made St. Louis an attractive alternative for the financial services industry.[29] Meanwhile, regional information sector job gains include niches in data processing, hosting, and related services, which increased their combined location quotient from 2.15 in 2009 to 2.43 in 2013.

Figure 7. Employment Trends in Financial and Information Services Cluster, St. Louis MSA, 2002 to 2013, Indexed 2002 = 1.0[30]

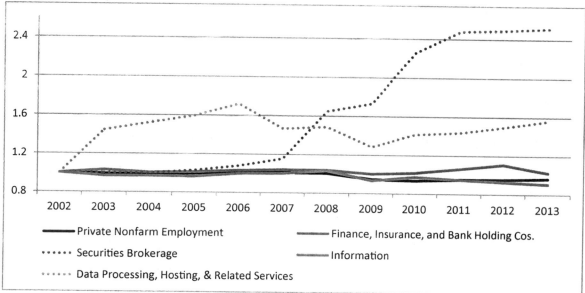

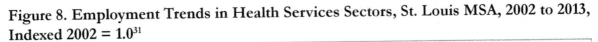

Health Economy

The Health Economy regional cluster is large and comprehensive, with businesses ranging from insurers to health care facilities to product manufacturers. This industry cluster consistently has added jobs since 2004, employing some 197,800 in more than 11,800 establishments in 2013. Its employment location quotient in metro St. Louis increased slightly from 1.06 in 2008 to 1.13 in 2013, as illustrated in Figure 9. This sector generally added employment even during the Great Recession.

Figure 8. Employment Trends in Health Services Sectors, St. Louis MSA, 2002 to 2013, Indexed 2002 = 1.0[31]

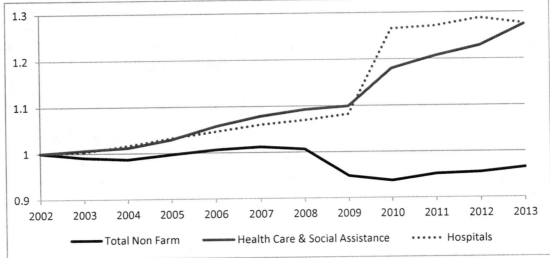

Hospitals are crucial drivers in the St. Louis economy, with about 72,200 employees in 2013 in 64 establishments. Hospitals added over 12,000 jobs between 2007 and 2013, and the employment location quotient increased from 1.34 to 1.57 over this period.

Multimodal Logistics and Advanced Manufacturing

The Multimodal Logistics and Advanced Manufacturing cluster is an integral part of the region's economy, because it is driven by the region's location and infrastructure assets, notably its geographic location, transportation network, workforce, and existing businesses. Transportation is a cost of doing business, so improvements in the transportation system and logistics management enhance the competitive position of many other sectors dependent upon moving goods and services.[32]

The cluster is a combination of industry sectors: manufacturing, wholesale trade, and transportation and utilities. Of those three, wholesale trade experienced net employment growth between 2002 and 2014 (see Figure 10) and, in fact, that sector did not drop below its year 2000 employment during the Great Recession. During that decade and a half, however, manufacturing continued its general employment decline, accentuated by the closing of three automobile assembly plants with resultant negative multiplier effects among suppliers and vendors. Much of the decline in the transportation sector, meanwhile, can be attributed to the decrease of hub activity at Lambert–St. Louis International Airport, as that industry reconfigured itself throughout the nation. Since about 2010, however, the manufacturing and transportation sectors have retained consistent employment now that those "shocks" have been absorbed by the economy.

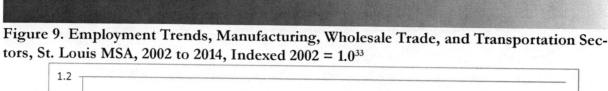

Figure 9. Employment Trends, Manufacturing, Wholesale Trade, and Transportation Sectors, St. Louis MSA, 2002 to 2014, Indexed 2002 = 1.0[33]

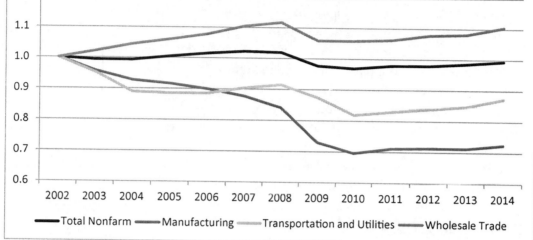

The strength of the cluster is also seen in the value and growth of the region's exports, which totaled $19.0 billion in 2012, ranking the region 18th in the nation. Despite having a smaller share of employment in manufacturing than the U.S., a larger share of the region's exports is for goods than for services (72.7 percent) than the nation as a whole (70.9 percent). Aircraft products and parts accounted for 14.3 percent of goods exported (e.g., Boeing) by value in 2012, while motor vehicles accounted for 6.8 percent of the goods exported even with only one assembly plant in the region.[34]

The value of this cluster prompted a major 2013 regional analysis sponsored by the East-West Gateway Council of Governments entitled *St. Louis Regional Freight Study*. As a result, the St. Louis Gateway District was formed to guide and align infrastructure investment with economic development strategies to expand freight-related economic growth. This public-private partnership includes participation by East-West Gateway, Bi-State Development Agency, which will oversee the new district, the Leadership Council Southwestern Illinois, and the St. Louis Regional Chamber.

Bioscience

With its world-renowned scientists, research institutions, and bioscience companies, St. Louis is a center of innovation, producing cutting-edge research in the medical and plant sciences. Growth has also been a result of substantial collaborative efforts, which presently center on an organization called BioSTL. St. Louis has long stood as a leader in scientific research in biomedical fields as well as agriculture, with such institutions as Washington University and Saint Louis University and multinational corporations like Monsanto and Sigma-Aldrich. BioSTL[35] is the latest evolution of strategic efforts to restructure the regional economy partly around the biosciences.

Prior to the more formal and better funded BioSTL, the Coalition for Plant and Life Sciences was formed in 2001 to make strides in commercializing bioscience innovation and to capture regionally the economic benefit of world-class medical and plant science entrepreneurship. Success of the coalition prompted creation of BioSTL in 2011 to lead ongoing efforts to build greater regional capacity in innovation, capital, and entrepreneurship. Much has been accomplished, including but not limited to the following:

- **The BioGenerator** was established in 2003 to work closely with universities, scientists, entrepreneurs, and investors to start new companies.
- **Cortex**, the Center of Research Technology and Entrepreneurial Exchange, was established in 2002 and is redeveloping more than 200 acres of urban land.
- In parallel, the **Bio-Research & Development Growth (BRDG) Park** on the Donald Danforth Plant Science Center campus has developed immensely successful multi-tenant buildings for emerging plant science companies.
- **Biosciences venture capital** has grown to over $1 billion under local management.
- Improved **university technology transfer** as well as attraction of increased **federal support** and **state tax credits** for Cortex, the BioGenerator, and the **Center for Emerging Technologies.**
- The **Missouri Biotechnology Association** (MOBIO), which advocates for pro-science policies in the state of Missouri.

Managing Strengths That Can Become Weaknesses

Economic specialization can also represent vulnerability if shifts in demand away from concentrated industries cause unwelcome shocks. Metro St. Louis recently experienced such shocks with the closures of the Ford and Chrysler automobile assembly facilities between 2006 and 2010. The region is also vulnerable to change in national defense policy and spending at Boeing Defense, Space & Security (BDS).

But St. Louis has successful experience in managing major shocks and changes. Working as a network of economic development agencies, the region was able to slow the demise of the Ford plant long enough to identify job opportunities for that workforce and to devise plans for reuse of the site. Included also were investments in transportation infrastructure to better accommodate future industrial growth opportunities.

Such regional efforts extend back much further. In the early 1980s, another auto industry recession triggered a collective focus to retain many of the workers so they would be less likely to leave for other regions. In the early 1990s, a defense industry recession also galvanized a regional response. The layoff of more than 10,000 workers at McDonnell-Douglas Corporation (now part of Boeing) inspired a metropolitan-wide effort that identified the skills of the laid-off workers and opportunities for them in other companies throughout the region. The result stimulated creation of several business incubators, and led to the formal creation of the World Trade Center of St. Louis (WTC). The WTC is one of three hundred global World Trade Centers. As St. Louis's international economic development organization, the WTC provides local businesses with the resources needed to be more competitive and strategic in their international business growth.

Business Management Expertise

St. Louis has had a deserved reputation as a "headquarters town" for a long time. As of the April 2014 issue of *Fortune* magazine, metro St. Louis had eighteen *Fortune 1000* companies headquartered in the area and a headquarters employment location quotient of nearly 2.0. This is not new. St. Louis has been a *Fortune 1000* leader for several decades even as the business landscape undergoes constant reinvention. Of the current *Fortune 1000* companies, some are new to St. Louis since 2000 (see changes in the *Fortune 500* list in Figure 10), several have fallen off the St. Louis list because of corporate takeovers but retain strong employment presences, while others have relocated their headquarters but maintain large St. Louis operations (e.g., Charter Communications).

Some have grown rapidly from within, like Express Scripts (now 20th on the *Fortune 500* list), while still others are stalwarts of the *Fortune* lists. Emerson, for instance, is the longest-standing St. Louis company on the *Fortune 1000* list, closely followed by Monsanto, which fell off for a short time when it sold off Solutia but quickly earned its way back.

Figure 10. Fortune 500 Companies Headquartered in Metro St. Louis since 1995 by Annual Ranking[36]

COMPANY	2014	2013	2012	2011	2010	2009	2008	2007	2006	2005	2004	2003	2002	2001	2000	1999	1998	1997	1996	1995
Express Scripts	20	24	60	55	96	115	135	132	134	137	151	147	210	276	371					
Emerson Electric	121	123	120	120	117	94	111	115	126	134	144	138	130	126	121	118	126	120	128	133
Monsanto	197	206	224	234	197	235	305	323	336	357	353				167	187	163	159	146	145
Centene	251	303	453	493	486															
Reinsurance Grp of America	274	275	289	290	321															
Peabody Energy	365	315	316	338	346	353	432	431	453	497										
Ameren	379	373	340	313	320	327	329	339	324	380	382	418	366	434	439	444	448			
Jones Financial (Edw Jones)	444	491																		
Graybar Electric	449	465	451	480	470	439	455	450	476	462	448	401	344	336	370	404	431	453	454	475
Charter Communications			351	333	332	385	409	409	413	390	358	362	417	492						
Smurfit-Stone						356	334													
Anheuser-Busch							149	146	146	139	142	142	159	159	151	150	141	127	87	85
May Department Stores										147	147	144	143	134	122	120	120	103	99	82
Premcor (Clark USA)													285	249	325	414	374			
TWA														463	468	454	433	383	374	337
Ralston Purina														543	342	293	252	236	180	152
GenAmerica															411	392	453	479		
Mercantile Bank															496					
Jefferson Smurfit																	440	397	310	351
McDonnell Douglas																		87	74	69
Boatmen's Bank																			415	485
No. of Companies	9	9	9	9	9	8	9	8	8	9	8	7	8	10	11	11	11	10	10	10

Entrepreneurship

The region recognizes that many of these corporate giants reflect St. Louis's rich history of entrepreneurial initiatives and the region's role as a launching ground for many of America's biggest public and privately held companies such as Express Scripts, Emerson, Monsanto, and Enterprise. While the importance of large employers cannot be underestimated, there is an important and growing focus on the influence of high-value start-ups on economic vitality and reinvention. According to the Kauffman Foundation, "the percentage of hiring based on job creation is much greater at startups than more mature firms. Four out of every 10 hires at young firms are for newly created jobs."[37] Another researcher pointed out that most of the nation's net new jobs every year are generated by new and small companies, leading an increasing number of economic developers to place emphasis on entrepreneurial activity and new business formation.[38]

St. Louis is building a robust entrepreneurial ecosystem to pick up the pace and success of this reinvention. In 2010 alone, the region had 4,600 births of businesses with 20 employees or less, although this was tempered by 4,900 deaths of small businesses.[39] In pre-recession years, business births outpaced business closures. The new businesses that start each year include traditional small businesses such as beauty salons, stores, and restaurants as well as high-technology start-ups that have the potential to bring new and innovative products and services to the market.

A 2014 study of St. Louis start-ups between 2006 and 2013,[40] while focused on the relatively narrow bioscience and technology cluster, found that there were 35 such start-ups in 2006,[41] a strong year that was helped in part by the growing Arch Angels organization (for early stage financing), two life sciences incubators, and robust programs of the National Institutes of Health (NIH). The number of companies reaching start-up status in bioscience or technology fell sharply through the Great Recession, but returned to pre-recession levels in 2011 with 34 new start-ups. The pace accelerated with 42 in 2012 and 52 in 2013.

The sources that supported new start-ups changed dramatically over this eight-year period. In 2006, 45 percent of the start-ups were funded through university licensing deals or Small Business Innovation Research (SBIR) awards from NIH, both with long commercialization horizons. One out of four (26 percent) of that year's start-ups was funded by accelerators (6 percent), incubators (14 percent), or business plan competitions (6 percent). By 2013, the composition of support changed significantly with 45 percent of the start-ups supported by incubators, 31 percent by business plan competitions, and 18 percent by accelerators.

> Launched in 2012, with the goal of attracting and retaining the best entrepreneurial talent to St. Louis, Arch Grants is a superb example of the flexibility of the private market to promote economic growth. Arch Grants holds an annual Global Start-Up Competition, offering $50,000 in equity-free grants to firms that relocate to St. Louis for at least a year. In addition to grant funding, contest winners receive support through free legal, accounting, and marketing services. Arch Grants winners often choose to locate in the downtown technology incubator, T-REX. Additional $100,000 funding grants are also available. Funding is raised almost entirely from private donors.

While there are many, and increasing, start up support programs of many sorts, there are also many deep connections among and between them. A classic example is T-REX, started in 2012 as a co-working space and technology incubator located in downtown St. Louis.[42] By early 2014, T-REX was home to more than one hundred start-ups as well as funders and support organizations including ITEN, Capital Innovators, Cultivation Capital, SixThirty, and Arch Grants (see sidebar), and many other entrepreneurial activities such as Startup Weekend and StartLouis.

The success of accelerators, incubators, and business plan competitions has created a large pipeline of companies at the earliest stages of funding, typically the first eighteen months. An indicator of the demand for this assistance from entrepreneurs has been an extraordinary increase in pressure on sources of seed capital in the regional economy, though this implies that even more investors might be attracted to further contribute to the region's growth and economic sustainability. Indeed, Accelerate St. Louis, a collaborative effort of more than fifty organizations staffed by the St. Louis Regional Chamber and the St. Louis Economic Development Partnership, is pursuing a shared regional agenda to increase St. Louis's ability to serve entrepreneurs and start up companies.[43]

Conclusion

The St. Louis metropolitan economy is, and has long been, large and diverse, though sluggish in its recovery from the Great Recession. While not growing as rapidly as the nation as a whole, it has nevertheless proven resilient in several crucial sectors, particularly as a financial services cluster, as a focus of business management talent, as a center for freight logistics, and as a research and development leader in health and biosciences.

But St. Louis continues to grapple with legacy issues. Large-scale manufacturing was once a source of good-paying jobs and strong profits. While the region continues to rid itself of such jobs in conformance with national trends, it falls behind in aggregate performance when compared to metro areas where manufacturing was never such a large part of the economy. Still, St. Louis steadily is becoming an "advanced manufacturing" economy that creates fewer manufacturing jobs, but they are more highly compensated and require advanced education, training, and skills.

St. Louis also is capitalizing quite successfully on its long leadership in the agriculture and food processing industries by evolving into a world-class bioscience research and production leader. Capital and wealth from legacy and emerging sectors is helping to fund future-oriented businesses and an incredible scale of entrepreneurialism.

The region lost population in the 1970s primarily because of net out-migration. Until the Great Recession, St. Louis narrowed the out-migration "gap" to almost zero while continuing to grow from within, but recent economic sluggishness seems to have encouraged more out-migration to perceived better opportunities in other places. Still, the city of St. Louis had the nation's highest growth rate in attracting 25- yo 34-year-olds with a four-year degree after the 2000 census.[44] It is critical to retain these people to raise families, run businesses, and contribute to stronger net growth potential over the coming decades. Present, and expanding, efforts to fund entrepreneurs may well have this effect.

Jobs of the future, of course, are brain-oriented. Critical thinkers, problem-solvers, collaborative workers, and good communicators are in increasing demand. St. Louis needs more people with skills honed in higher education environments—bachelor's and master's degrees, if not higher. The labor force of legacy industries has difficulty adapting to such a future, but efforts are underway. Moreover, the present initiative to raise sharply the share of the region's workforce with college degrees is not just a good idea, it is absolutely necessary for the St. Louis economy to retain a leadership role in the world. That said, St. Louis is not really behind the nation in college degrees, but it could have many more degreed employees which, in turn, will lead to a far more sustainable and adaptable economy.

St. Louis struggles with change, as almost everyone does. But it has its own amazing economic assets: strongly growing sectors even as others fade; astounding empowerment and leadership in start-up businesses; affordable housing for all classes coupled with as rich a cultural environment as can be found anywhere; wealthy families and businesses willing to invest in St. Louis; a hardworking labor force, albeit with many members needing assistance to adapt to new opportunities; high-quality colleges and universities and many excellent elementary and high schools.

What may be lacking is a belief in ourselves—that we are far more capable than we often admit. Reinvention of the economy is hard work. Reinvention challenges the successes of the distant and recent pasts. Those successes, of course, confronted their own pasts while building on them. There are ample examples today of similar forces. Proclaiming our successes, taking chances with promising ideas, and preparing the population to see and grasp more opportunities are the important next steps to sustainable prosperity.

Endnotes

1. The St. Louis Metropolitan Statistical Area comprises Bond, Calhoun, Clinton, Jersey, Macoupin, Madison, Monroe, and St. Clair Counties in Illinois, and Franklin, Jefferson, Lincoln, St. Charles, St. Louis, and Warren counties and the independent City of St. Louis in Missouri.

2. IMPLAN Group, LLC, IMPLAN System (2013 data and software),16740 Birkdale Commons Parkway, Suite 206, Huntersville, NC 28078, www.IMPLAN.com

3. The Bureau of Labor Statistics defines Goods-Producing and Services-Providing Sectors as follows:

   Goods-Producing

   Natural Resources and Mining
   - Agriculture, Forestry, Fishing and Hunting (NAICS 11)
   - Mining, Quarrying, and Oil and Gas Extraction (NAICS 21)

   Construction
   - Construction (NAICS 23)

   Manufacturing
   - Manufacturing (NAICS 31-33)

   Services-Providing

   Trade, Transportation, and Utilities
   - Wholesale Trade (NAICS 42)
   - Retail Trade (NAICS 44-45)
   - Transportation and Warehousing (NAICS 48-49)
   - Utilities (NAICS 22)

   Information
   - Information (NAICS 51)

   Financial Activities
   - Finance and Insurance (NAICS 52)
   - Real Estate and Rental and Leasing (NAICS 53)

   Professional and Business Services
   - Professional, Scientific, and Technical Services (NAICS 54)
   - Management of Companies and Enterprises (NAICS 55)
   - Administrative and Support and Waste Management and Remediation Services (NAICS 56)

   Education and Health Services
   - Educational Services (NAICS 61)
   - Health Care and Social Assistance (NAICS 62)

   Leisure and Hospitality
   - Arts, Entertainment, and Recreation (NAICS 71)
   - Accommodation and Food Services (NAICS 72)

   Other Services (except Public Administration)
   Other Services (except Public Administration) (NAICS 81)

4. GDP, Bureau of Economic Analysis http://www.bea.gov/regional/index.htm, and Nonfarm Payroll, U.S. Bureau of Labor Statistics, http://www.bls.gov/data/#employment. The rest of the metropolitan economy is found in "goods providing industries."

5. "GDP by Metropolitan Area (millions of current dollars)," Bureau of Economic Analysis, http://www.bea.gov/iTable/iTable.cfm?reqid=70&step=1&isuri=1&acrdn=2#reqid=70&step=1&isuri=1

6. Resilience Capacity Index, Building Resilient Regions Network, University of California Institute of Governmental Studies, http://brr.berkeley.edu/rci/

7. U.S. Bureau of Labor Statistics, Quarterly Census of Employment and Wages, 2013 http://data.bls.gov/pdq/querytool.jsp?survey=en

8. U.S. Census Bureau, Population Division, Annual Estimates of the Resident Population: April 1, 2010, to July 1, 2014 https://www.census.gov/popest/data/index.html

9. *New York Times*, "How the Recession Reshaped the Economy, in 255 Charts," June 6, 2014, http://www.nytimes.com/interactive/2014/06/05/upshot/how-the-recession-reshaped-the-economy-in-255-charts.html?_r=2

10. Economic Policy Institute, http://www.stateofworkingamerica.org/charts/job-loss-in-prior-recessions/

11. Brookings Institution, Metro Monitor—March 2015, http://www.brookings.edu/research/interactives/metromonitor#/M10420

12. Bureau of Economic Analysis, Wage and Salary Employment, 1969 to 2013; and Bureau of Labor Statistics, Current Employment Statistics, 2013 to March 2015.

13. Bureau of Economic Analysis, Wage and Salary Employment Not Seasonally Adjusted.

14. University of Georgia, shift share of regional employment, St. Louis MSA, 2010–2013 using online calculator, http://georgiastats.uga.edu/sshare1.html

15. The United States Conference of Mayors, *Update and 2015 Metro Jobs Forecast*, January 2015, Page 1. http://www.usmayors.org/83rdWinterMeeting/media/012115-release-MetroEconomies.pdf

16. Bureau of Economic Analysis, Real GDP by Metropolitan Area (millions of chained 2009 dollars). http://www.bea.gov/regional/index.htm

17. Area Development Online, "28th Annual Survey of Corporate Executive: Availability of Skilled Labor New Top Priority," http://www.areadevelopment.com/Corporate-Consultants-Survey-Results/Q1-2014/28th-Corporate-Executive-RE-survey-results-6574981.shtml and "10th Annual Survey of Site Selection Consultants: Economy on a More Continuous Growth Track," http://www.areadevelopment.com/Corporate-Consultants-Survey-Results/Q1-2014/10th-site-selection-consultants-corporate-RE-survey-1167098.shtml

18. The formula for calculating the unemployment rate is to first determine the "labor force," which consists of people who are over age 16 and who are either working or are actively looking for work. Unemployed people are considered part of the labor force if they are looking for work. If people opt for school or retirement during sluggish economic times, they effectively drop out of the labor force (though they might later reenter) and thus are no longer considered unemployed.

19. Moody's Analytics, Précis U.S. Metro-St. Louis MO-IL, February 2015

20. "U.S. Bureau of Labor Statistics, Local Area Unemployment Statistics, http://www.bls.gov/data/#unemployment

21. Federal Reserve Bank of New York, "Job Polarization and Rising Inequality in the Nation and the New York–Northern New Jersey Region," Current Issues in Economics and Finance, http://www.newyorkfed.org/research/current_issues/ci18-7.html

22. U.S. Bureau of Labor Statistics, Occupational and Wage Estimates, 2007 and 2014, http://www.bls.gov/oes/tables.htm. **Occupations in Low-Skill Group:** Food Preparation and Serving-Related Occupations; Personal Care And Services Occupations. **Lower-Middle Skill Group:** Farming, Fishing, and Forestry; Building and Grounds Cleaning and Maintenance; Healthcare Support; Transportation and Material Moving; Office and Administrative Support; Production (manufacturing) Occupations; Sales and Related; Protective Service; Community and Social Service; Installation, Maintenance, and Repair Occupations. **Upper-Middle Skill Group:** Arts, Design, Entertainment, Sports, and Media; Education, Training, and Library; Construction and Extraction; Life, Physical, and Social Science; Healthcare Practitioners and Technical Occupations. **High-Skill Group:** Business and Financial Operations; Architecture and Engineering; Computer and Mathematical; Legal; Management Occupations.

23. St. Louis Is Headed to the Top Ten; Catalogue of College Completion Programs, May 2013, draft.

24. Brookings Institution, "The Hidden STEM Economy," June 4, 2013, http://www.brookings.edu/research/reports/2013/06/10-stem-economy-rothwell

25. Moody's Analytics, Précis U.S, Metro, Midwest, February 2015

26. Moody's Analytics, Précis U.S, Metro, Midwest, February 2015

27. Brookings, "The Geography of Immigrant Skills: Educational Profiles of Metropolitan Areas," June 2011, http://www.brookings.edu/research/papers/2011/06/immigrants-singer

28. St. Louis Mosaic Project, http://www.stlmosaicproject.org/

29. "Meet Them in St. Louis: Bankers Move," *Wall Street Journal*, December 13, 2014, http://online.wsj.com/news/articles/SB10001424127887324296604578177710219203782

30. U.S. Bureau of Labor Statistics, Quarterly Census of Employment and Wages, http://data.bls.gov/pdq/querytool.jsp?survey=en, and St. Louis Federal Reserve Bank of St. Louis and St. Louis Regional Chamber.

31. U.S. Bureau of Labor Statistics, Quarterly Census of Employment and Wages, http://data.bls.gov/pdq/querytool.jsp?survey=en, and St. Louis Regional Chamber.

32. AECOM, St. Louis Regional Freight Study, June 30, 2013. http://www.ewgateway.org/pdffiles/library/trans/freight/freightstudy_summary-final.pdf

33. U.S. Bureau of Labor Statistics, Employment, Hours, and Earnings—State and Metro Area (Current Employment Statistics—CES), http://www.bls.gov/data/#employment

34. Brookings Global Cities Initiative, "Export Nation 2013" http://www.brookings.edu/research/interactives/export-nation

35. Adapted for this report from http://biostl.org/about/history/.

36. *Fortune* magazine, Fortune 500, 1995–2014.

37. Kaufman Foundation, Business Dynamics Statistics Briefing: Job Creation, Worker Churning, and Wages at Young Businesses, http://www.kauffman.org/newsroom/2012/11/young-firms-lead-recovery-in-hiring-and-job-creation-according-to-kauffmanfunded-census-brief

38. *Washington Post*, "How an Oft-Used Economic Development Tactic May Actually Be Hurting the Economy," July 9, 2014, http://www.washingtonpost.com/business/on-small-business/how-an-oft-used-economic-development-tactic-may-actually-be-hurting-the-economy/2014/07/08/700017aa-06d7-11e4-8a6a-19355c7e870a_story.html

39. U.S. Census Bureau, "Statistics of U.S. Businesses," http://www.census.gov/econ/susb/index.html

40. St. Louis Regional Chamber, *Accelerate St. Louis: St. Louis Start-up & Capital Report 2014*, http://www.stlregionalchamber.com/docs/default-source/default-document-library/2014-startup-capital-report-with-attachment.pdf?sfvrsn=2

41. Start-ups were included if they were one of the following: an accelerator investment, funded by outside equity, an incubator client, university-license with fewer than 200 employees, SBIR Phase I or II awardee, winner of a business plan competition, a presenter at Invest MidWest, or high-tech equity-backed firm that have relocated or is new-to-market self-financed firm within the high-tech NAIC & revenues exceeding $100K, Joint-venture or spin-off of major corporation, in development stage with capitalization. See report for methodology used to develop database of startups.

42. http://downtowntrex.com/

43. http://www.acceleratestlouis.org/

44. CEOs for Cities, "Young and Restless 2011."

About the Authors

Robert M. Lewis, AICP, CEcD, is principal and president of Development Strategies, an economic development research firm. He is both an urban planner and regional economist, evaluating the economic feasibility of development projects within the context of the city planning process. Mr. Lewis holds a master's degree in city and regional planning from Southern Illinois University Edwardsville and a bachelor's degree in business economics from Miami University in Oxford, Ohio. He is a certified economic developer (CEcD) within the International Economic Development Council. He is a member of several professional associations, including the American Institute of Certified Planners of the American Planning Association.

Ruth Sergenian is the director of economic research and analysis for the St. Louis Regional Chamber. She conducts economic impact studies; designs and analyzes surveys; assesses and monitors industry clusters; and transforms and summarizes demographic, business, and economic data. Her work supports the chamber's staff, members, investors, community partners, and the community at large to better understand regional and national economic trends and strengths. Ms. Sergenian has more than twenty-five years of real estate market research and economic and community development consulting experience. She earned a bachelor's degree in psychology from SUNY at Stony Brook and a master's degree in urban planning from the University of Michigan.

ST. LOUIS
CURRENTS

Rebounding Neighborhoods

If there is a theme to urban redevelopment in the twenty-first century, it is that success is found at the neighborhood level. St. Louis is a city—a region—of neighborhoods.

Todd Swanstrom and Hank Webber examine closely what's working and where it could lead. By studying the region's performance over the last forty years, the authors identify five places in the region that exhibit the ability to rebound from dire conditions, with special attention on the Central West End. They also identify eight key elements involved in neighborhood success.

By understanding what elements create a rebounding neighborhood, we are given a roadmap by which success can be spread to other areas. This study will help focus effort and leverage capacity in a time when resources are so very limited.

Rebound Neighborhoods in St. Louis:
Causes and Consequences

Todd Swanstrom, Ph.D. and Hank Webber, M.P.P.

American cities are currently experiencing a resurgence not seen since the early 1900s. For the first time since the 1920s, central cities in America's largest metropolitan areas are growing faster than their surrounding suburbs.[1] This revitalization is particularly welcome in older industrial cities like Baltimore, Pittsburgh, and St. Louis, where thriving neighborhoods are successfully attracting new populations back into the urban core. Young people are moving in and renovating historic homes, and neighborhoods are enjoying a new urban vitality. Despite these success stories, each of these cities still contains desperately poor neighborhoods that have remained so for decades.

For the past several years, we have been working to identify the factors that determine why some neighborhoods in St. Louis have revitalized while others have stagnated or declined. In particular, we were interested in determining how local actors can influence neighborhood trajectories. What are the necessary and sufficient conditions of neighborhood revitalization and which of these factors can local governments, nonprofits, and residents control? How can local actors help ensure that neighborhood revitalization, when it occurs, benefits the low-income and minority residents who have lived in these areas for many years? What lessons can be learned from successful neighborhood revitalization in St. Louis that can be applied to other neighborhoods in other cities?

Our first task was to characterize neighborhood changes in St. Louis over the past forty years. To do so we constructed a database that follows neighborhoods in the St. Louis region over a forty-year period (1970–2010). Using a three-part Neighborhood Vitality Index (NVI) we devised a methodology for grouping neighborhoods in three categories: (1) neighborhoods that were strong at the beginning of our study period and remained strong until the end, (2) neighborhoods that were weak at the beginning of our study period and remained weak or declined further, and (3) neighborhoods that bounced back from urban decline in the past twenty years.

Next, we wanted to find out *why* certain neighborhoods were able to rebound and what role local actors and institutions played in the process. So many factors vary simultaneously in neighborhoods that it is difficult to determine the causes of decline or renewal. Our quantitative data were useful in identifying rebound neighborhoods but it did not help to identify the causal factors driving neighborhood change. For this reason, we decided to conduct qualitative case studies of five different rebound neighborhoods. In this chapter we draw on one case study to illustrate the key factors behind neighborhood revitalization. Readers may find all five case studies and more details of our quantitative analysis in our original white paper on the topic.[2]

Data and Methodology

Our unit of analysis is the neighborhood. Neighborhoods are often easier to describe than define, but for our purposes we define a neighborhood as an identifiable section of a city where social networks are stronger within rather than across neighborhood boundaries and where residents identify with the area.[3] Neighborhoods are often defined by a common history and by political boundaries, such as wards. Unfortunately, no national database tracks data by neighborhood, so we relied on census tract data as our means of following neighborhood trends. In our analysis we used census tract data to trace neighborhood change in the St. Louis metropolitan area from 1970 to 2010. Census tract boundaries can change over time. In order to ensure that we were tracking uniform geographies over this time period, we utilized the US2010 Longitudinal Tract Data Base (LTDB), which normalizes data from each census into 2010 tract boundaries.[4]

Given our interest in why some older neighborhoods in the urban core rebounded from decline, we decided not to examine the entire metropolitan area. Our database consisted of the 218 census tracts that make up the area of the St. Louis region defined in 1950 as "urbanized" by the U.S. Census Bureau.[5] This area, shown in the palest yellow in Figure 1, includes the city of St. Louis and the immediately surrounding counties to the east and west that are roughly inside the region's outer-ring highway, I-270. In 1950, the study area's 1,400,000 people represented 72 percent of the region; by 2010, the study area population had shrunk to 802,000 people, making up only 28 percent of the growing regional population.[6] Today's definition of the St. Louis metropolitan area includes many counties outside this area, but those counties were primarily developed after 1950 and are therefore not included in our analysis. Figure 1 shows the growth of the urbanized area since 1950.

Figure 1. Change in Urbanized Area, 1950–2010

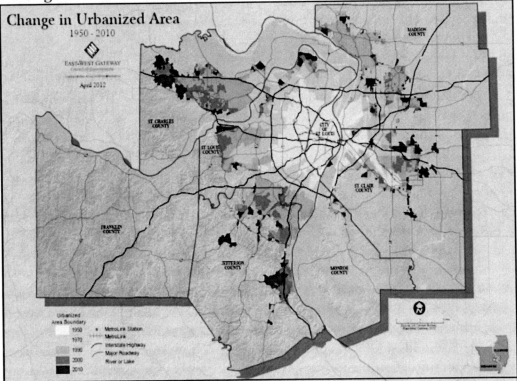

Figure 2 shows the median performance of census tracts in the urban core of St. Louis from 1970 through 2010. The general pattern is decline over time, although the rate of decline has slowed somewhat. On average, census tracts have seen shrinking populations, increased poverty rates, decreased occupancy rates, fewer children, and some white flight. The college-educated population and per capita income (in 2012 dollars) have increased. Neighborhoods that have rebounded since 1970 clearly were not lifted by a rising tide of increased prosperity; they succeeded despite area-wide decline.

Figure 2. Means of All Study Area Census Tracts, 1970–2010

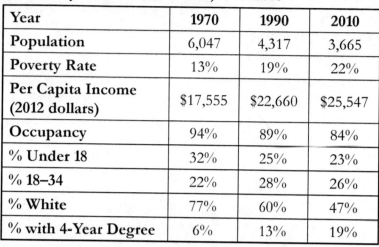

Year	1970	1990	2010
Population	6,047	4,317	3,665
Poverty Rate	13%	19%	22%
Per Capita Income (2012 dollars)	$17,555	$22,660	$25,547
Occupancy	94%	89%	84%
% Under 18	32%	25%	23%
% 18–34	22%	28%	26%
% White	77%	60%	47%
% with 4-Year Degree	6%	13%	19%

Index of Neighborhood Vitality

To compare the performance of neighborhoods in St. Louis, we created a measurement tool called the Neighborhood Vitality Index (NVI) that rates census tracts on their relative strengths. The index looks at three data points for each census tract: per capita income, poverty rate, and vacancy rate. These three data points were picked to represent a census tract's economic (per capita income), social (poverty rate), and physical (vacancy rate) performance. The NVI score is the sum of the standardized values for each of these three variables. Index scores range from around 10 to 260, with a higher score representing stronger performance and 150 representing the study area median. Index scores were calculated for each tract in 1970, 1980, 1990, 2000, and 2010.

Our particular focus was identifying neighborhoods that improved after an earlier period of decline. We call these "rebound" neighborhoods. Rebound census tracts are defined as those that meet the following three requirements:

1. The census tract increased at least 10 percentiles in its ranking among all 218 census tracts in our data set, either from 1990 to 2000 or from 2000 to 2010.
2. The census tract's NVI score was once below the median of all study area tracts.
3. If the census tract improved from 1990 to 2000, we excluded it as a rebound tract if it declined from 2000 to 2010.

Figure 3. Rebound Census Tracts

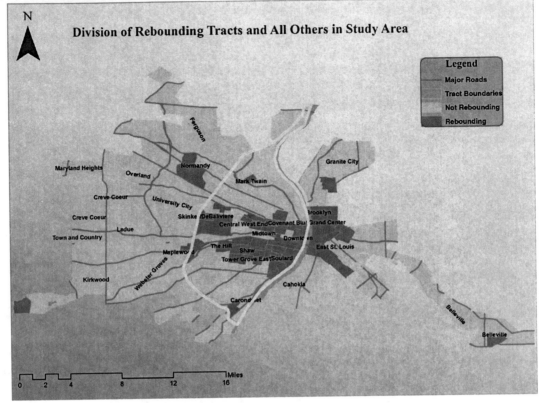

The full set of rebound neighborhoods can be seen highlighted in orange in Figure 3. As the map shows, the rebounding tracts are primarily located within the city of St. Louis (outlined in yellow), with particular concentration in the central corridor of the city. The area between Delmar Avenue and I-64 is where most of the region's key urban amenities are located, including universities, a hospital, the major regional park, and the theatre district. Rebound neighborhoods in the central corridor fit the general theory that "neighborhood improvement" will occur in areas that are close to clusters of professional employment and that have historically significant housing stock. The wealthy in St. Louis migrated directly west from their original settlement along the river to avoid industry's noise and pollution. Much of the housing stock in the central corridor consists of substantial brick-frame structures with unique architectural details. Areas well outside the central corridor, however, also rebounded, including tracts in East St. Louis, a few in North St. Louis City and County, and some far from the urban core, such as Belleville, Illinois. Even within the central corridor of the city of St. Louis, neighborhood improvement was not universal. While some neighborhoods improved, others did not.

Throughout our research we had a number of questions about rebound neighborhoods. How do rebound neighborhoods differ from other neighborhoods in the older parts of the region? Are the residents of rebound neighborhoods different from the residents of other neighborhoods in our data set? Has neighborhood improvement produced communities that are economically and racially diverse or has gentrification occurred, with middle class whites driving out low-income residents of color?

Market theory predicts that the demand for housing in older urban neighborhoods will be driven by increased demand for urban living among the growing number of single and childless households, as well as older empty nesters. Our data analysis, displayed in Figure 4, shows that rebound neighborhoods did have significantly higher percentages of young people and single households than non-rebound census tracts. The low quality of most St. Louis public schools has undoubtedly contributed to the low number of households with children under the age of eighteen in our St. Louis City rebound census tracts.[7] Surprisingly, however, rebound tracts actually had lower percentages of elderly and married couples without children than non-rebound tracts. Young single households are the primary driving force behind neighborhood revitalization in St. Louis.

Figure 4. Residential Demographics in Rebounding and Non-Rebounding Tracts

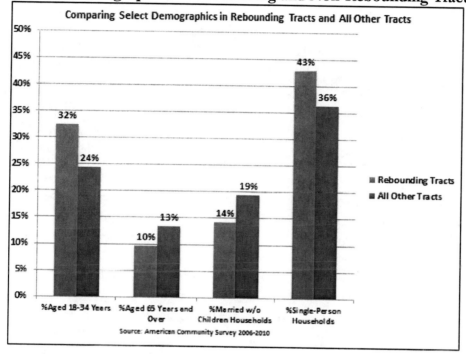

A particular area of interest for us was whether neighborhood improvement would lead to gentrification, with an exodus of minorities and the poor as neighborhoods improved. To test this hypothesis, we constructed two measures of diversity. Our racial diversity index measures the probability that two individuals randomly selected from a single census tract will be of different races. Essentially, this attempts to measure the degree to which a place facilitates interaction among individuals of different races—assuming that racial interaction is random and based on spatial propinquity.[8]

Somewhat surprisingly we found that rebound tracts on average were more diverse than non-rebound tracts. As shown in Figure 5, rebound tracts had a mean diversity score of .40 and a median score of .49, compared to mean and median scores for non-rebounding tracts of .30 and .27. (A higher diversity score indicates a higher level of racial diversity.) A diversity score of .40 could be generated by a neighborhood that was 73% white and 27% black. Conversely, a diversity score of .30 could be generated by a neighborhood that was 82% white and 18% black. Rebounding does not appear to be associated with low racial diversity.

Figure 5. Diversity Index Scores, Rebounding and Non-Rebounding Tracts

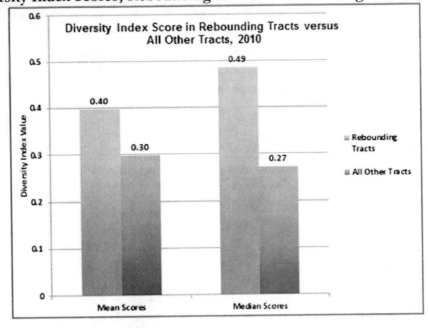

We were also interested in understanding whether the rebound neighborhoods were less economically diverse than non-rebound neighborhoods. To study this question, we computed a score for each census tract based on the percentage of residents in professional occupations and the percentage of residents below the federal poverty level, in both cases using census data. We used this measure of economic diversity to provide a preliminary test of the proposition that the in-movement of young professionals pushes out the poor. As shown in Figure 6, compared to non-rebound neighborhoods, our rebound neighborhoods were much more likely to have higher than median poverty rates and higher than median number of residents with professional occupations. In other words, many of our rebound neighborhoods have both more professionals and more poor people than non-rebounding neighborhoods.

Figure 6. Economic Diversity of Rebounding and Non-Rebounding Tracts

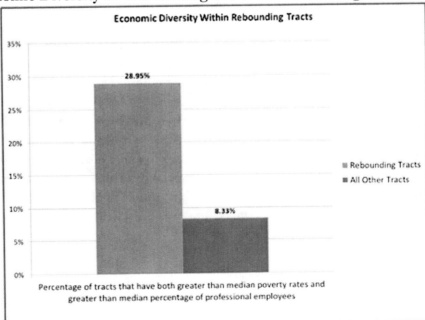
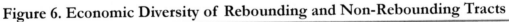

Our findings clearly contradict the classic image of gentrification. The continued racial and economic diversity of rebound neighborhoods in the St. Louis metropolitan area suggests that there has not been large-scale involuntary displacement at the census tract level. Our findings are consistent with a study of six corporate-sponsored redevelopment areas in St. Louis, which concluded that the areas were more economically and racially diverse after redevelopment. "[The] improvements they have seen look very little like gentrification."[9]

There are some important limits, however, to our analysis. Our analysis cannot speak to what might happen in these neighborhoods in the future; we do not have a way of knowing whether the rebound neighborhoods are approaching a point at which they will become less diverse, or if the non-rebound neighborhoods will in the future become more diverse. Second, the racial and economic diversity indices are census tract–level measures; this analysis does not reflect the diversity of individual streets, but rather looks at whether the census tract as a whole is diverse. Individuals may be priced out of living on a specific block, but this analysis suggests that rebounding neighborhoods at least contain areas that are still accessible to lower-income and minority residents.

Moreover, we cannot be sure that the apparent diversity of rebounding neighborhoods reflects a constant population. Census data provides a snapshot of residents every ten years, but it does not track which residents have remained in the same location year after year. Because of this, our analysis does not enable us to determine if longtime minority and low-income individuals have been able to remain in rebound neighborhoods. Therefore it is possible that neighborhoods could appear to be as or more diverse as they were in the past, but the individuals that make up those neighborhood statistics could be an entirely new set of residents. It could also be the case that neighborhoods became less diverse as they rebounded but remained relatively more diverse than other neighborhoods.[10]

The quantitative analysis we have described tells us much about what happened in rebounding neighborhoods in St. Louis. It provides very little if any insight into *why* these changes occurred, however. What factors led some neighborhoods to attract young professionals while others did not? In order to explore these questions, we conducted detailed case studies of five rebounding neighborhoods in St. Louis: the Central West End, Botanical Heights, Shaw, Mark Twain, and Maplewood. The following case study of the Central West End provides one powerful example of how neighborhood revitalization can occur.

The Central West End: Lessons for Leveraging Assets

The Central West End (CWE) is probably the most successful rebound neighborhood in our study area. Many have forgotten that the area shared in the precipitous decline of the city of St. Louis in the 1960s and 1970s. The Chase Park Hotel became vacant, older houses fell into disrepair, the commercial area declined, and the neighborhood was viewed by many as a dangerous place to go at night. Now, it is a vibrant neighborhood with well-maintained homes, crowded sidewalk cafes, and new housing and commercial developments. A Whole Foods grocery store, a symbol of urban neighborhood success, is under construction. Located next to one of the region's major employment centers and one of the great urban parks in the nation, the Central West End enjoys a kind of "place luck" equaled by few other older neighborhoods. Despite this, the Central West End can provide lessons to other neighborhoods in the way its local citizens and institutions leveraged its assets. The Central West End demonstrates the potential of rebound neighborhoods in an older industrial city like St. Louis.

Figure 7. The Location of the Central West End

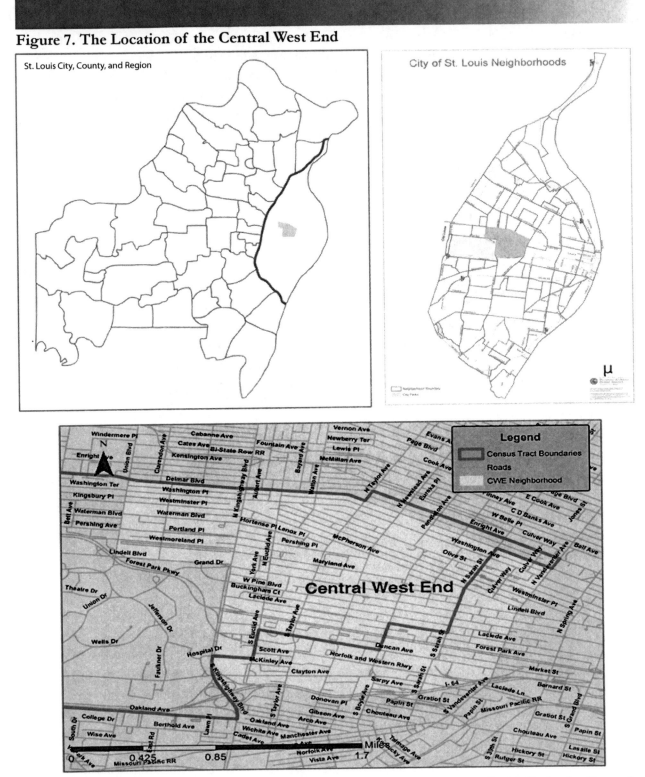

Located in the central corridor of the city of St. Louis, adjacent to Forest Park, the Central West End neighborhood is bordered by Delmar Boulevard to the north, Interstate 64 to the south, Union and Kingshighway to the west, and Vandeventer to the east (see Figure 7). The quantitative analysis conducted for this study utilizes census tracts, which, as shown in Figure 7, omit a small section of the eastern and southern portions of the neighborhood and include a few blocks north of Delmar and west of Union. The exclusion of some of the southern area likely has little effect on the quantitative analysis as the area is dominated by a large medical center and has few residents. In St. Louis, neighborhoods north of Delmar Avenue tend to be much poorer than their neighbors south of Delmar. The inclusion of several blocks north of Delmar therefore has the effect of modestly depressing the average income and increasing the poverty rate for our Central West End data.

Table 1. Central West End, 1970–2010[11]

Year	1970	1990	2010
Population	25,859	17,282	15,518
Poverty Rate	24%	22%	24%
Per Capita Income	$23,078	$38,690	$43,406
Occupancy	85%	86%	86%
% Under 18	20%	10%	7%
% 18–34	28%	35%	44%
% White	54%	59%	58%
% with 4-Year Degree	18%	45%	63%
Index Score	101	164	192

The Central West End, like most of the city of St. Louis, experienced population decline from 1970 to 2010. Poverty rates in the CWE have stayed relatively stable since 1970. While a 24 percent poverty rate is not low by national standards, we estimate that at least half of the population classified as poor by the census in this area is made up of students currently attending Washington University and Saint Louis University. Per capita income in the CWE rose consistently from 1970 to 2010. Occupancy rates remained strong and stable. Reflecting the ongoing weakness of St. Louis's public schools and a location near two major universities, the Central West End has seen a sharp decline in children and a concomitant increase in young adults. The white population has risen slightly since 1970, although the neighborhood has retained considerable racial diversity.

Background: Prior to 1970

The Central West End was traditionally among the most attractive and affluent neighborhoods in the city of St. Louis. During the time of the World's Fair in 1904, the CWE blossomed and attracted many famous individuals and families, inspiring development of numerous grand mansions. The neighborhood is densely populated, featuring attractive single-family homes mixed with higher-end rentals and condominiums. The Chase Hotel, which dominates the skyline of the neighborhood, was for decades a major attraction for the rich and famous visiting St. Louis. Maryland Plaza, immediately adjacent to the Chase Hotel, was considered a stylish shopping area prior to the 1970s, hosting Saks Fifth Avenue and other luxury shops.[12]

The major employment center in the Central West End has long been the Washington University Medical Center, which historically included Barnes, Jewish, St. John's, Shriners, and Children's Hospitals, as well as the Washington University School of Medicine. Many of these institutions have long had national and international reputations and serve as some of the largest employers in the St. Louis region.[13]

Despite an attractive location, strong anchor institutions, and an excellent housing stock, the Central West End was not immune to the decline of the city of St. Louis during the years following World War II. The decline of the Central West End began with suburban flight. From 1950 to 1970 the city of St. Louis lost 27 percent of its residents.[14] The next twenty years brought little relief from this pattern of decline. Many residents who owned homes in the Central West End moved elsewhere or died, and few came to take their place due to fear of crime and difficulty in obtaining home loans. Much of the neighborhood was red-lined with few banks offering home mortgages.[15] The neighborhood's housing stock was impressive, but it included many old homes that began to deteriorate, becoming more expensive to maintain. Commercial spaces were also threatened. Despite the grand history of the Chase Hotel, it fell into disrepair, closed in 1989, and remained vacant for a decade. With the development of malls outside the city of St. Louis, Maryland Plaza became largely vacant despite several attempts at redevelopment.[16]

The Central West End was also impacted by the decline of nearby Forest Park, traditionally the great city park of St. Louis and the home of the St. Louis Zoo, Saint Louis Art Museum, and other cultural and athletic venues. Starting in the 1950s, the quality of Forest Park was threatened by poor maintenance and inadequate funding for improvements.[17]

Partial Rebirth: 1970 to 1990

The institutional and civic forces in the Central West End responded to the challenges facing the neighborhood with skill and dedication. There was much they could not control, but many groups in the Central West End worked effectively to promote the neighborhood and capitalize on its strengths.

The single largest factor contributing to the CWE's success was the decision of Washington University's School of Medicine, the Central Institute for the Deaf, and Barnes, Jewish, and Children's Hospitals to remain in place and launch a concerted effort to improve the surrounding neighborhoods.[18] This decision to stay and improve the environment was not true of all of the medical center's institutions—St. John's Hospital and Shriners Hospital relocated to the suburbs—but the largest institutions stayed and invested. Investments were aimed at increasing safety and livability for students, faculty, staff, physicians, and visitors to the medical complex.[19]

In order to coordinate their neighborhood improvement activities, the institutions in the Washington University Medical Center District combined to create the Washington University Medical Center Redevelopment Corporation (WUMCRC), a nonprofit corporation.[20] Among its duties were physical planning, land acquisition, developer recruitment, and development management in the Central West End. Formed in 1973, WUMCRC sponsored and raised $432 million of investments from 1975 to 1985, creating 641 new housing units and rehabilitating 685 housing units.[21] WUMCRC also attracted commercial developers and businesses to the corridor surrounding the medical complex, creating a thriving commercial district.[22]

Much of this development was aided by Chapter 353, a Missouri statute that provides incentives such as tax abatement to developers of blighted areas. This statute also allowed the use of eminent domain, a policy that facilitated the purchase of underutilized land. Some argue that without Chapter 353, the WUMCRC developments would not have been possible and much of the Central West End would not have been redeveloped. In addition, the city's support of the developments helped to secure $2.2 million in Community Development Block Grants, which are still an essential source for development in the city.[23]

The decision of these anchor institutions to stay and invest in the neighborhood led other employers to invest as well. Blue Cross and Monsanto located substantial facilities in the CWE, adding 1,350 new jobs, and the medical center itself grew by 3,540 employees from 1975 to 1985.[24] With growing employment, new businesses and retailers chose to locate in the CWE. Many historic buildings were refurbished rather than torn down, much to the relief of many vocal neighborhood residents.[25]

WUMCRC was not the only developer active in the neighborhood. By 1988, the Union-Sarah Economic Development Corporation, an organization formed in 1969 by several long-term neighborhood residents, had stimulated more than $55 million in residential and commercial developments in one of the previously most desolate parts of the neighborhood. McCormack Baron Salazar (previously McCormack Baron), a development company that would become a national leader in mixed-income housing developments, also developed housing in the CWE.[26]

One of the issues facing the Central West End through the 1980s was the conflict between preservation and new construction. Preservation of the neighborhood's historic legacy was important to many residents and with the help of the Landmarks Association a large portion of the CWE was declared a local historic district in 1974. The Landmarks Association also helped to get many buildings on the National Register of Historic Places.[27] The decision to make preservation an important part of the CWE neighborhood strategy was rewarded over time as increasing numbers of home buyers valued historic property.

The creation of the local historic district and the listings of buildings on the National Register also allowed residents and developers to access investment tax credits and federal and Missouri state historic tax credits. Investment tax credits provide incentives to developers to preserve rather than tear down historic buildings.[28] Federal historic tax credits were widely used throughout the CWE by developers and owners of income-producing property (commercial or residential rentals) interested in rehabilitating and reusing historic buildings.[29] Missouri historic preservation tax credits are a more recent development, instituted in 1998, which can be used by home or property owners to revitalize historic buildings. When used together, state and federal historic tax credits can reduce the cost of building renovations by 25–40%.[30] Local developers were also skillful in using the federal low-income housing tax credit, to preserve affordable housing in the neighborhood.

The presence of anchor institutions and supportive public policies were two of the three major forces fighting neighborhood decline in the CWE in the 1970s and 1980s. The third was local activism, which was led primarily by the Central West End Association (CWEA). Formed by concerned residents in 1958, the CWEA was particularly active in the 1970s and 1980s and engaged many residents from the neighborhood. The CWEA sought to preserve the historic character of the neighborhood while improving the safety and vitality of the area. Residents involved in the CWEA created their own newsletter, the *West End Word*, as a means for disseminating important information about events, crime, meetings, and other neighborhood news.[31] Leaders of the CWEA included both long-term CWE residents and urban pioneers who moved into the city from the suburbs.[32] Among the many achievements of residents of the Central West End was the creation of the New City School, a high-quality private school that kept many families in the neighborhood.[33]

Local churches and religious institutions were another source of support for residents and the neighborhood. Three local churches—Second Presbyterian, First Unitarian, and Trinity Episcopal—formed the Joint Community Board in the early 1970s to help address decay in the surrounding neighborhood. The board brought residents together and offered tutoring programs and emergency food services, as well as other community resources.[34] Another organization called TW3, sponsored by a donation from Second Presbyterian Church and representing the streets of Taylor, Westminster, Walton, and Washington, was formed with the help of local residents and offered forgivable loans to nearby residents for home improvements. All these efforts helped to strengthen the fabric of the neighborhood on a block-by-block basis.[35]

Strong political leadership was essential to the success of the CWE. In 1986, Alderwoman Mary Stolar was tasked with directing rehabilitation of Forest Park. She created Forest Park Forever, the not-for-profit entity responsible for fundraising and planning for the park's future development and maintenance. Prior to her death in 1987, Stolar raised over $400,000 for the park's development, laying the foundation for the revival that has made Forest Park the jewel that it is today.[36]

Continued Revitalization: 1990 to Present

The initiatives for neighborhood improvement in the Central West End, which began in the 1970s and 1980s, flourished after 1990. The anchor institutions in the Washington University Medical Center grew in quality and size, reflecting national growth in the education and health care sectors. Today, almost 30,000 people work daily at the Washington University Medical Center, and Barnes-Jewish Hospital (Barnes and Jewish Hospitals merged in 1992) and Children's Hospital are regularly ranked among the top ten hospitals in the U.S.[37]

The two most visible improvements in the CWE after 1990 were commercial revitalization and the rebirth of Forest Park. The Chase Hotel reopened successfully in 1999 as the Chase Park Plaza, which now includes a four-star hotel and luxury condominiums as well as a movie theater and upscale restaurants and bars. Commercial development around the Washington University Medical Center and the Chase Park Plaza also boomed. The bars, restaurants, and shops along Euclid Avenue are among the more attractive urban destinations in the country, serving local residents, visitors, students, and employees. Maryland Plaza has once again become an upscale commercial and residential area, with attractive condominiums adjacent to unique shops.[38]

Pedestrian-friendly mixed-use areas like Euclid Avenue are a valuable asset in the Central West End.

The rebirth of Forest Park is among the great success stories of urban redevelopment in the nation. A long and extensive public process led to an award-winning master plan. Responsibility for funding this plan was shared by Forest Park Forever and the city of St. Louis.[39] Thanks to the adoption of this master plan in 1995 and a strategic plan for the post-restoration era in 2009, Forest Park is now a thriving destination hosting bike trails, the newly expanded art museum, zoo, Missouri History Museum, thirty-six holes of golf, restaurants, the Muny theater, and numerous community events.[40]

In 1993, much of St. Louis benefited from the introduction of improved public transportation through the creation of the MetroLink Light Rail system.[41] The Central West End MetroLink stop is directly adjacent to the medical center, improving access to the neighborhood and other parts of the city. Since the area surrounding the MetroLink stop was developed with pedestrians in mind, people can now easily access the CWE without a car.

Security in the neighborhood improved due to the combined efforts of WUMCRC and the CWEA. The two groups established special business districts within their respective areas in the late 1980s and early 1990s, but the districts operated independently of each other with little or no communication. (Special business districts are property owner approved property tax increases that provide funding for enhanced services, such as increased patrolling by off-duty police officers, crime monitoring, and other security efforts.) In 2007, WUMCRC and the CWEA came together to develop a joint Neighborhood Security Initiative, which allowed the districts to pool their security resources together and become more efficient and effective. Since the creation of the CWE NSI, crime rates have decreased over 40 percent and cost savings have allowed for increased investment in security services.[42] Neighborhood beautification has also been a priority, with the introduction of the CWE Community Improvement District (CID) in 2009 providing an increase in sales taxes for beautification and marketing efforts.[43] The Central West End Midtown Development Corporation was founded in 2001 and has had a significant impact on the marketing and physical development of the eastern portion of the neighborhood. More recently, the group changed its name to Park Central Development and expanded its footprint to include several neighborhoods south of the CWE, including Botanical Heights; this expanded organization now provides centralized marketing and development review for this collection of midtown neighborhoods.[44]

From 2000 to the present, the Central West End has undoubtedly become one of the most desirable and affluent urban neighborhoods in the St. Louis region. Housing prices in the neighborhood have increased substantially, with homes that sold for under $30,000 in the early 1970s now costing over $500,000, even as the area has maintained racial and economic diversity.[45] As with all of the rebounding neighborhoods in the central corridor, the neighborhood has been particularly successful in attracting young people.

Conclusion: Prospects for Rebound Neighborhoods in St. Louis

Our case studies of the Central West End and four other neighborhoods identified eight factors that are strongly associated with rebound neighborhoods:

1. strong anchor institutions;
2. excellent housing stock;
3. thoughtful commercial development;
4. thoughtful residential development;
5. resident civic engagement;
6. successful public policy;
7. strong public schools; and
8. good location

Every rebound neighborhood does not need to be strong on every factor. For example, many neighborhoods have rebounded with a modest housing stock. But the more assets a neighborhood has, the greater the likelihood of success. The Central West End, the most clear-cut example of neighborhood rebound in our sample, is strong in seven of the eight success factors. The area is not generally viewed as having strong public schools but even here there are signs of strength.[46] While few, if any, neighborhoods in the older parts of the region have as many factors working in their favor as the CWE, other neighborhoods can learn from how the CWE leveraged its considerable assets.

A key principle of neighborhood revitalization is building upon the unique character of the community. "Thoughtful" commercial and residential development is development that respects the historical and physical character of the community. If older urban neighborhoods try to imitate suburbs, they will fail. The older parts of the region were developed before zoning codes separated uses and they have advantages in developing mixed-use, pedestrian-friendly, amenity-rich urban environments.

The Central West End has been remarkably adept at utilizing public policies to support development, especially physical development. The neighborhood utilized a variety of policies, from Missouri Chapter 353 to historic tax credits and low-income tax credits. The use of low-income housing tax credits was particularly important in maintaining the neighborhood's economic diversity.

In an age when the resources of government are limited, mobilizing the resources of anchor institutions is crucial to success. An "anchor institution" is any institution that is tied to a specific location "by reason of mission, invested capital, or relationships to customers or employees . . ."[47] Few neighborhoods have an anchor with the resources of Barnes Jewish Hospital and the Washington University Medical Center, but every neighborhood has anchors, such as churches, major employers, or cultural institutions, and community success requires the engagement of these institutions.

One factor that was present in every one of our case studies was robust civic engagement by local residents, suggesting that this is the one factor that is necessary for success. The Central West End mobilized early and it mobilized often, producing a vibrant voluntary neighborhood association and its own newsletter. Even though local citizens, by themselves, cannot turn a neighborhood around, they can certainly stop inappropriate developments from happening. Developers in the CWE know that if their developments are not "thoughtful" and respectful of the unique context, they will be opposed by the citizens. The development of local civic capacity is necessary to defend a neighborhood over the long run and support the positive social connections that are necessary for neighborhoods to function well on a day-to-day basis.

Neighborhoods have no control over "good location." As a quick glance at the map of rebound neighborhoods (Figure 3) shows, being located in the central corridor in St. Louis greatly increases a neighborhood's chances of rebounding. This is the area where many higher-paying professional jobs, significant cultural and recreational amenities, and the most expensive older housing stock are located. With the success of the Cortex bio-tech initiative and other major investments on the horizon, there is evidence that the real estate market in the central corridor is continuing to improve. For many this raises the specter of gentrification—the worry that the influx of higher-income professionals in the central corridor will push out the low-income persons and minorities who have lived there for decades. As we noted, our research suggests that this has not yet happened in St. Louis to a great extent. In St. Louis's relatively weak housing prices have not increased enough to cause mass displacement, and the presence of modest rental housing and affordable housing programs has enabled most rebound neighborhoods to remain diverse. This does not mean that as the housing market heats up in St. Louis, longtime residents will not be displaced.

The major issue currently facing St. Louis is not how to control gentrification but how to spread the prosperity of the central corridor south and particularly north into areas of concentrated poverty and racial segregation. We find it encouraging that our data suggest that racial diversity is not a barrier to rebounding; in fact, it appears to be an asset. It is discouraging, however, that all-black neighborhoods were much less likely to rebound.[48] St. Louis's challenge going forward will be to strengthen the civic capacity of all communities, enable all neighborhoods to leverage their unique assets, and begin to connect the separate pockets of success currently emerging in the region.

The authors acknowledge the contributions of the following individuals who assisted with the research on this project: Laura Jenks, Leslie Duling, and Miriam Keller at Washington University and Dean Obermark and Derrick Redhead at the University of Missouri–St. Louis.

Endnotes

1. Will Oremus, "For the First Time Since the 1920s, U.S. Cities are Growing Faster Than Suburbs," *Slate* (June 28, 2012). Retrieved from: http://www.slate.com/blogs/future_tense/2012/06/28/new_census_data_show_us_cities_growing_faster_than_suburbs.html.

2. Hank Webber and Todd Swanstrom, *Rebound Neighborhoods in Older Industrial Cities: The Story of St. Louis, a White Paper* (Public Policy Research Center, UMSL, and Center for Systems Dynamics, Washington University, August 2014).

3. Kent P. Schwirian, "Models of Neighborhood Change," *Annual Review of Sociology* 9 (1983), 83–102.

4. For more information on the data go to: http://www.s4.brown.edu/us2010/Researcher/Bridging.htm.

5. The urbanized area generally consists of contiguous territory that is part of a metropolitan area of at least 50,000 people that has a density of at least 1,000 persons per square mile. For a more complete explanation of how the Census Bureau defines urbanized area, see U. S. Bureau of the Census, Urban and Rural Definitions, October 1995; available at: http://www.census.gov/population/censusdata/urdef.txt. We only included census tracts that were wholly within the urbanized area as of 1950; small parts of the urbanized area in 1950, therefore, are not included in our data set.

6. U.S. Bureau of the Census, "Census of Population 1950–2000" (Washington, D.C.: U.S. Bureau of the Census, various years); U.S. Bureau of the Census, "American Community Survey 2006–2010" (Washington, D.C.: U.S. Bureau of the Census).

7. The St. Louis public schools lost state accreditation in 2007 but gained provisional accreditation in 2012.

8. Our racial diversity index was computed using the following formula based on four racial groups: $D = 1 - (w^2 + b^2 + h^2 + o^2)$ Where D= racial diversity index, w= % white non-Hispanic, b= % black non-Hispanic, h= % Hispanic and o= % other races. The highest diversity score possible is .75 (25 percent in each racial category); the lowest possible score is zero (entire population of one race).

9. Daniel J. Monti Jr. and Daniel Burghoff, "Corporately Sponsored Redevelopment Campaigns and the Demographic Stability of Urban Neighborhoods: St. Louis Revisited," *Journal of Urban Affairs* 34 (5) (2012), p. 528.

10. In our five case studies we did not find any case where a rebound neighborhood became significantly less diverse, with the exception of Botanical Heights, which saw a significant drop in the poverty population between 1990 and 2010. This was probably due to the demolition of properties in the McRee Town development.

11. All per capita income figures are inflation-adjusted to 2012 levels.

12. Suzanne Goell, ed., *The Days and Nights of the Central West End: An Affectionate Look at the Last 20 Years in the City's Most Exciting Neighborhood* (St. Louis, MO: Virginia Publishing Company, 2007).

13. Goell, 2007.

14. Brady Baybeck and E. Terrence Jones, eds., *St. Louis Metromorphosis: Past Trends and Future Directions* (St. Louis, MO: Missouri Historical Society Press, 2004).

15. Goell, 2007; *West End Word*, About the West End Word, retrieved from: http://www.westendword.com/CallPage-9609.114137-Company-History.html#axzz2kRjODTxP; Jim Dwyer, personal interview, August 13, 2013; Nicki Dwyer, personal interview, August 8, 2013.

16. Goell, 2007.

17. Ibid.

18. Goell, 2007; Casey Croy, "The Ten-Year Turnaround: Washington University Medical Center Redevelopment Corporation Brings Back the Neighborhood," *Outlook, Washington University School of Medicine* (Summer 1983), 2–7.

19. Croy, 1983.

20. Ibid.

21. Goell, 2007; Croy, 1983; Rachelle L. Levitt, *Cities Reborn* (Washington, D.C.: Urban Land Institute, 1986).

22. Goell, 2007; S. Jerome Pratter and William G. Conway, *Dollars from Design*, National League of Cities, Office of Membership Services (1981).

23. Pratter & Conway, 1981.

24. Levitt, 1986.

25. Goell, 2007; Pratter & Conway, 1981.

26. Goell, 2007.

27. Ibid.

28. Ibid.

29. Goell, 2007; The City of St. Louis, Missouri, "Historic Preservation Tax Credit Programs" (2013), retrieved from: https://stlouis-mo.gov/government/departments/planning/cultural-resources/national-register-historic-places/Historic-Preservation-Tax-Credit-Programs.cfm.

30. The City of St. Louis, Missouri, Historic Preservation Tax Credit Programs.

31. Goell, 2007.

32. J. & N. Dwyer, personal interviews.

33. Goell, 2007.

34. Goell, 2007.

35. Arthur Perry, personal interview, August 30, 2013.

36. Goell, 2007.

37. "Barnes-Jewish Hospital/Washington University Rankings," *U.S. News and World Report* (2013), retrieved from: http://health.usnews.com/best-hospitals/area/mo/barnes-jewish-hospitalwashington-university-6630930.

38. Goell, 2007.

39. Goell, 2007; Forest Park Forever, "History" (2013), retrieved from: http://www.forestparkforever.org/learn/forest_park_forever/.

40. Forest Park Forever, 2013.

41. Metro Transit–St. Louis, "Metrolink History" (2013), retrieved from: http://www.metrostlouis.org/About/History/The1990s.aspx.

42. Central West End Neighborhood Security Initiative, "About CWE NSI" (2013), retrieved from: http://cwensi.com/.

43. "About the CWE North CID," *Central West End Scene* (2014), retrieved from: http://cwescene.com/about-the-cwe-north-cid/.

44. Brian Phillips, email communication, June 19, 2014.

45. Goell, 2007.

46. A Language Immersion Charter School (Spanish and Chinese) is located not far from the CWE and there are a number of well-respected private schools, including New City, Crossroads College Prep, and Rosati-Kain Catholic High School.

47. Henry S. Webber and Mikael Karlstrom, *Why Community Investment Is Good for Nonprofit Anchor Institutions: Understanding Costs, Benefits, and the Range of Strategic Options* (Chicago: Chapin Hall at the University of Chicago, 2009), p. 1.

48. Richard Florida, "Gentrification and the Persistence of Poor Minority Neighborhoods," *The Atlantic CityLab* (August 7, 2014); available at: http://www.citylab.com/housing/2014/08/gentrification-and-the-persistence-of-poor-minority-neighborhoods/373062/.

ST. LOUIS
CURRENTS

About the Authors

Todd Swanstrom, Ph.D., is the Des Lee professor of community collaboration and public policy administration at the University of Missouri–St. Louis. He has a master's degree from Washington University and a Ph.D. from Princeton. His first book, *The Crisis of Growth Politics: Cleveland, Kucinich, and the Challenge of Urban Populism,* won an award as the Best Book in Urban Politics by the Urban Section of the American Political Science Association (APSA). Swanstrom's co-authored book, *Place Matters: Metropolitics for the Twenty-First Century* (3rd ed., 2014) won the Michael Harrington Award as the best book by the Urban Politics Section of the APSA. As part of the MacArthur Foundation's Building Resilient Regions Network, he published research on local responses to the foreclosure epidemic and efforts to increase employment of women, minorities, and low-income persons in construction.

Henry S. Webber is executive vice chancellor for administration at Washington University in St. Louis. Mr. Webber serves as the chief administrative officer at Washington University, where he oversees administrative and external affairs areas with combined operating and capital budgets exceeding $400 million annually and more than 1,000 university and contracted employees. Mr. Webber is a professor of practice at the Brown School of Social Work and an adjunct professor at the Sam Fox School of Art and Architecture. Since coming to St. Louis in 2008, Mr. Webber has led major initiatives to make Washington University a stronger anchor institution in St. Louis. Mr. Webber serves as vice-chair of the board of directors of Cortex, an urban research park that is currently the largest economic development initiative in St. Louis. Mr. Webber graduated with honors from Brown University and has a master's degree in public policy from Harvard University's John F. Kennedy School of Government.

Community Development

"Neighborhoods matter," begins the essay by Karl Guenther and Todd Swanstrom. Neighborhoods require networks, and those networks build community. The system of community is complex and fluid, with regional, state, and national components along with public, private, and nonprofit actors.

Guenther and Swanstrom map this complex and changing network of community development. This is a glimpse of what successful redevelopment will look like across the region. The actors are varied, but each is making an important contribution to overall success.

Community development in St. Louis is in transition. With continued coordination and emphasis on creating successful networks, St. Louis can avoid worrisome trends by building capacity and leveraging resources.

The Community Development System in St. Louis: The Times, They Are A-Changing

Karl Guenther, M.S.W., and Todd Swanstrom, Ph.D.

Introduction

Neighborhoods matter. They matter to individual life outcomes for those who grow up and live there. They also matter for the region through the attraction of new residents and retention of existing residents with opportunity-rich, high-quality-of-life places to live. *For the Sake of All*, a research initiative by the Washington University and Saint Louis University Schools of Public Health, found that where you live in St. Louis can reduce your life expectancy by eighteen years compared to the highest life expectancy neighborhoods in the region.[1] An opinion piece in the St. Louis Community Builders Exchange newsletter by Brian Phillips, executive director of Washington University Medical Center Redevelopment Corporation, pointed out that in a sea of population losses on the city of St. Louis's Northside are islands of regeneration made possible by "developing and implementing a funding infrastructure to partner with the existing neighborhood development stakeholders in the area" on community-oriented plans.[2] Where you live matters and it is possible to change the trajectory of neighborhoods. So how is the St. Louis region doing in creating strong neighborhoods?

A recent report by Henry Webber, Washington University in St. Louis, and Todd Swanstrom, University of Missouri–St. Louis, explored neighborhood change in the St. Louis region. They found the older parts of the region are home to communities with many different trajectories: many have steadily lost population and investment over the last forty years, some have remained stable, and some have rebounded from urban decline. The core of the region lost over 20% of its population in the 1970s and has yet to stem the population loss, though the loss rate has slowed down considerably. Almost half of the census tracts in the study area had poverty rates over 20% in 2010.[3] St. Louis County has seen a 150% increase in high poverty areas since 2000.[4] On the other hand, many communities in the central corridor of the city of St. Louis and St. Louis County from the river to I- 170 are enjoying population growth and new investment.[5] A few communities in Illinois and north and south of the central corridor in Missouri have also fared better than their peer neighborhoods.[6] These trends demonstrate that neighborhoods can rebound from urban decline.

The region is faced with important questions around how we strengthen neighborhoods in all parts of the region, spread growth outward from strong communities, and decrease the number of neighborhoods of concentrated poverty. How do we as a region develop whole communities that "have a diverse housing stock that meets the needs of the area's workforce, as well as households at different life stages and walks of life; provide access to jobs, services, and goods through multiple transportation options, including autos, transit, bicycles, and walking; have effective schools; use sustainable energy/resource practices; incorporate vibrant public spaces; and encourage civic engagement by all parts of the community?"[7] Carrying out this type of successful community revitalization in slow growth regions such as St. Louis requires:

- **Market Savvy**: Interventions must be appropriate to the market strength of each community.[8]

- **Sufficient Scale**: In order to move a community's market and change the investment psychology, a critical mass of investments is needed.[9]
- **Cross-Silo**: Especially in weak market communities (where housing supply exceeds demand), comprehensive, cross-silo community development plans are necessary to rebuild the market and connect residents to sustained opportunity and resources. Cross-silo planning addresses the many facets a community needs for success—housing, health, education, jobs and business development, social services, safety, community building, transportation options, and public spaces.[10]
- **Civic Engagement**: Input and buy-in from area residents and businesses is essential.
- **Cross-Sector Collaboration**: The public sector cannot do the job alone; collaboration among public, private, and nonprofit actors is necessary.
- **Marketing**: Image-building and marketing of neighborhoods are crucial components of successful community revitalization.[11]

Putting these best practices into action in communities requires strong community organizations and a supportive policy and investment environment. How the St. Louis region supports the practice of these key principles will determine whether or not neighborhoods have an easier or harder time revitalizing and sustaining gains. What would an ideal community development system look like?

First, well-managed, professionally staffed, community-based development organizations are needed. They need the capacity to conduct deep community engagement, develop market-sensitive comprehensive community plans, and coordinate a multitude of funding streams, programs, and partnerships to implement plans at the scale needed for neighborhood change.

Community-based organizations need a supportive environment that incentivizes best practices in community economic development. A supportive environment comprises governments, lenders, businesses, and philanthropic organizations committed to coordinating funding across the life cycle of comprehensive community development initiatives from planning to implementation, investing in organizational capacity of community development organizations and intermediaries, and requiring merit-based, nonpolitical funding decisions. Lastly, cross-sector associations and intermediaries are needed to assist leaders in building strong relationships with one another, connect regional plans and initiatives to neighborhood revitalization, and support policy innovation and change.

To be sure, this ideal does not presently exist. As important as neighborhoods are for individual economic mobility, health, and education—and as much as research has identified practices that are effective in generating community economic development—regions' community development systems vary in their ability to support successful community development. They vary in the number and quality of community development nonprofits, the strength of capacity-building support, the efficiency and effectiveness of cross-sector investment, and sector-wide associations' ability to create space for leaders to collaborate and innovate.[12] Building a better regional community development system is essential to improving our neighborhoods. A study of the Living Cities National Community Development Initiative (NCDI) in the 1990s found that improvements in community development corporation (CDC) practices during that decade had measurable impacts on neighborhood markets, but the majority of improvement was attributable to stronger community development *systems*. Those regions that saw sustained impact shifted community development funding and policy from being "ad hoc and poorly coordinated" to more rational, institutionalized, and impactful practices.[13]

What is happening in each part of the region's community development system? Just as neighborhoods change, so does the system that supports their success. This essay examines the changing community development system in the St. Louis region, including the roles played by CDCs, governments, lenders, businesses, and philanthropy—along with the cross-sector leadership in community development.

Figure 1. Activities of CDCs (percent engaging in each activity)

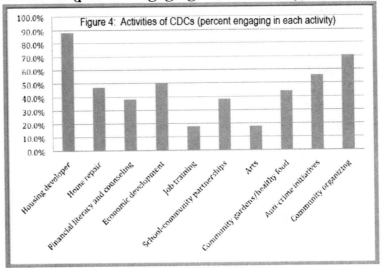

Community Development Organizations

The field of community development organizations encompasses a wide range of actors from community development corporations (CDCs), neighborhood associations, business districts, and for-profit community development organizations. While community-based nonprofits are not the only community development actors in neighborhoods, they are central to many systems as organizations committed to place-based community improvement. CDCs are often integral because they address the "double bottom line": addressing social and economic equity at the same time that they meet the demands of the marketplace. CDCs can respond more quickly to opportunities than government departments, coordinate disparate programs across government and philanthropy, and guide community plans over the long run often in the face of shifting political winds.[14] CDCs carry out a range of activities in the neighborhoods they serve. Besides housing development and repair, CDCs' activities include financial literacy, economic development, community gardens and healthy food, anti-crime initiatives, community organizing, and more (see Figure 1).[15] The breadth of activities indicates that St. Louis CDCs have embraced the movement toward a more comprehensive approach to community improvement and are able to apply local knowledge of what matters in the neighborhoods they serve. CDCs are also able to leverage funds from government grants, foundations, corporations, and fees for service, as well as mobilize volunteers to address community concerns.[16] Lastly, through a commitment to community engagement and resident empowerment, CDCs can help create more inclusive communities.

Figure 2. Map of respondents to 2011 report on St. Louis region's community development system

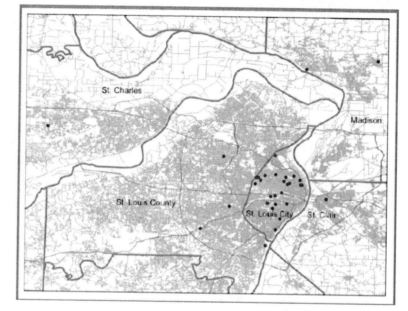

While individual CDCs have strengths, the CDC industry in the St. Louis region has a number of weaknesses. CDCs are mainly located in the city of St. Louis with a small number located in distressed parts of St. Louis County and St. Charles County in Missouri, and St. Clair County and Madison County in Illinois (see Figure 2).[17] This concentration of CDCs leaves many distressed communities without the organizational capacity to develop and implement community improvement strategies. This is especially troubling for the disadvantaged communities in north St. Louis County whose challenges were highlighted by the turmoil in Ferguson. Many municipalities in North County are too small to lead effective community planning. In any case, governments are much more effective when they partner with a community-based nonprofit to do this work. Addressing the gap in community development nonprofits, Christian Northeast Hospital, St. Louis County Planning, and the Economic Development Partnership provided funding to establish a CDC in Spanish Lake, a community in far north St. Louis County.

Another weakness is that too many CDCs lack capacity and are overly dependent on government funding. For example, according to a 2011 study 40% of CDCs have two or fewer employers and 60% have four or fewer employees, making organizational management and comprehensive community initiatives with sufficient scale difficult to undertake successfully.[18] CDCs are also over-reliant on government funding, philanthropic support is currently scarce for this work, and commercial lending for community development lags behind other metropolitan areas.[19]

Figure 3. Percent of community development nonprofits with a certain number of staff

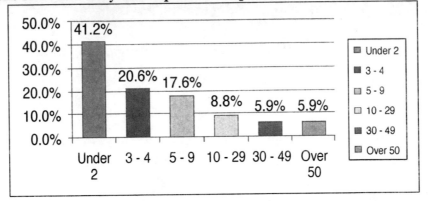

Despite the capacity issues in the community development nonprofit industry, St. Louis is home to larger organizations and initiatives like Beyond Housing's nationally recognized 24:1 initiative, a comprehensive community development initiative in the inner-ring suburban school district of Normandy.[20] Beyond Housing has been working with the twenty-four municipalities that are in the Normandy School Collaborative's footprint to develop and repair housing, build a grocery store and bank, strengthen early childhood education, and more.[21] Habitat for Humanity St. Louis has been a national leader in building LEED platinum housing. Some smaller community development nonprofits are intentionally trying to address low staff capacity through collaboration and consolidation. In 2014, three one-staff-person organizations in south St. Louis City consolidated into a new organization called the Tower Grove Neighborhoods CDC, providing them with more staff capacity to address issues in multiple contiguous neighborhoods. Four new place-based collaborations, each involving three CDCs, are in the midst of developing joint initiatives, supported by the Community Builders Network of Metro St. Louis, an association of community building nonprofits.

While the region does not have consistent local funding sources for community planning and implementation, St. Louis has been able to win federal dollars to aid this work and in some cases has made considerable progress with local resources. The region received a three-year $4.7 million HUD Sustainable Communities Regional Planning grant in 2010, which has resulted in the OneSTL plan for sustainable community development. St. Louis County, along with other local partners, won a federal Choice Neighborhoods Planning grant in 2014, which will support comprehensive planning in Wellston, an inner-ring suburb of St. Louis County.[22] Urban Strategies also was awarded a Choice Neighborhoods Planning grant in 2015 for the near-north side of the city of St. Louis.[23] Beyond Housing, with support from an anonymous donor, undertook a full year of community engaged planning before finalizing their 24:1 plan. Lemay Housing Partnership and Lemay Development Corporation partnered with St. Louis County to develop a community plan. Carondelet Community Betterment Federation created a planning room to showcase community development opportunities to for-profit developers. Skinker-Debaliviere Community Council recently completed a master plan for their neighborhood.

Lastly, for-profit development organizations are also leaving their mark on St. Louis Communities. National mixed-income community developers, McCormack Baron and their nonprofit partner Urban Strategies, are headquartered in St. Louis and have partnered locally with communities to do large-scale mixed-income revitalization throughout north St. Louis City and East St. Louis.

Northside Regeneration, an effort by developer Paul McKee, aims to redevelop 1,500 acres in north St. Louis City.

In short, community-based nonprofits in the St. Louis region often lack the size and capacity to engage in the scale of community development work that is needed. Nevertheless, many communities are devising and implementing neighborhood plans. Successful community planning in the St. Louis region tends to be patchwork, with some communities doing cutting-edge work and other needy communities not even in the game. If a community is lucky enough to have a strong CDC with a strong and even charismatic leader, they can succeed at the revitalization game. However, if we want to insure that every disadvantaged community has the chance to revitalize itself, we will need a stronger community development infrastructure, supported by public, private, and philanthropic organizations.

Government and Nongovernment Infrastructure

Community development organizations and their partners rely on investment and policy support from government, lenders, business, and philanthropy to undertake comprehensive community development initiatives. Funding community development in the St. Louis region has mostly fallen to the public sector, whether through Community Development Block Grant funds, HOME Investment Partnership funds, tax credits, or federal programs such as Choice Neighborhoods and Promise Neighborhoods.[24] Community development nonprofits on average (un-weighted) had 50% of their budgets coming from government funds in a 2011 study on the state of community development in the St. Louis region. Foundation and private sector grants accounted for only 15% and 16% of budgets, respectively. Thirteen of the thirty-plus nonprofit community development organizations participating in the 2011 study relied on government for 75% or more of their funding.[25] These statistics illustrate the heavy reliance on government funding for community development in the region.[26]

Figure 4: Percent of community development nonprofit income for past three years from different sources (un-weighted averages)

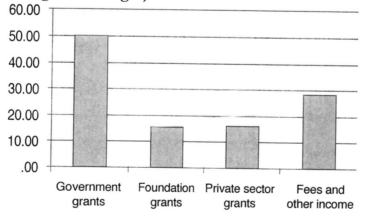

Government Support

The St. Louis metropolitan area had the third-highest level of municipal fragmentation in the nation in 2007.[27] St. Louis County alone has ninety municipalities. Fragmented jurisdictions have meant fragmented use of public funds and often encouraged competition instead of collaboration.[28] Fragmented use of funds has made amassing large amounts of capital difficult. This limited fund size in any one community has meant that larger community development initiatives at a scale capable of impacting markets have been hard to support. Many of the government funding and investment streams are currently declining, capped, or threatened. Despite these barriers, recent developments in the government landscape are changing how the region uses the resources it has.

Revitalization tools include a wide range of items like tax abatement, tax increment financing (TIF), grant programs, and tax credits like New Markets tax credits. The dominant programs used by nonprofit community development organizations in the region, which face cuts, caps, and threats, are federally funded programs like the Community Development Block Grant (CDBG) and HOME Investment Partnership, state low-income housing and historic preservation tax credits, and affordable housing trust funds.

The counties in the inner core of the metropolitan area that have faced the most headwind since the 1970s have seen large decreases in the federal programs often used to support community improvement. While funding may go up and down from year to year, in 2015 dollars, St. Louis City, St. Louis County, St. Clair County, and Madison County are receiving $24,121,301 fewer CDBG dollars in 2014 than they did eleven years earlier and received $6,883,133 fewer Home Investment Partnership dollars in 2013 than they did in 2003. [29]

Table 1. Community Development Block Grant Funding Levels, 2003–2014

County	2003 CDBG	2014 CDBG	Percent Change
St. Louis City, MO	$32,218,542	$16,469,826	- 48.88%
St. Louis County, MO	$8,513,794	$4,765,818	- 44.02%
St. Clair County, IL	$2,204,975	$1,159,500	- 47.41%
Madison County, IL	$4,728,756	$1,149,622	- 75.69%
Total	$47,666,067	$23,544,766	- 50.60%
Grant amounts were adjusted for inflation and are in 2015 dollars.			

Table 2. Home Investment Partnership Funding Levels, 2003–2013

County	2003 HOME	2013 HOME	Percent Change
St. Louis City, MO	$5,990,365	$2,320,464	- 61.26%
St. Louis County, MO*	$4,492,454	$2,811,755	- 37.41%
St. Clair County, IL*	$1,344,541	$616,070	- 54.18%
Madison County, IL	$1,543,922	$739,859	- 52.08%
Total	$13,371,282	$6,488,148	- 51.48%
*Figures represent HOME consortiums in both counties Grant amounts were adjusted for inflation and are in 2015 dollars.			

The St. Louis region is a leader in tax credit real estate development, especially using the historic preservation and low-income housing tax credit programs. The St. Louis metropolitan area ranked 6th in the nation for number of federal LIHTC projects completed through 2012.[30] One of the reasons is that the state of Missouri has state low-income and historic tax credits that can be piggybacked on the federal credits. The Missouri House and Senate have debated cutting the state low-income housing tax credit in recent years. The House passed a measure in 2014 to curb the state

LIHTC program from $140 million to $110 million, but the measures to curb housing tax credits have not become law.[31] The future of these development tools remains uncertain.

While Missouri debates the size of its housing tax credit programs, the Illinois legislature has for the most part supported housing programs but increasingly uses the Illinois Affordable Housing Trust Fund to support programs that formerly were supported by general revenue.[32] Affordable housing trust funds have been developed by states and counties across the country. St. Louis City and St. Louis County both have locally controlled affordable housing trust funds. These local trust funds supply another revenue stream to invest in building strong communities, but the St. Louis County trust fund is narrowly focused on addressing homelessness and St. Louis City's trust fund was capped at $5 million a year in 2003.[33] Capping the affordable housing trust fund limits one of the only local sources of community development funds in the region.

Table 3. Top Ten Metropolitan Statistical Areas for Low-Income Housing Tax Credits

Rank	Metropolitan Area
1	New York–Newark–Jersey City, NY-NJ-PA Metro Area
2	Los Angeles–Long Beach–Anaheim, CA Metro Area
3	Philadelphia-Camden-Wilmington, PA-NJ-DE-MD Metro Area
4	Chicago-Naperville-Elgin, IL-IN-WI Metro Area
5	Kansas City, MO-KS Metro Area
6	St. Louis, MO-IL Metro Area
7	Washington-Arlington-Alexandria, DC-VA-MD-WV Metro Area
8	Seattle-Tacoma-Bellevue, WA Metro Area
9	Boston-Cambridge-Newton, MA-NH Metro Area
10	Atlanta–Sandy Springs–Roswell, GA Metro Area

In an era of decreasing public resources, three positive trends are noteworthy: 1) the St. Louis region has recently done a better job of garnering competitive grant resources from the federal government; 2) recent pushes for more strategic, transparent, and objective grant processes open the possibility of making current public funding more effective; 3) the St. Louis Port Authority's Community Reinvestment Fund has added a new source of revenue. As mentioned previously, the region won a HUD Sustainable Communities Regional Planning grant and two Choice Neighborhoods Planning grants. The city of St. Louis received a Strong Cities Strong Communities grant that is designed to increase local government's ability to apply for and integrate federal funding into more impactful community revitalization initiatives.[34] New developments in how the city of St. Louis allocates its CDBG and HOME funds have created opportunities for more merit-based funding decisions. HUD has worked with the city of St. Louis to transition its Community Development Block Grant (CDBG) process from ward-based funding into a more transparent competitive city-wide funding process with priorities based in part on a market value analysis that enables communities to have a data-based understanding of local housing markets.[35] This change allows the city of St. Louis to deal with the limitations of fragmentation and incentivize best practices. In 2011, East St. Louis's mismanaged Community Development Block Grant Program switched to being managed by St. Clair County's Intergovernmental Grants Department, which had more capacity to run federal government grant programs.[36] Lastly, around 2010, St. Louis County and the St. Louis Port Authority created a fund dedicated to community and economic development from lease payments paid by the River City Casino.[37]

Nongovernmental Infrastructure

The region has not yet developed a consistent or coordinated approach to nongovernmental funding. Very few local foundations focus on community development. Since the Danforth Foundation pivoted away from its St. Louis 2004 initiative and spent down its endowment, there has been no large local community development funder like the Cleveland Community Foundation, Zilber Family Foundation in Milwaukee, or Kresge Foundation in Detroit.[38] While the Rockefeller Foundation recently made the city of St. Louis one of their Resilient Cities, enabling the city to hire a staff person to work on resiliency efforts,[39] the St. Louis region does not have a robust connection to large national community development funders or intermediaries like the Local Initiatives Support Corporation (LISC), MacArthur Foundation, Kellogg Foundation, Annie E. Casey Foundation, or Rockefeller Foundation. Through Rise Community Development, the region's leading community development intermediary, the metropolitan area has been able to remain connected to Enterprise Community Partners but Enterprise does not have an office in the St. Louis region. St. Louis has not participated in national opportunities, such as the National Community Development Initiative, which invested $253.8 million ($152.5 million in loans and $101.3 million in grants) across twenty-three cities in the 1990s.[40] Lastly, commercial lending in St. Louis has historically lagged behind other regions like Cleveland and Indianapolis.[41]

This lack of philanthropic funding creates a dearth of entrepreneurial funding for strategic collaborative community development initiatives, managing coordination across silos (education, health, job training, etc.) and sectors, managing community engagement and neighborhood marketing, and providing subsidy, through program-related investments, or other creative models for attracting private capital into communities. Whether through pooled funds or coordinated investment, other regions have developed models to effectively blend investment from the corporate, lending, and philanthropic sectors. Healthy Neighborhoods, pioneered in Baltimore, is a model of collaboration between the philanthropic and banking community that targets favorable home mortgage and home improvement loans to bolster "middle market" communities that could fall into decline.[42]

A growing number of Community Development Financial Institutions (CDFIs) in recent years are developing or have expanded into the St. Louis region, each with its own focus. Founded in 2009, Gateway CDFI focuses on housing development and consulting services, and IFF, which expanded into the St. Louis market in 2006, focuses on nonprofit facilities, community centers, schools, and grocery stores. The St. Louis Equal Housing and Community Reinvestment Alliance (SLEHCRA) has been using the Community Reinvestment Act and fair housing laws to negotiate with banks for increased investment in minority and distressed communities. As a result, area banks have begun to increase loans in needy communities, hire new, often minority, community investment staff, and develop new loan products for low-income persons.[43] The Greater Saint Louis Community Foundation has worked with young professionals to launch Invest STL, a crowd funding approach to building investment for communities.[44] Anchor institutions, like Washington University in St. Louis, the BJC Hospital System, Bellefontaine Cemetery, the Missouri Botanical Garden, and the University of Missouri–St. Louis, have invested in neighborhoods around their institutions. These institutions have provided funding to community development nonprofits and invested directly in communities. Anchor institutions represent a growing part of the changing nongovernmental funding landscape.[45]

The development of new solutions to nongovernmental funding may come out of conversations underway between the nonprofit, banking, and philanthropic communities.. The Metropolitan St. Louis CRA Association and the Community Builders Network of Metro St. Louis have formed a task force that includes representatives from the Greater St. Louis Community Foundation, United Way, and IFF, to develop recommendations on how to build a stronger community development system. The task force report calls for pooling funds for community development investments and capacity building.[46] Also, the Greater Saint Louis Community Foundation worked with the University of Missouri–St. Louis, the Gateway Center for Giving, and others on forums during the fall of 2013 to engage the philanthropic sector around issues of place and people. Broader conversations and recommendations across the sectors increases the likelihood that the St. Louis region will enhance nongovernmental support for community development .

Capacity-Building Environment

Not only do governments, corporations, and philanthropies support community development activity but they also support capacity building for individual organizations. Given the prominence of small community development nonprofits and their reliance on a few funding sources, supporting their growth and increased expertise is especially important. Capacity building involves pairing professional development with operating support to increase organizational effectiveness.[47]

Operating Support

Metropolitan areas with impactful capacity-building systems such as Cleveland, Portland, Oregon, and Washington, D.C. have in the past developed funding collaboratives that pool and coordinate funding across government, foundations, banks, and businesses to provide multiyear financial support, contingent on performance, to community development organizations with clear business plans and comprehensive neighborhood plans.[48] While this multisector, multiyear model of supplying operating support has not been fully realized in St. Louis, Rise Community Development has managed for a number of years a CDC capacity-building and collaborative grant funding program supported by local banks to build the capacity of community development nonprofits.[49] Given low levels of nongovernmental funding, some communities have turned to special taxing districts to support their work, such as Park Central Development Corporation and South Grand Community Improvement District.[50]

Professional Development

Complementary to operating support is technical assistance and professional development for community development organizations. The St. Louis region is witnessing a growth in training and professional development opportunities for community development professionals. Below are examples of the offerings currently in the region:

- Rise offers technical assistance to individual organizations, like strategic planning or development consulting, and provides informational trainings four times a year that are open to the public.
- The Community Builders Network of Metro St. Louis with support from the University of Missouri–St. Louis Des Lee Collaborative Vision has delivered intensive capacity-building programs that take community development nonprofits from workshops to project implementation on issues like financial sustainability and collaboration, and offer scholarships to trainings and encourage peer-to-peer learning.

- The St. Louis Association of Community Organizations is rebuilding to more strongly support neighborhood associations and returned to offering its yearly neighborhoods conference.
- The Brown School at Washington University in St. Louis developed a partnership with Neighborworks America to offer a series of three trainings that culminate in a certificate of affordable housing and mixed-income community management.
- The University of Missouri–St. Louis and the University of Missouri Extension offer the Neighborhood Leadership Academy.
- Community development financial institutions like the Gateway CDFI are offering technical assistance services.
- The city of St. Louis's Community Development Administration is holding monthly trainings on issues facing community development nonprofits.
- The city of St. Louis has also received support through the federal Strong Cities Strong Communities program which will aid those working in the city to learn how to apply for and weave together federal programs to strengthen communities.
- The Metropolitan St. Louis Community Reinvestment Act (CRA) Association provides peer-to-peer learning and assistance to members in understanding best practices in CRA and community development.
- The region's universities, along with Rise, have community data analysis capacity and experts on community development that are able to assist community development nonprofits in evaluation. Led by Rise, St. Louis is a member of the National Neighborhood Indicators Partnership coordinated by the Urban Institute.

The training and technical assistance component of St. Louis's capacity-building system is rather strong. These professional development assets are provided on top of a rich set of general nonprofit management and leadership offerings throughout the region. Government, nonprofit intermediaries and associations, and universities are all involved in making sure professionals in the sector have access to professional training.

Cross-Sector Relationships and Activity

Associations, task forces, working groups, and funder/lender collaboratives are structures that regions employ to ensure that the connectivity of leaders and practitioners in a field can be maintained and regions can develop solutions to barriers facing the field. Connectivity within and across sectors is crucial for creating the space needed to work continuously on the social relationships between leaders, to fostering collaboration and coordination between different community development actors.[51] The St. Louis region is seeing growth in associations and increased attempts at collaboration within and across sectors.

Growth in Associations

The St. Louis region has a long-standing history of associations and councils in the business community (Regional Chamber and Regional Business Council), education (Regional Early Childhood Council, Maternal Child and Family Coalition, St. Louis Graduates, etc.), philanthropy (Gateway Center for Giving), and even cross-sector organizations like the Leadership Council Southwestern Illinois. Two new associations and one reviving association are strengthening the ability for the community development sector to get more organized and engage with other sectors. The twenty-seven-member Community Builders Network of Metro St. Louis was formed in September 2011 as an association of nonprofit community building organizations dedicated to organizational capacity building, civic capacity building, and public awareness of the importance of community revitalization.[52] The thirty-five-member Metropolitan St. Louis Community Reinvestment Act Association formed in February 2012 to support professional development and collaboration among CRA officers in banks.[53] The St. Louis Association of Community Organizations (SLACO), a long-standing association of neighborhood associations, hired a new part-time executive director in 2013, hired a neighborhood organizer in 2014, and has since begun more recruitment of new members.[54] SLACO members now represent 25 percent of the population of the city of St. Louis. The statewide Missouri Workforce Housing Association, formed in the later part of the first decade of the century, has brought together developers, nonprofits, architects, and others to advocate for affordable workforce housing at the state level.[55]

Increasing Attempts at Collaboration

Having formal networks of community development organizations, banks, and neighborhood associations is making it easier for organizations within sectors to attempt collaborations. Members of the Metropolitan St. Louis Community Reinvestment Act Association have partnered together to coordinate their participation in resource fairs, work to support member professional development, and explicitly work to form a collaborative environment across institutions.[56] The Community Builders Network of Metro St. Louis (CBN) has invested heavily in collaboration. In March 2013, CBN began a formal initiative to develop collaboration among its members. As of July 2014, four groups of three organizations each are finalizing their collaborative initiative plans, which range from safety to housing to entrepreneurship support for beautification efforts. Outside this formal process, a CBN member has partnered with educational institutions to develop a community health initiative; three organizations consolidated into one to achieve greater staff capacity; and some CDCs have begun to collaborate through pooled purchasing of printing services for their neighborhood newspapers.

Potential for Common Understanding, Collaborative Solutions, and Coordination Across Sectors

Evaluation of the National Community Development Initiative found that systems with agreement to neighborhood revitalization strategies across public, corporate, banking, philanthropic, and nonprofit community development sectors were stronger than those without a shared understanding.[57] Developing a common commitment to neighborhood revitalization strategies will take civic dialogue and intentional conversation across sectors. Area universities, local radio stations, reporters, and associations have been focusing on neighborhood revitalization issues in public forums, articles, radio shows, and television shows. The University of Missouri–St. Louis and Washington University in St. Louis have put on two forums in the last two years on neighborhood change with subsequent radio appearances on *St. Louis on the Air. Stay Tuned*, a local program on the region's public television network, has focused a number of programs on neighborhood issues. The University of Missouri–St. Louis has held six community forums, called "What's Brewing?," to examine the local actions that helped to create "rebound neighborhoods." The Department of Housing and Urban Development's interjection of the market value analysis tool into the city of St. Louis's grant process sparked conversation about real estate development strategy in different types of market strength communities.[58] The philanthropic community in 2013 explored the interaction between place-based and people-based issues over a three-part series. In 2014, representatives from the

Metropolitan St. Louis Community Reinvestment Act Association, Community Builders Network of Metro St. Louis, IFF, United Way of Greater Saint Louis, and the Greater Saint Louis Community Foundation created the Strengthening St. Louis Neighborhoods Task Force and released a report in December 2014 on how St. Louis could build a regional community development system.[59] The recommendations in that report are a starting point to get agreement among civic actors on strategies and systems that support neighborhood revitalization.

Lastly, coordination across sectors for community development activity, especially to link regional initiatives and trends to neighborhood improvement, has yet to become a mainstay in the metropolitan area. Tackling coordination is essential on issues like economic development. Often regional action is required to create growing economic strength. But a commitment is needed by regional economic development and neighborhood revitalization practitioners to tie regional growth to distressed communities.[60] Transit-oriented development around MetroLink stations, such as that being planned by Beyond Housing for the St. Charles Rock Road Station, could be an effective strategy for linking disadvantaged communities to regional opportunity structures.

Conclusion: A system in Flux with Discrete Areas for Growth

The situation of neighborhoods in the St. Louis region varies tremendously. On the one hand, the central corridor is taking off, turning around neighborhood's that once were in rapid decline. The strength of the central corridor is spreading south to neighborhoods like the Grove, Botanical Heights, and Shaw. But the neighborhoods north of the infamous "Delmar Divide" are struggling. Some, like Old North, Mark Twain, and the West End, have made some progress but much more needs to be done. Beyond Housing is doing some of the most comprehensive community development work in the nation, but few neighborhoods have the generous anonymous donor that has made this work possible. Growing poverty in the inner-ring suburbs of St. Louis County is especially worrisome. These communities generally lack both community-based nonprofits and strong municipal governments to address their issues. In short, the St. Louis region needs a stronger community development system so that every community can develop and implement revitalization plans.

St. Louis's community development system is in a period of change. The region has new assets and practices that are counterweights to system weaknesses. The following highlights the status of different parts of the St. Louis region's community development system.

- Community development organizations in general 1) have limited staff capacity, 2) are concentrated in the city of St. Louis and not in outlying counties, 3) are over-reliant on government funding, 4) do more comprehensive community development than just housing development, and 5) are beginning to do more community-engaged planning.
- Government, lender, business, and philanthropic support for community revitalization is marked by 1) often-used government funding being cut, capped, or threatened, 2) increased professionalism in government grant processes, 3) limited and uncoordinated nongovernment funding, 4) no consistent investment for comprehensive community planning, 5) limited operating support for CDCs, and 6) increasingly robust professional development offerings.
- Within and across sector connectivity is typified by 1) growth in associations, 2) growth in attempted collaborations within sectors, and 3) potential for a common understanding of community development, collaboration, and coordination across sectors.

With all the changes that have taken place recently and the potential for more, the next five to ten years of community development activity in the region will be interesting to watch. Given where the region is today, the following are areas to focus on in the coming years.

- Fostering sufficiently staffed and well-managed community development organizations with sufficient scale to cover a wider range of disinvested geographies.
- Creating nongovernmental funding streams, including pools of funding for investment and capacity building, for multiyear community development initiatives.
- Developing creative ways to coordinate and leverage funding streams, ultimately attracting national foundations to invest in the St. Louis community development system.

Endnotes

1. *For the Sake of All* investigated social determinants of health in the St. Louis African American community. This report looked heavily at how communities effect health outcomes. Washington University in St. Louis and St. Louis University. (2014). *For the Sake of All: A report on the health and well-being of African Americans in St. Louis and why matters for everyone.* Retrieved from https://forthesakeofall.files.wordpress.com/2014/05/for-the-sake-of-all-report.pdf

2. B. Phillips, "The 2010 Census: A Wake-Up Call for Community Development in St. Louis." *Community Builders Exchange E-Newsletter.* (2012). Retrieved from < http://www.communitybuildersstl.org/index.php/the-2010-census-a-wake-up-call-for-community-development-in-st-louis/ >.

3. H. Webber & T. Swanstrom, "Rebound Neighborhoods in Older Industrial Cities: The Story of St. Louis" (Unpublished white paper). Washington University in St. Louis and University of Missouri St. Louis, St. Louis, MO. (2014).

4. St. Louis County Government. "Snapshot of Strategic Plan: Imagining Tomorrow for St. Louis County" (2013). Retrieved from <http://www.stlouisco.com/Portals/8/docs/document%20library/Planning/strategicplan2013/stakeholder_handout.pdf >.

5. T. Bryant, "Anchors and Transit Spur Growth of St. Louis corridor," *St. Louis Post-Dispatch* (2014 January 26). Retrieved from< http://www.stltoday.com/business/local/anchors-and-transit-spur-growth-of-st-louis-corridor/article_f095688e-11b9-5819-9bc7-14292595c47a.html >.

6. H. Webber & T. Swanstrom, 2014.

7. Description of whole communities is defined on page 3 of T. Swanstrom & K. Guenther. (2011). Creating Whole Communities: Enhancing the Capacity of Community Development Nonprofits in the St. Louis Region. Public Policy Research Center, University of Missouri–St. Louis, St. Louis, MO. Retrieved from <http://pprc.umsl.edu/pprc.umsl.edu/data/EnhancingCapacity2011.pdf >.

8. P. C. Brophy & K. Burnett, "Community Development Partnership Network." *Buildling a New Framework for Community Development in Weak Market Cities.* Denver, CO: (2003). Retrieved from < http://community-wealth.org/_pdfs/articles-publications/cdcs/paper-brophy-burnett.pdf >.

9. G. Galster, P. Tatian & J. Accordino, "Targeting Investment for Neighborhood Revitalizaiton." *Journal of the American Planning Association,* 72 (4) (2006). 457–473.

10. On the importance of cross-silo, comprehensive community development practices, see the Low Income Support Corporation's (LISC's) Sustainable Communities Initiative: http://www.lisc.org/sustainable/; and Ann C. Kubisch, Patricia Auspos, Prudence Brown & Tom Dewar, *Voices from the Field III: Lessons and Challenges from Two Decades of Community Change Efforts.* Washington, D.C.: Aspen Institute.

11. Key principles quoted from policy brief written by Professor Todd Swanstrom, University of Missouri–St. Louis, and members of the Community Builders Network. See Community Builders Network of Metro St. Louis. (2012). *Improving the Community Development System in the City of St. Louis.* St. Louis, MO. Retrieved from< http://www.communitybuildersstl.org/wp-content/uploads/2013/01/CBN_STLCityGov_Recommendations_2_22_13.pdf >.

12. See Table 2.3 on page 20 regarding CDC industry, page 30–31 regarding production systems, page 44 regarding capacity-building systems, and page 52–53 regarding leadership systems in C. Walker, 2002. Community Development Corporations and Their Changing Support Systems. Washington, D.C.: Urban Institute.

13. C. Walker, 2002, pages 1-2

14. C. Walker, 2002 page 1

15. T. Swanstrom & K. Guenther, based on a survey of 34 community-based nonprofits in the region. (2011). Pages 5–15. (Figure 1 from page 10.)

16. T. Swanstrom & K. Guenther (2011). Pages 15–21

17. T. Swanstrom & K. Guenther (2011). Figure 2 is from page 4.

18. T. Swanstrom & K. Guenther (2011). Pages 15–21 (Figure 3 from page 16.)

19. Pages 3 and 14–15 in W. T. Bogart (2003). Civic Infrastructure and the Financing of Community Development (Discussion paper). Brookings Institution Center on Urban and Metropolitan Policy, Washington, D.C.; graph of origins of income on page 19 of T. Swanstrom & K. Guenther (2011).

20. Beyond Housing was highlighted on page 6 of White House Report. (2011). Building Neighborhoods of Opportunity: White House Neighborhood Revitalization Initiative Report. Washington, D.C. Retrieved from http://www.whitehouse.gov/sites/default/files/nri_pb_agencies_final_9.pdf

21. Beyond Housing (2011). The 24:1 Initiative Community Plan: Strong Communities, Engaged Families, Successful Children. St. Louis, MO. Retrieved from http://www.beyondhousing.org/wordpress/wp-content/uploads/2012/08/24-1-Community-Plan-Final-7-18-11.pdf

22. M. Hales (2011–2012). Planning Grant Tries to Ready St. Louis for a Sustainable Future. *Bridges*, Winter 2011–2012.; for HUD press release listing St. Louis County's Choice Neighborhoods Planning Grant U.S. Department of Housing and Urban Development. (2013). HUD Awards Nearly $4 Million to Spur Next Generation of Housing, Neighborhood Transformation (HUD No. 13-175). Washington, D.C. Retrieved from http://portal.hud.gov/hudportal/HUD?src=/press/press_releases_media_advisories/2013/HUDNo.13-175

23. T. Bryant, Urban Strategies Gets Neighborhood Planning Grant. stltoday.com (2015 January 16). Retrieved from <http://www.stltoday.com/business/columns/building-blocks/urban-strategies-gets-neighborhood-planning-grant/article_cb18074b-6419-5ad0-b4c8-7318002af79a.html >.

24. Examples and definitions of federal, state, and local community development programs can be found at <http://ded.mo.gov/Programs.aspx,><http://www.missouridevelopment.org/Community%20Services/Local%20Finance%20Initiatives.html,>< http://www.mhdc.com/nofa/,> and <http://portal.hud.gov/hudportal/HUD?src=/hudprograms/toc.>. Many of the funding streams used locally are federal grants that come to local jurisdictions like the Community Development Block Grant and HOME Investment Partnership or state/federal programs.

25. T. Swanstrom & K. Guenther (2011). Pages 16–21. (Figure 4 from page 19.)

26. St. Louis is not alone. Over the last twenty years researchers estimate that government spent $9 billion on community development compared to only $1 billion for philanthropy. A.C. Kubisch, P. Auspos, P. Brown & T. Dewar, (2010). Voices from the Field III: Lessons and Challenges from Two Decades of Community Change Efforts. Washington, D.C.: Aspen Institute, p. 10..

27. Dreier, Mollenkopf, and Swanstrom, from the 2007 Census of Governments as compiled. 2014, p. 38.

28. Living Cities and the Initiative for Responsible Investment at Harvard University (2013). Expanding the Geographic Reach of Community Investment: The IFF Case Study. Retrieved from http://www.livingcities.org/knowledge/media/?action=view&id=152

29. Calculations on CDBG and HOME fund allocations in text and in the tables use data from U.S. Department of Housing and Urban Development. Grant amounts were adjusted to 2015 dollars. Community Planning and Development Allocations and Awards [Data File]. Available from https://www.onecpd.info/grantees/cpd-allocations-awards/

30. Metropolitan Statistical Area (MSA) rankings come from analysis of the Low Income Housing Tax Credit Database and was conducted on data entries that had geographic information recorded for the project. The ranking is based on number of projects and not number of units produced. If the ranking was based on units produced, St. Louis would be ranked 22nd. The database is available at the U.S. Department of Housing and Urban Development. Low Income Housing Tax Credit Database [Data File]. Available from http://www.huduser.org/portal/datasets/lihtc.html#data

31. J. Rosenbaum, "Under the Microscope: Questioning Low-Income Housing Tax Credits Impact and Future." St. Louis Public Radio. (2014 March 12). Retrieved from< http://news.stlpublicradio.org/post/under-microscope-questioning-low-income-housing-tax-credits-impact-and-future >.

32. Housing Action Illinois. Illinois General Assembly Session Wrap Up (2014). Retrieved from <http://housingactionil.org/2014/06/02/illinois-general-assembly-session-wrap-up/ >.

33. For information on St. Louis's affordable housing trust funds and the city of St. Louis's trust fund, see the following: pages 16 and 17 in Focus St. Louis (2005). Affordable Housing for the Region's Workforce. Retrieved from< http://c.ymcdn.com/sites/www.focus-stl.org/resource/resmgr/policy_report/affordable_housing_for_the_r.pdf; > St. Louis City, Missouri. St. Louis City Ordinance 65132. Retrieved from< http://www.slpl.lib.mo.us/cco/ords/data/ord5132.htm;>St. Louis City, Missouri. St. Louis City Revised Code Chapter 3.59 Affordable Housing Commission. Retrieved from< http://www.slpl.lib.mo.us/cco/code/data/t0359.htm >.

34. U.S. Department of Housing and Urban Development (2014). Obama Administration Announces Seven Additional Cities Participating in the Strong Cities, Strong Communities Initiative (HUD No. 14-006). Washington D.C. Retrieved from http://portal.hud.gov/hudportal/HUD?src=/press/press_releases_media_advisories/2014/HUDNo.14-006.

35. T. Logan, "Feds Forcing St. Louis to Rework Community Development Grants." *St. Louis Post-Dispatch*. (2013 October 25). Retrieved from< http://www.stltoday.com/business/local/feds-forcing-st-louis-to-rework-community-development-grants/article_c87b4e3c-64c9-5582-a218-78ee1775be01.html >.

36. Associated Press. County Takes over East St. Louis Grant. St. Louis Public Radio. (2011 October 25). Retrieved from< http://news.stlpublicradio.org/post/county-takes-over-east-st-louis-grant-program >.

37. For information about the community reinvestment fund, see http://www.stlpartnership.com/port-authority-reinvestment-fund.html; and a news article about its grant making in 2012, for more background information seeBinns, E. (2012 March 6). St. Louis County Port Authority Awards $2.6 Million to 8 Community Groups. *St. Louis Business Journal*. Retrieved from http://www.bizjournals.com/stlouis/news/2012/03/06/st-louis-county-port-authority.html.

38. Editorial overview of the Danforth Foundation can be found in Editorial Board. (2011, January 12). "Loyal Sons: Danforth Foundation 'Dared' St. Louis to Be at Its Very Best. *St. Louis Post-Dispatch*. Retrieved from http://www.stltoday.com/news/opinion/columns/the-platform/loyal-sons-danforth-foundation-dared-st-louis-to-be-at/article_b117adc6-1ea9-11e0-88af-00127992bc8b.html; overall trend in St. Louis nongovernmental funding discussed on page 15 in Living Cities and the Initiative for Responsible Investment at Harvard University (2013); and for a discussion of philanthropic support of community development nonprofits see pages 18 and 19 in T. Swanstrom & K. Guenther, (2011).

39. Associated Press, "St. Louis Named a 'Resilient' City by Rockefeller Foundation." CBS St. Louis (2014 December 2). Retrieved from < http://stlouis.cbslocal.com/2014/12/02/st-louis-named-a-resilient-city-by-rockefeller-foundation/ >.

40. C. Walker & M. Weinheimer, *Community development in the 1990s*. Urban Institute: Washington, D.C. (1998). See page X in the preface for summary of investment.

41. W. T. Bogart, 2003.

42. For more information on the Healthy Neighborhoods program in Baltimore, visit their website at http://www.healthyneighborhoods.org/. For the theory and discussion of Healthy Neighborhoods design, view two reports by the Goldseker Foundation (2012). Paul C. Brophy, *Great Neighborhoods Great Cities: Strategies for the 2010s*. (Baltimore, MD: Goldseker Foundation, 2004). D. Boehlke, *Great Neighborhoods Great City: The Healthy Neighborhoods Approach in Baltimore*.

43. M. D. Leonard, "Banks Have Increased Efforts in Minority Areas, but More Needs to Be Done, Say Advocates." *St. Louis Beacon* (now St. Louis Public Radio) (2012 October 1). Retrieved from <https://www.stlbeacon.org/#!/content/27267/fair_lending_advocates_say_banks_have_stepped_up_efforts >.

44. K. Hare, "Put Your Money Where Your Heart Is: Two New Groups Challenge St. Louisans to Step Up." *St. Louis Beacon* (now St. Louis Public Radio) (2013 January 30). Retrieved from <https://www.stlbeacon.org/#!/content/28985/more_crowdfunding_overfundit_investl >.

45. View neighborhood case studies in H. Webber & T. Swanstrom (2014) to see the role of anchor institutions in St. Louis communities

46. Strengthening St. Louis Neighborhoods Task Force, *Building a Regional Community Development System;* available at https://gallery.mailchimp.com/7603a99d4426c770c2b088b4b/files/StrengtheningNeighborhoodsTaskForceFinalDecember2014.pdf.

47. C. Walker discusses characteristics of high-quality capacity building systems (2002), page 42.

48. C. Walker showcases regions with high-quality capacity-building systems (2002), page 45.

49. Rise. CDC Capacity Building and Collaborative Grant Program. St. Louis, MO. Retrieved from <http://www.risestl.org/what/support/#collaborative>.

50. For information on the proliferation of special taxing districts and the different ways they are used, see East West Gateway (2012). "The Use of Development Incentives in the St. Louis Region—Update" (St. Louis, MO). Retrieved from http://www.ewgateway.org/dirr/comrpts/DevIncentivesRpt.pdf; T. Logan (2012 September 9). "Pennies Add Up as Special Taxing Districts Proliferate." *St. Louis Post-Dispatch*. Retrieved from http://www.stltoday.com/business/local/pennies-add-up-as-special-taxing-districts-proliferate/article_95f59066-f923-11e1-a8aa-0019bb30f31a.html.

51. C. Walker (2002).

52. K. Guenther & T. Swanstrom, "Community Builders Network of Metro St. Louis." St. Louis, MO. 2011–2012 annual review. Retrieved from< http://www.communitybuildersstl.org/wp-content/uploads/2013/01/cbnannualreview_nov2012.pdf >.

53. D. R. Noble, "The Metropolitan Saint Louis CRA Association." *Community Builders Exchange E-Newsletter*. (2013 April 3). Retrieved from< http://www.communitybuildersstl.org/index.php/the-metropolitan-saint-louis-cra-association/ >.

54. Nancy Thompson, formerly with Great Rivers Greenway, assumed the executive director position at SLACO in 2013 and has been working to expand the capacity of SLACO. St. Louis Association of Community Organizations (2014). SLACO Hiring Neighborhood Organizer. SLACO News and Events. Retrieved from http://us5.campaign-archive2.com/?u=8e801fa845f1633bac5644683&id=9b18408752&e=4f705d5940; The Rome Group (2013). The People Section. *The Rome Group Newsletter*. Retrieved from http://www.theromegroup.com/news/Newsletters/july2013.aspx.

55. For news and organizational information about the founding of the Missouri Workforce Housing Association see: Brown, L.R. (2007, January 28). Developers take action, form lobby. *St. Louis Business Journal*. Retrieved from http://www.bizjournals.com/stlouis/stories/2007/01/29/story4.html ; Missouri Secretary of State. Missouri Workforce Housing Association. Missouri Online Business Filing. Retrieved from https://bsd.sos.mo.gov/BusinessEntity/BusinessEntityDetail.aspx?page=beSearch&ID=2912619.

56. D. R. Noble (2013 April 3).

57. C. Walker (2002), page 49, details different components of strong leadership systems in community development.

58. To learn more about the market value analysis and initial conversation about it in the region, see J. Rosenbaum (2014 February 3). Market Values Analysis Could Provide Roadmap for Development Funds. St. Louis Public Radio, retrieved from http://news.stlpublicradio.org/post/market-values-analysis-could-provide-roadmap-development-funds.

59. Strengthening St. Louis Neighborhoods Task Force, *Building a Regional Community Development System;* available at <https://gallery.mailchimp.com/7603a99d4426c770c2b088b4b/files/StrengtheningNeighborhoodsTaskForceFinalDecember2014.pdf.>

60. A. C. Kubisch, P. Auspos, P. Brown & T. Dewar, review how economic development involves regional and neighborhood actors (2010), page 25.

About the Authors

Karl Guenther, MSW, is a community development specialist at the Public Policy Research Center at the University of Missouri–St. Louis (UMSL). Guenther is lead staff for the Community Builders Network of Metro St. Louis. The network is a professional association of nonprofit community building organizations whose goal is to build vibrant neighborhoods where people want—and can afford—to live, creating a stronger and more competitive regional economy. In addition, he staffs the Creating Whole Communities initiative at UMSL, a partnership between the university, the University of Missouri Extension, and the St. Louis region's neighborhoods, while helping advance research and data-driven decision making related to the region's community development sector.

Guenther is also a co-founder of Invest STL, a fund at the Greater Saint Louis Community Foundation dedicated to supporting great neighborhood development in the St. Louis region. He holds a Masters Degree from the Brown School of Social Work at Washington University in St. Louis focused on social & economic development and research, and was named one of the St. Louis Business Journal's 30 under 30 in 2013.

Todd Swanstrom, Ph.D., is the Des Lee professor of community collaboration and public policy administration at the University of Missouri–St. Louis. He has a master's degree from Washington University and a Ph.D. from Princeton. His first book, *The Crisis of Growth Politics: Cleveland, Kucinich, and the Challenge of Urban Populism*, won an award as the Best Book in Urban Politics by the Urban Section of the American Political Science Association (APSA). Swanstrom's co-authored book, *Place Matters: Metropolitics for the Twenty-First Century* (3rd ed., 2014) won the Michael Harrington Award as the best book by the Urban Politics Section of the APSA. As part of the MacArthur Foundation's Building Resilient Regions Network, he published research on local responses to the foreclosure epidemic and efforts to increase employment of women, minorities, and low-income persons in construction.

ST. LOUIS CURRENTS

Planning for Long-Term

The idea of "sustainable" development sounds wonderful. Most citizens would agree with the concepts involved in long-term, stable, and renewable development. Making it happen is quite a different story.

Mary Rocchio and Medora Kealy were involved deeply in the region's recent Regional Plan for Sustainable Development called OneSTL. Their essay captures that process, the outcomes if the region does it correctly and the challenges to do so.

It is difficult for a region to have a unified mindset when decision making is so dispersed. Decentralized decision making allows for many priorities to come forward, each with institutional backing. However, it also creates diversity of approach and allows for many small contributions to larger indicators. In the end, sustainability will require many hands working together for the benefit of all.

Sustainability in St. Louis: Regional Plan, Local Action

Mary Rocchio, M.P.P.A. and Medora Kealy, M.S.

Introduction

The regional plan for sustainable development, OneSTL, tracks over fifty performance indicators with the purpose of measuring the region's progress toward sustainability. The hope is that these data points will be used to evaluate the plan, guide local and regional decisions, and help local actors understand the challenges and opportunities of the region.

OneSTL was developed during a three-year planning process that brought together residents, local governments, businesses, and nonprofits from across the eight county region[1] to articulate and work toward a vision for a sustainable future. The OneSTL plan document was completed in December 2013, and now the plan is being carried out by a variety of groups and individuals.

Performance measurement is a key part of the plan. The data can help us understand what is happening in the region—where we have made improvements and where we are falling behind. For the most part, tracking these data points is not new to the region. The Regional Chamber reports on many indicators of the economy, East-West Gateway Council of Governments reports data that are important to consider in transportation planning, and many other organizations report on environmental conditions in the region.

What makes OneSTL unique is that it pulls together data on multiple topics of importance to the St. Louis region to try to provide a more comprehensive picture of how the region is performing and where our priorities need to be. This is particularly relevant when evaluating sustainability, since no one measure can completely capture the economic, environmental, and equity aspects of sustainable development. On its own, escalating economic activity appears to be a good thing, but if coupled with worsening air and water quality or income inequality, we are not meeting the sustainability goals of the region. OneSTL attempts to address this by providing data points that indicate how the region is performing in a range of topic areas as well as some measures that provide an indication of how the region is performing in multiple theme areas.

However, data can only move the region so far in achieving the sustainability goals. To understand the OneSTL performance measures, we need to look at additional information. In this essay we contribute to a more complete picture of how the region is advancing on sustainability by providing appropriate context to the data, including trend data, comparisons with other regions and national data, and highlighting local efforts.

The regional-level data being tracked for OneSTL supplemented with the local action stories indicate that the St. Louis region is making the connections and taking the steps to be more sustainable, but there is plenty of work to be done. Based on this analysis, we conclude that the region needs to continue to push ahead on all areas of the OneSTL plan. There is not one area of the plan that can be ignored or set aside. That being said, of the three e's of sustainability (equity, economy and environment), the region appears to be lagging farthest behind on equity. We are seeing improvement in the overall economy of the region but those improvements are not reaching everyone. To be a region that thrives, we need to do more so that all residents have access to quality education, a healthy environment, and a job that can support a family.

Performance of the St. Louis Region

This essay is organized around the nine themes of OneSTL—Collaborative, Prosperous, Distinctive, Inclusive, Green, Prepared, Connected, Efficient, and Educated. These nine words are meant to identify what is important to the people of St. Louis in building a sustainable region. For each theme area we provide a brief description of the goals of the themes and analysis of how St. Louis is preforming on the indicators in the theme area. In the analysis we provide some contextual information that is important to understanding the data. Part of this context is what is happening on the ground. To help provide this part of the region's story, we spotlight a local government program for each theme area. These are examples of the many programs that are happening throughout the region that are contributing to the sustainability of the region. There are many more. It is important that as we analyze the performance indicators, we also tell these local stories. They are what will help us make progress in achieving the OneSTL goals and see progress on the measures of our performance.

Collaborative

Collaboration is a key element to developing sustainably in the St. Louis region. To be sustainable we need to consider all aspects of planning a community together. Recognizing that working collaboratively has many benefits, and that it is an area with which the St. Louis region often struggles, collaboration takes a central role in OneSTL. The goals under this theme recognize that more coordinated efforts are needed at every level and are essential to accomplishing the goals in all areas of the plan. If we do not work collaboratively we will miss opportunities, duplicate efforts, and miss important elements that need to be considered together as we work toward our goals. The Collaborative measures indicate that the region is positioned to make progress in being more collaborative through growing support for the regional plan, increased sharing of resources, and through the work of neighborhood-based organizations. One of the ways the region can improve our performance on collaboration is through efforts such as the 24:1 Initiative in St. Louis County. We spotlight this effort as one that is moving the region forward in reaching sustainability goals by working across jurisdictional boundaries to increase the efficient use of resources.

Membership in the OneSTL Network is one way the plan seeks to measure the level of collaboration in the region. The consistent increase in membership over the first year of the network's existence is a sign of increased collaboration. In the first year after the adoption of OneSTL, 108 organizations and 75 individuals joined the network.[2] The OneSTL Network is a group for local governments, organizations, businesses, and residents who support the OneSTL plan. Anyone can join the network to share their own successes and learn how other members are implementing the plan's strategies. One member, the city of Belleville, Illinois, joined the network to increase its access to resources and knowledge so that the city can serve the community better.[3] Entities from across the region and from a variety of sectors have become network members, indicating that OneSTL has a broad base of support, and is creating opportunities for new collaborative efforts. The St. Louis region will be more sustainable by increasing the number of organizations and individuals connecting and sharing ideas through the OneSTL Network.

The other indicator for which data are currently available measures the percent of residents living within the service area of an active Community Development Corporation (CDC). CDCs are nonprofits that work to revitalize neighborhoods through community organizing, economic development projects, affordable housing, and other activities. In 2011, 34 percent of St. Louis–area residents lived within the service area of an active CDC.[4] While we do not expect all St. Louis residents to live in the service area of a CDC, and more research is needed on the capacity and success of these CDCs, tracking this measure over time will indicate the level of support in the region for strengthening neighborhoods.

The Access to Information indicator will measure the percent of local governments that use two of the web-based OneSTL resources—the Sustainable Solutions Toolkit and the St. Louis Regional Data Exchange. These two resources provide information such as best practices, case studies, and local data to help organizations, local governments, and residents implement OneSTL. Data are not currently available for this indicator, but we know that the OneSTL Toolkit was visited by over six hundred individuals in 2014. The use of this resource indicates that there are more organizations in the St. Louis region that are learning from each other, sharing information, and building capacity to work together.

The last indicator in this theme is Interjurisdictional Cooperation, which will catalogue the number of agreements and programs established between two or more local governments in the St. Louis region. Data are not yet available for this indicator, in part because it is difficult to track. Despite the lack of available data, this measure is included because it gets at the core of OneSTL—the need for collaboration to achieve shared goals.

The 24:1 Initiative is a prime example of a program that is helping the region achieve the goals under Collaborative. The initiative is a community partnership among the twenty-four municipalities located in the footprint of the Normandy Schools Collaborative, a school district in north St. Louis County. The 24:1 Initiative is facilitated by Beyond Housing, a regional community development organization. The idea for the initiative grew out of discussions in 2008 between several communities and Beyond Housing about the growing foreclosure crisis. Over time, the discussions expanded to address a broad range of topics. One component of the initiative is the 24:1 Municipal Government Partnerships Committee, which consists of mayors and key municipal staff who meet regularly to discuss sharing resources to improve services and reduce costs. One of the efforts of the committee was a collective trash bid, in which several communities utilized the same bid for trash services that resulted in a savings of over $80,000 and improved services for residents.[5] According to Kevin Buchek, an elected official for the village of Bel-Nor and member of 24:1, it took a while to build trust among the communities, but now members are looking to share multiple types of resources, including information on vendors and costs, shared purchases, joint grant proposals, and perhaps even shared facilities or staff.[6]

Prosperous

Throughout the OneSTL planning process employment and economic development were brought up time and again by residents as one of the most important factors affecting the future of the St. Louis region. The goals under Prosperous seek to provide residents with quality job opportunities and an economy that is resilient to change. The measures tracked under this theme include some typical measures of the health of a region's economy—GMP and employment—but also consider the equitable distribution of the economic benefits. These are all important pieces of a sustainable region.

Together, the measures in this section indicate that the region's economy is not sustainable. If we looked only at the typical measures, the economy looks like it is doing okay, or at least improving from the Great Recession, but by looking at the other measures we see that the region needs to take action to be more equitable and resilient. One program that is a good example of how the region can do this is the workforce inclusion program in the city of St. Louis.

The measures of Employment, Unemployment, Gross Metropolitan Product (GMP), and Income indicate the region is improving in the area of prosperity. Employment increased from 1.12 million full-time equivalent workers in 2009 to 1.14 million in 2013, but is still lower than the 1.18 million employed in 2008.[7] The unemployment rate decreased from 9.9 percent to 7.2 percent over the same time period, but remains higher than the 6.3 percent unemployment rate in 2008.[8] The GMP, a measure of overall economic activity in the region, increased from $132.6 billion in 2009 to $136.5 billion in 2013, slightly higher than the GMP in 2008, at $136.3 billion (in chained 2009 dollars).[9] Personal income per capita bottomed out in 2010 in the St. Louis region, at $44,861 per capita in 2013 dollars and increased over the next three years but saw a small decrease from 2012 ($46,021) to 2013 ($45,992).[10] Compared to 34 peer metropolitan regions, the St. Louis economy is not doing well with the 10th largest decrease in personal income per capita from 2008 to 2013, and the 6th lowest GMP per capita in 2013. All four of these measures point to the region's progress, yet continued struggle to recover from the Great Recession.

Additionally, the region is seeing some improvement in the resilience and diversity of the economy. The region's economic resiliency improved slightly in 2012 compared to 2010.[11] Economic resiliency is a measure of the diversity of employment in the region relative to the diversity of employment at the national level, with the idea that a region with employment in many sectors will be able to adapt if employment in a single sector declines. Historically, manufacturing was the largest employment sector in the region, but employment in manufacturing declined substantially from 1970 to 2010. The increase in economic diversity since 2010 is due in part to an uptick in manufacturing employment in recent years as well as an increase in jobs in the health care industry.

But three measures indicate that the region's economic gains are not reaching all residents. The first of these measures, Poverty, has remained about the same over the past few years. In 2013 the rate was 13.0 percent, a slight decrease from 13.9 percent in 2012 and about the same as the rate of 12.9 percent in 2010. Since 2000 the poverty rate has increased 3.8 percentage points and the number of individuals in poverty increased 46 percent.[12] The percent of jobs with a median wage higher than self-sufficiency wage (quality jobs) also remained about the same from 2010 (42.7 percent) to 2013 (42.8 percent).[13] And the gap between white median household income and that of black households widened from white households making 1.88 times that of black households in 2010 to 1.96 times in 2013.[14]

The city of St. Louis is taking action to address a critical portion of the prosperous goals—workforce diversity—through an initiative that increases skills and work opportunities for disadvantaged residents. Mayor Francis Slay made workforce inclusion a priority for the city of St. Louis by signing Executive Order No. 46 and by making implementation a priority action item on the Sustainable Action Agenda.[15] In 2013 the Board of Aldermen updated the workforce inclusion ordinance with the passage of ordinance 69427 to include the language of the executive order.[16] The workforce inclusion ordinance requires the St. Louis Agency on Training and Employment (SLATE) to work with local unions and community organizations to build labor resources so contractors are able to achieve the diversity goals of the ordinance. The ordinance also requires public works contracts, city bonded projects, and tax increment financing projects with an estimated base value of at least $1 million dollars to employ apprentices for a minimum of 15 percent of the contract's labor hours, minorities for 25 percent, women for 5 percent, and city of St. Louis residents for 20 percent.[17] The ordinance is increasing diversity and equality in the construction industry and providing valuable skills to minority residents and women. Additionally, the ordinance is increasing the partnerships among SLATE and the St. Louis Development Corporation (SLDC) with private employers, public agencies, organized labor, and social organizations.[18] Targeted programs like this can increase the likelihood that all residents will be included in economic growth.

Distinctive

The Distinctive theme area appears to be somewhat of a hodgepodge of goals—with goals on everything from reducing crime to increasing housing opportunities to improving health. But this variety of goals recognizes the many components of what is important to people and how the built environment has an impact on people's day-to-day lives. The goals in the Distinctive theme focus on the importance of strong local communities to regional sustainability.

The region's mixed performance on the measures under Distinctive indicates that this is an area that is important for the region's focus. One example of a local effort contributing to the Distinctive goals is the city of St. Charles's adoption of a form-based code for the 5th Street Corridor. The program's goal of creating a safer and more inviting corridor for people using all modes of transportation clearly aligns with the goals of OneSTL.

One of the key areas under Distinctive is crime. The data indicate that the St. Louis region's crime rate is improving but, from what we heard from residents, reducing crime is still a top priority. The region has seen a 29 percent decrease in the crime rate from 2003 to 2013.[19] This decrease is better than the nationwide decline of 23 percent over the same time period, and the region's current crime rate is slightly lower than its peer region average.[20] Safe communities provide many benefits to a sustainable region. A community with lower crime rates is more appealing to potential employers and provides a more enjoyable environment for residents that could lead to a higher rate of physical activity.

Another aspect of strong local communities is the health of residents. OneSTL tracks the percent of adults meeting the recommended exercise standard as an indication of the health and amount of activity of residents in the region. In 2011 just under half of St. Louis region residents (49.5 percent) met the standard, which calls for 150 minutes or more of physical activity in a week.[21,22] A change in the definition used to collect these data makes it difficult to look at how this has changed over time. But it appears to be holding steady over the last decade with only about half of residents meeting this standard. Further, a comparison with peer regions indicates St. Louis is doing poor on this measure, ranking 26th out of 35 peer regions.

Another OneSTL strategy that seeks to increase the health of residents is to increase residents' access to parks. Based on the Access to Open Space performance measure residents in the St. Louis region have fairly good access to parks. Based on data for the 2007–2011 time period,[23] 74.5 percent of residents in the St. Louis region live near a public open space (within ½ mile in urban areas and 1 mile in rural areas).[24] Although the region appears to do well on this indicator, the quality and extent of the open space is not assessed and may vary substantially.

The St. Louis region is commonly considered to be an affordable place to live with reasonably priced housing. However, to fully assess housing affordability the cost of transportation must also be included, since housing located far from job centers or other services may cost less, but residents will need to spend more money on transportation to reach destinations. The H+T Affordability indicator provides a comprehensive measure of housing and transportation costs in the region. On average, a household making the area median income spends 54.8 percent of their income on housing and transportation costs, exceeding the 45 percent threshold that is commonly considered affordable.[25] Almost 60 percent of households spend over 45 percent of their income on housing and transportation. Compared to 34 peer metropolitan regions, St. Louis is slightly more affordable than most, ranking 26th.

The city of St. Charles's use of a form-based code will help the region meet the goals under Distinctive by creating strong communities with built environments that promote active and healthy lifestyles. In the spring of 2012 the city of St. Charles adopted a form-based code, also known as a SmartCode, for the 5th Street Corridor and hospital district. Form-based codes differ from conventional zoning because they focus on the scale and relationship of buildings to create a more cohesive built environment, and tend to promote mixed-use development that is compact and walkable. The code is a long-term strategy to increase access to destinations for residents, relieve traffic congestion, and preserve open lands.[26] The code also includes provisions for a ten-foot-wide sidewalk and a bicycle lane along 5th Street, which will increase transportation options and opportunities for exercise.

Inclusive

As touched on in the Prosperous section, inclusiveness is an important aspect of a sustainable region. The OneSTL goals in the Inclusive section address the need for equitable services and opportunities for all residents as well as the need for diversity in creating an entrepreneurial and resilient economy. All three measures tracked under this theme indicate that the St. Louis region's performance is worsening on this aspect of sustainability. Some may say that St. Louis does not need data to tell us that the region needs to be more inclusive. But these measures can help us better understand some of the challenges in the region and help convey those challenges. The St. Louis HOME Consortium is one local program that is making the region more inclusive by creating housing opportunities for low-income residents in three counties.

One way we can measure inclusiveness is by the number of residents living in concentrated areas of poverty. When we segregate poor people from others, we exclude them from accessing the same opportunities, such as quality schools and health care, as their middle-or high-income counterparts. The percentage of poor residents living in areas of concentrated poverty increased slightly over the last decade, from 12.4 percent in 2000 to 13.2 percent for the 2007–2011 time period.[27] Though the percentage increase in this measure was fairly small, the actual number of poor residents living in concentrated poverty increased over 20 percent, from around 33,000 residents in 2000 to over 40,000 in 2007–2011.[28] The substantial increase in the number of affected residents is due to the increase in the poverty rate over the last decade.

A second measure of inclusiveness, income inequality, is also increasing in the St. Louis region. The Gini Index measures the distribution of income, with a score of one representing the most unequal situation (one household earns all of the income), and a score of zero representing complete equality (each household earns the same amount). Since 2006, income inequality in the St. Louis region increased from 0.451 to 0.463 in 2013. This increase mirrors the national trend, which experienced an increase from 0.464 in 2006 to 0.481 in 2013.[29] Though the increases appear small, both are statistically significant and reveal growing economic disparities in the St. Louis region and the nation. The only bright note is that the St. Louis region ranks 22nd among 35 peer regions with slightly less income inequality than most of the peers.

The last measure we track under Inclusive looks at whether or not housing is available to low-income residents in the region at an affordable price. We find that low-to moderate-income households are able to afford 35.2 percent of the available housing, which represents a shortage of around 130,000 affordable housing units. The region does provide a higher percentage of affordable housing units than most of our peer regions,[30] but with a shortage of 130,000 units the region needs to focus on providing more housing options.[31]

There are many organizations in the region that are trying to make the region more inclusive and equitable. The St. Louis HOME Consortium is one initiative that counties and municipalities in the region have been collaborating on since 2003 to provide more affordable housing opportunities. The counties of Jefferson, St. Charles, and St. Louis joined with the cities of Florissant, O'Fallon, and St. Charles to become eligible for funding from the HOME Investment Partnerships Program, a Housing and Urban Development (HUD) initiative to create affordable housing for low-income households. The HOME funds can be used for down-payment assistance for low-income, first-time homebuyers or to rehabilitate or develop affordable housing. In 2013 around 250 households received down-payment assistance through the program, helping them purchase their first homes.[32] The consortium is helping the region achieve the goals in the Inclusive theme of OneSTL by increasing access to home ownership and affordable housing for low-income residents. The hope is that these increased options could lead to more economically and racially integrated communities that will provide residents with access to more opportunities and a higher quality of life.

Green

The Green theme is the section of the plan that is dedicated to the health of the natural environment. Goals in this area of the plan focus on protecting and enhancing the quality of water, air, land, and biodiversity in the region. This is an important aspect of sustainability because preserving the natural environment is beneficial for healthy ecosystems and it supports a strong economy and high quality of life for residents. The performance measures under Green indicate that the region has made noticeable efforts to address environmental challenges, but it needs to strengthen these efforts because the quality of the air, water, and land use is still poor. One example of such a successful effort is the city of Alton's implementation of stormwater management practices to address the water quality of a polluted river.

The seven measures under the Green can be divided into two categories of indicators. The first four are measures of inputs or actions being taken to address environmental challenges. The seven measures under Green can be divided into two categories of indicators. or the overall quality of the environment. Essentially, the first set are actions local governments can take that should help improve the region's performance on the second set of measures.

One of the input measures is Rainscaping, which tracks practices that reduce stormwater overflow and improve water quality. Rainscaping includes things such as rain gardens and permeable pavers, which enable stormwater to soak into the ground close to where it falls, minimizing erosion in streams, preventing localized flooding, and enhancing water quality by allowing the soil to filter out pollutants. Beginning in 2000, the EPA's Phase II stormwater program required many areas in the St. Louis region to control stormwater runoff from new developments, and many projects are using rainscaping practices to fulfill these requirements. The number of acres treated for stormwater runoff using rainscaping practices in the St. Louis region has doubled in the past two years to over three thousand acres in 2012.[33]

Watershed planning is also on the rise, with seventeen watersheds in the St. Louis region benefiting from a watershed plan and/or an active watershed-based organization as of 2013, which is an increase from eight in 2010.[34] Watershed plans seek to identify and control or eradicate pollutants that drain into our streams, rivers, wetlands, and other bodies of water. The existing plans and organizations cover about 41 percent of the land area in the region.

The Tree City USA program offered by the Arbor Day Foundation certifies municipalities for properly managing their trees. As of 2013 around 20 percent of municipalities—40 in total—in the St. Louis region are certified, which is a slight decrease from the 41 that were certified in 2010.[35] Sustainable Codes is another measure of local government action, tracking the number of local governments adopting the International Energy Conservation Code (IECC). The IECC sets energy efficiency standards for new buildings and renovations. At least 80 percent of the local governments in the region have adopted some version of the IECC or are subject to statewide standards for IECC compliance (all communities in Illinois).[36] The most energy efficient version available at the time of analysis is the 2012 IECC, which is the standard adopted by the state of Illinois as well as by two communities in Missouri: Richmond Heights and University City.

The OneSTL measures on air, water, and land reveal potential strains on the region's environmental assets. The long-term trend for ozone-related air quality shows improvement, with fewer days of unhealthy air quality due to ozone. The short-term trend has also improved from 17.3 days of poor air quality per year (for the 2007–2009 time period) to 16.3 days per year (for 2012–2014),[37] but ozone is a critical air pollutant and the region is currently classified as nonattainment[38] for the ozone standard set by the EPA. The Water Quality measure documents that 36.2 percent of the assessed rivers and streams in the region are impaired (polluted), slightly lower than the national figure of 39 percent.[39] Regarding land use, the St. Louis region has more developed land per population than most of the other peer regions, ranking 5th in 2011 with 0.30 acres of developed land per capita.[40] In addition, the amount of developed land per capita increased between 2006 and 2011 by 0.9%, whereas the majority of peer regions (29) experienced decreases over the same time frame. The increase in developed acres per capita in St. Louis is resulting in loss of agricultural and natural resource land, impacting the region's ecosystem.

The city of Alton, Illinois, is one community in the region that is taking steps to improve water quality and reduce stormwater runoff. In 2010 the city collaborated with Heartlands Conservancy and was awarded an Illinois Green Infrastructure Grant. The grant funded a stabilization project for a stream corridor that receives stormwater runoff from a business district and releases into the east fork of the Wood River, which is an impaired (polluted) body of water. The stream's banks were eroding, contributing to the pollution in the river downstream. The project stabilized the stream using a two-stage channel design and by planting deep-rooted native plants, which increase water infiltration. The stream now treats an estimated 250 million gallons of stormwater annually, removing 200 tons of suspended solids.[41] In addition, a pedestrian trail was added to increase recreational opportunities for residents. The city is currently planning a mixed-use development for the area with requirements for sustainable stormwater management. The city of Alton's project is furthering the goals of the Green theme by improving water quality through the use of green infrastructure.

Prepared

The Prepared theme focuses on improving resources and strengthening partnerships to be better prepared for natural and man-made disasters. To be sustainable the region needs to be proactive in creating an environment that mitigates threats, and needs to take measures to be prepared for disasters when they do happen. The St. Louis region's performance in this area is mixed. More local governments are taking action to mitigate against flooding and severe weather and to address climate change, but the numbers are still fairly low. Meanwhile, there has been a decrease in hazard mitigation planning and a greater percentage of development is located in potentially hazardous areas, increasing residents' exposure to risk. The city of Creve Coeur is one community that is leading the region in becoming more resilient by adopting policies and programs to mitigate the effects of climate change.

Three measures that indicate the region is improving on being Prepared are Stormready, Floodplain Management, and Addressing Climate Change. The National Weather Service's Storm-Ready® program helps communities strengthen local safety efforts, reduce fatalities, and minimize property damage from severe weather. Nine local governments in the St. Louis region were certified StormReady® as of 2013, almost double the number that were certified as of 2010 (five).[42] In a region with 204 local governments, nine certified communities may not seem significant, but given that three of the certified communities are counties, it turns out that over 65 percent of residents in the St. Louis region live in a certified StormReady® community. There has also been an increase in the number of local governments participating in a floodplain management program called the Community Rating System (CRS), which provides discounts to flood insurance policyholders. The number of participating communities increased from one in 2010 to four as of 2013; however, those four only cover about 6.8 percent of residents in the region.[43] By participating in the CRS, these communities are reducing the risk of flooding through enhanced floodplain management techniques while saving money for their residents.

Between 2010 and 2013 the percent of local governments addressing climate change increased from 9.8 percent to 11.3 percent with a total of 23 local governments addressing climate change.[44] These local governments have addressed climate change by conducting greenhouse gas inventories, completing climate action plans, or joining programs that support and encourage local efforts to address climate change. Though the percent of governments taking action is not very high, those that have taken action in the past are continuing their efforts. For example, in 2005 the mayor of the city of Maplewood, Missouri, signed the U.S. Conference of Mayors Climate Protection Agreement. And in 2013 a greenhouse gas inventory was completed for the city.

The last two measures in this area—Hazard Mitigation and Development in Potentially Hazardous Areas—indicate the region needs to take steps to be more prepared. The majority of local governments in the St. Louis region participate in local hazard mitigation planning, but between 2010 and 2012 the percentage of participating communities dropped from 84.3 percent to 72.5 percent.[45] Hazard mitigation planning helps reduce or eliminate long-term risk to people and property, and communities that participate in the plan are eligible for hazard mitigation grant funding through FEMA. Hazard mitigation plans are valid for five years, after which they must be updated. The decrease from 2010 to 2012 was due to the expiration of two county plans, and reveals a gap in preparedness in the region.

Development such as housing, offices, and retail is increasingly located in potentially hazardous areas, including floodplains; on soils susceptible to earthquake liquefaction; and in areas susceptible to landslides. In the Missouri portion of the St. Louis region, the percent of development in potentially hazardous areas increased from 15.5 percent in 2006 to 16.1 percent in 2011.[46] The upward trend of this indicator represents increased risk for the residents of St. Louis.

One of the communities taking action to address climate change is the city of Creve Coeur, Missouri. In 2008 Mayor Harold Dielmann signed the U.S. Conference of Mayors Climate Protection Agreement, showing support for reducing greenhouse gas (GHG) emissions. Also in 2008, Creve Coeur conducted a GHG inventory, which calculated energy use and GHG emissions for municipal operations and for the entire community. The city followed up in 2010 with a Climate Action Plan, outlining strategies for reducing energy use and GHG emissions and established an emissions reduction goal of 20 percent from 2005 levels by 2015. In 2011 the city took on the EPA's Green Power Community Challenge, which requires that at least 3 percent of community-wide energy use comes from renewable sources. Through the participation of businesses, schools, non-profits, and residents, the city exceeded the challenge requirements in 2013 by offsetting 3.77 percent of energy through green power.[47] The city of Creve Coeur continues to work toward mitigating climate change, providing a model for other local governments.

Connected

The focus of the connected theme area is the transportation system. The transportation system is an integral component of a sustainable region because of its role in facilitating economic development, providing access to jobs and other opportunities, and because of its important impact on the quality of our environment. The goals of the Connected theme address maximizing efficiency of existing transportation assets, increasing access to transit and active transportation (e.g., walking and biking), stimulating economic development, increasing safety, and integrating land use planning with transportation planning. The eight performance indicators focus on reducing transportation-related emissions and increasing access to destinations. In recent years the St. Louis region has made progress on several measures related to non-auto modes of transportation; however, the increase in workers commuting by automobiles diverges from the other trends in this theme. The local spotlight showcases the Great Streets Initiative, which has facilitated several communities taking steps to expand the way they think about their streets and designing roadways that are more lively and accessible.

Several measures under this theme indicate the region is becoming more connected, including Bikeability, Transit Ridership, Complete Streets, and VMT per Capita. The St. Louis region has around 744 miles of bike facilities as of 2015.[48] There are many organizations, including Great Rivers Greenway and the Metro East Park and Recreation District, that continue to advance trail projects and increase access for bicyclists.

Transit ridership on the Metro and Madison County transit systems is increasing; up from 43.0 million trips in 2010 to 49.9 million trips in 2013; however, transit ridership was even higher between 2006 and 2009.[49] The decline in ridership from 2009 to 2010 was caused by the March 2009 service reductions by Metro and the impact of the economic recession.

More local governments are adopting complete streets policies, which promote safe access for people of all ages and abilities and for all modes of transportation. Complete streets policies ensure that local governments are considering all types of modes when designing and constructing streets. As of 2014, eighteen local governments in the St. Louis region have a complete streets policy, up from seven local governments in 2010.[50]

Transportation by personal vehicles has high personal and public costs, contributes to congestion, and emits more pollution than other transportation modes. Due to these reasons, the number of miles traveled by automobiles—also called "VMT" for vehicle miles traveled—is a key indicator of sustainability. VMT per capita grew steadily in the last several decades, in St. Louis and in the nation, but beginning around 2005 VMT per capita started to decline. In the St. Louis region, VMT per capita declined almost every year since 2006, from 28.0 miles per day to 25.4 miles per day in 2013.[51]

While there has been improvement in many of the measures for the Connected theme, there has not been progress for Transportation Choice, the indicator that measures how many people commute to work by walking, biking, transit, or carpooling. These modes are not always available for workers, but when available they provide a lower-cost commute with fewer emissions than single occupant vehicles. The percent of commuters traveling via one of these modes held steady from 2010 to 2012 at about 12.4 percent and decreased to 11.9 percent in 2013. Over the last decade, the region reached a peak rate of 14 percent in 2000 and 2008.[52] There was a slight decline in commuting via transit over this time period, possibly related to the Metro service cuts in 2009, but most of the decrease in this measure is due to a decline in carpooling.

One program that contributes to the Connected theme is the Great Streets Initiative. Since 2006, East-West Gateway has worked with local communities throughout the region to promote interesting, lively, and attractive streets that serve all types of users, including pedestrians, bicyclists, and vehicles. Four projects have been planned and constructed, and another four have completed plans. The projects are located in a range of places, from South Grand in the city of St. Louis to the main street of Labadie, a small rural community in Franklin County. In both Labadie and on South Grand, improvements included enhanced stormwater drainage, narrowing of streets, and the addition or expansion of sidewalks to increase access for pedestrians. The Great Streets Initiative works with the local communities to meet their needs, and helps create safer corridors with an aesthetically pleasing sense of place, both of which can help stimulate economic activity. Great Streets helps the region meet the Connected goals related to increasing transportation choice as well as goals of creating more distinctive communities.

Efficient

The Efficient theme area focuses on the region's needs to efficiently use limited resources. The section covers a range of topics that are concerns of St. Louis residents, including rising energy costs and the way government resources are spent. These are important elements of a sustainable region because these resources are limited and we want to get the most out of our public funds. The St. Louis region is headed in the right direction on all four of the Efficient indicators for which trend data are available. We spotlight the city of Maplewood for their efforts to reduce waste, energy use, and costs in their business district.

The measures Energy Use, Energy Diversity, Building Energy Efficiency, and Waste Diversion Rate all indicate the region is more efficiently using the region's natural resources than before, but there is still plenty of room for improvements. Residential energy use declined in St. Louis from 111.4 million British thermal units (BTUs) per household in 2010 to 106.6 million BTUs in 2011,[53] an amount of energy that cost about $1,900 per household in 2011. The St. Louis region is headed in the right direction, but residential energy use in the region remains much higher than the national average, which was 89.6 million BTUs in 2009.[54]

The use of renewable energy, predominantly from wind power and hydropower, is increasing in the St. Louis region, from 3.2 percent of electricity in 2010 to 4.2 percent in 2012.[55] The states of Missouri and Illinois both have renewable energy requirements that are ratcheting up the percent of energy coming from renewable resources—with requirements of 25 percent by 2026 in Illinois and 15 percent by 2021 in Missouri.[56] The increase in renewable energy in the St. Louis region from 2010 to 2012 reflects the rising renewable energy standards in each state.

Since buildings account for nearly 40 percent of energy use in the United States,[57] building energy efficiency is very important for reducing overall energy use. The St. Louis High Performance Building Initiative is a regional effort to increase the amount of green-certified buildings and spaces. The square footage of certified green buildings and space increased from 15.0 million square feet in 2012 to 18.3 million square feet in 2013.[58] The initiative is now challenging the region to reduce building energy use by 25 percent by 2020, calling for businesses, organizations, and local governments to benchmark their energy use and aim for the 25-percent reduction target.

Materials use and disposal is another critical component of the Efficient theme. In the state of Missouri the amount of waste that is diverted from landfills through source reduction, recycling, reuse, or composting is on the rise. The waste diversion rate increased from 40.7 percent in 2002 to 55.5 percent in 2012.[59] Data for St. Louis County show a similar trend, increasing from 29.0 percent in 2003 to 55.9 percent in 2010.[60] The amount of waste generated by Missourians increased steadily throughout most of the first decade of this century, but dipped slightly in recent years. As of 2012 the average Missourian generated 7.0 pounds of waste per day,[61] while in Illinois the average resident generated 5.7 pounds of waste per day in 2007,[62] both of which are higher than the national average of 4.4 pounds per day in 2010.[63]

The city of Maplewood provides a good example of how a community can work with businesses to advance many of the goals of OneSTL, including increasing waste diversion, reducing energy use, reducing costs, and promoting a healthy and vibrant commercial district. The Marietta parking lot, located behind the 7300 block of Manchester Avenue, provides parking for customers of a variety of businesses and restaurants in the Maplewood business district. Prior to the city's involvement, there were nine to twelve trash haulers that served the businesses in this area, and thirty-eight unscreened dumpsters that produced offensive odors, blocked pedestrian walkways, and limited parking availability. In addition, hardly anything was being recycled due to lack of space and cost.[64] The city worked with the individual businesses to determine their trash and recycling needs, and developed a plan to consolidate services. Now, only one trash hauler is needed to serve this area, and the thirty-eight unscreened dumpsters were replaced with seven screened enclosures for trash, recycling, and composting. Composting and recycling rates increased dramatically, and businesses are saving money, with costs about 10 to 50 percent lower due to the economies of scale. Maplewood made additional improvements by using pervious materials in the new parking areas to reduce stormwater runoff, installing LED lighting to increase energy efficiency, and laying infrastructure to prepare for future electric vehicle charging stations.[65]

Educated

The Educated theme recognizes the importance of many aspects of an educated community, including quality educational institutions that produce a skilled workforce as well as the value of well-rounded adults who are engaged in the local community. The sustainability of the region relies on educated, knowledgeable, and involved residents. The St. Louis region's performance in this area is split, with improvements in three indicators and declines in the other three. The city of Maryland Heights provides one example of how a local community is advancing the Educated goals by hosting a program that increases the knowledge and civic involvement of residents.

Three Educated measures—School Quality, High School Graduation, and College Attainment—indicate the region's performance in providing educational opportunities. School Quality, as measured by the percent of third grade public school students who meet or exceed reading proficiency standards, decreased over the last four years from 53.4 percent in 2010 to 46.6 percent in 2014.[66] Part of this decrease is due to the state of Illinois using higher testing standards starting in 2013.[67] Between 2012 and 2013, the percent of third grade students meeting the reading standards decreased 19.0 percentage points for the Illinois districts in the St. Louis region. But the percent of students meeting standards also decreased in the Missouri districts in our region in 2014.[68] Third grade reading proficiency is a critical measure, since students who do not read proficiently by this age are four times more likely to drop out of high school.[69]

High school graduation rates are rising in the St. Louis region, increasing from 79.3 percent in 2011 to 87.3 percent in 2014.[70] However, graduation rates vary substantially based on race and income, with African American, Hispanic, American Indian, and low-income students graduating at below average rates, and White and Asian students graduating at above average rates.[71]

College attainment is also on the rise in the St. Louis region. In 2000, 25.3 percent of adults over age 25 had a bachelor's degree or higher, which rose to 30.0 percent by the 2009–2011 time period. Compared to 34 peer regions, however, the St. Louis region is lower than average, ranking 23rd out of 35.[72]

Voter Participation and Volunteer Rate are two measures that indicate the level of civic engagement in the region. Turnout among registered voters in the St. Louis region increased for presidential and congressional elections between 2000 and 2008, but fell short in 2010 and 2012. Turnout for the congressional election declined from 51.0 percent in 2006 to 47.2 percent in 2010, while turnout for the presidential election declined from 69.5 percent in 2008 to 67.9 percent in 2012.[73] Even with the recent declines, the St. Louis region had higher voter turnout than the nation for every general election between 2000 and 2012. The volunteer rate is also relatively high in the St. Louis region. In 2013 about 28.2 percent of St. Louis residents volunteered, compared with 25.4 percent for the nation. St. Louis ranks higher than most of its peers, with the 12th highest volunteer rate out of the 35 peer regions. However, the volunteer rate is not as high as it was in 2010, when 32.1 percent of residents volunteered.[74]

Lastly, Cultural/Arts Institutions is an indication of the capacity of arts and cultural programming. The St. Louis region benefits from a growing arts and culture sector, which has seen increases in inflation-adjusted revenue per capita over the last couple of years. Arts and cultural institution revenue in St. Louis increased from $100.57 per capita in 2009 to $111.37 per capita in 2011 (both in 2011 dollars).[75]

Maryland Heights University is an example of a program that furthers the goals under Educated by fostering civic engagement. For the past six years the city of Maryland Heights has provided a free citizens' academy to teach residents about city government and the operation of city departments. Participants tour city facilities, learn about topics such as finance and budgeting, planning and zoning, parks and recreation, and public works, and discover ways to get involved in the community. The program makes city government more accessible and understandable to its residents, helping residents become more involved in their local community.[76]

Conclusion

The OneSTL performance measures indicate the St. Louis region is performing well in some areas of sustainability while lagging behind in others. By looking at specific initiatives in the St. Louis region, we see that many efforts are moving the St. Louis region in the desired direction, even in areas where the region is performing poorly. Continued monitoring of the performance measures as well as recognition of these local efforts is important to understanding how the region is performing on the sustainability goals and in moving the region in the right direction.

Although the focus of this essay is on the role of local governments in the implementation of the regional sustainability plan, local public agencies are not the only ones responsible for implementation. Local nonprofit organizations, residents, and private entities all have an important role. All must do their part by communicating what they are doing, becoming civically involved, connecting with others, and taking bold steps to improve the region's outcomes. The OneSTL performance measures can be employed by all to learn, evaluate, prioritize, motivate, budget, promote, celebrate, and move the region forward in becoming a better place to live today and in the future.

Endnotes

1. The eight county region used by OneSTL is the one used by the region's Council of Governments, and is different from the St. Louis Metropolitan Statistical Area established by the Census Bureau.

2. East-West Gateway Council of Governments.

3. E. Fultz, city of Belleville, personal communication, July 1, 2014.

4. E. Tutt, Rise, personal communication, November 8, 2013.

5. Beyond Housing (2013). The 24:1 Initiative November 2013 Impact Report. Retrieved 8 July 2014, from http://www.beyondhousing.org/wordpress/wp-content/uploads/2013/12/24-1-Annual-Report-to-the-Communityfor-2013.pdf.

6. K. Buchek, Village of Bel-Nor, personal communication, July 1, 2014.

7. Bureau of Labor Statistics (2008–2013). Current Employment Statistics.

8. Bureau of Labor Statistics (2008–2013). Local Area Unemployment Statistics (LAUS).

9. Bureau of Economic Analysis (2008–2013).

10. Bureau of Economic Analysis (2010–2013).

11. U.S. Census (2010–2013). County Business Patterns.

12. U.S. Census Bureau (2010–2013). Small Area Income and Poverty Estimates.

13. Bureau of Labor Statistics (2010–2013). Occupational Employment Statistics; Poverty in America (2010–2013). Living Wage Calculator.

14. U.S. Census Bureau (2010). U.S. Census Bureau (2013). American Community Survey.

15. The Mayor's Action Agenda refers to the ordinance as "Board Bill 297," https://stlouismo.gov/government/departments/mayor/documents/upload/Mayor%20Slay%20Sustainability%20Aon%20Agend%202013--2018.pdf.

16. In 2009 the Board of Aldermen passed ordinance 68412. The new ordinance expanded the Community Jobs Board, introduced penalties for noncompliance, and added redevelopment projects supported by tax increment financing to those required to comply with the ordinance.

17. St. Louis (Mo.). City Board of Aldermen (2013). St. Louis City Ordinance 69427. Retrieved 14 July 2014, fromhttp://www.slpl.lib.mo.us/cco/ords/data/ord9427.htm.

18. E. Strauther, Jr., SLATE, personal communication, July 11, 2014; St. Louis Agency on Training and Employment (2013). St. Louis City Ordinance 69427 Annual Report. Retrieved 11 July 2014, from https://stlouismo.gov/government/departments/slate/documents/loader.cfm?csModule=security/getfile&pageid=374629.

19. Federal Bureau of Investigation (2003-2013). Uniform Crime Reports.

20. In 2013 there were 3,102 crimes per 100,000 residents in the St. Louis region compared to 3,451 crimes per 100,000 residents on average for 29 metropolitan peer regions.

21. Centers for Disease Control and Prevention (2011). Behavioral Risk Factor Surveillance System.

22. Measures of exercise for previous years utilized a slightly different exercise standard, making recent trend analysis problematic. But when the former standard was in use from 2003 to 2009, the percent of adults meeting the exercise standard increased steadily from 44.6 percent to 52.2 percent, indicating a strong upward trend.

23. A portion of the data are from the American Community Survey five-year estimate, which provides an estimate based on survey data for the five-year period.

24. U.S. Census Bureau (2007–2011). American Community Survey; East-West Gateway Council of Governments.

25. U.S. Census Bureau (2005–2009). American Community Survey; U.S. Census Bureau. Longitudinal Employer-Household Dynamics; AAA (2011). Your Driving Costs Brochure. Calculations by East-West Gateway.

26. City of Saint Charles (9 April 2012). Saint Charles Gateways Smartcode, Version 9.2. Retrieved 20 June 2014, fromhttp://www.stcharlescitymo.gov/Portals/0/Public%20Works/Fifth%20Street%20Project/Fifth%20StreetHospital%20Area%20SmartCode.pdf.

27. U.S. Census Bureau (2007–2011). American Community Survey; U.S. Census Bureau (2000).

28. Ibid.

29. U.S. Census Bureau (2006 and 2013). American Community Survey.

30. Compared to 34 peer metropolitan regions, the St. Louis region provides a higher percentage of affordable housing units than most of its peers, ranking 15th out of 35.

31. U.S. Department of Housing and Urban Development (2006–2010), Comprehensive Housing Affordability Strategy; U.S. Census Bureau (2006–2010). American Community Survey.

32. St. Louis County (Mo.) County Department of Planning Office of Community Development (2013). St. Louis County Fiscal Year 2013 Consolidated Annual Performance and Evaluation Report. Retrieved 2 July 2014 from

http://www.stlouisco.com/Portals/8/docs/Document%20Library/planning/community%20development/Draft_CAPE2013.pdf.

33. R. Biehl, Metropolitan St. Louis Sewer District, personal communication, August 28, 2013.

34. East-West Gateway Council of Governments (2013).

35. Tree City USA—The Arbor Day Foundation. Retrieved 7 July 2014 from http://www.arborday.org/programs/treeCityUSA/; N. Kuhn, Missouri Department of Conservation, personal communication, October 11, 2013.

36. International Code Adoptions. Retrieved 16 June 2014 from http://www.iccsafe.org/gr/Pages/adoptions.aspx; East-WestGateway Council of Governments.

37. U.S. Environmental Protection Agency (2007–2013). Air Quality Index; East-West Gateway Council of Governments.

38. Areas of the country where air pollution levels persistently exceed the national ambient air quality standards may be designated "nonattainment" by the U.S. Environmental Protection Agency.

39. U.S. Environmental Protection Agency (6 March 2012). How Is the Quality of Our Waters Determined? Retrieved 14 July 2014 from http://water.epa.gov/learn/resources/quality.cfm.

40. National Land Cover Database, Multi-Resolution Land Characteristics (MRLC) consortium; U.S. Census Bureau, Population Division.

41. Moody, Jeff (March/April 2013). Green Stream: Illinois Watershed Controls Storm Water Using Green Infrastructure. StormWater Solutions. Retrieved 9 July 2014 from http://www.estormwater.com/sites/default/files/24_00.13_Vegetation_Williams%20Creek.pdf.

42. NWS StormReady Program, Weather Safety, Disaster, Hurricane, Tornado, Tsunami, Flash Flood, Lightning, Heat, Cold. Retrieved 10 July 2014 from http://www.stormready.noaa.gov; M. Magnus, NOAA, personal communication, July 30, 2013.

43. Federal Emergency Management Agency (2010–2013). The National Flood Insurance Program Community Status Book. Retrieved 9 July 2014 from http://www.fema.gov/national-flood-insurance-program/national-flood-insuranceprogram-community-status-book.

44. Sierra Club, U.S. Conference of Mayors, Resilient Communities for America, and East-West Gateway Council of Governments.

45. Missouri State Emergency Management Agency, Illinois Emergency Management Agency, and Local Multi-Jurisdictional Hazard Mitigation Plans (2010–2012).

46. Federal Emergency Management Agency; Missouri Department of Natural Resources; and National Land Cover Database, Multi-Resolution Land Characteristics (MRLC) consortium.

47. Missouri Green Power Communities (2011), Creve Coeur. Retrieved 14 July 2014 from http://www.mogpc.com/creve-coeur/.

48. Great Rivers Greenway, Metro-East Parks & Recreation, HeartLands Conservancy, and East-West Gateway Council of Governments.

49. National Transit Database (2006–2013).

50. Smart Growth America; East-West Gateway Council of Governments.

51. Federal Highway Administration Highway Performance Monitoring System and East-West Gateway Council of Governments (2005–2013).

52. U.S. Census Bureau (2000–2013). American Community Survey.

53. M. Chell, Ameren Corporation, personal communication, October 11, 2013; R. Hipp, personal communication, August 28, 2013; United States Energy Information Administration; and U.S. Census Bureau. American Community Survey.

54. U.S. Energy Information Administration (2009). Residential Energy Consumption Survey (RECS) Data. Retrieved 10 December, 2013 from http://www.eia.gov/consumption/residential/data/2009/index.cfm?view=consumption#undefined.

55. Ameren Corporation (2010–2012).

56. United States Department of Energy. Database of State Incentives for Renewables & Efficiency. Retrieved 10 July 2014 from http://www.dsireusa.org/incentives/incentive.cfm?Incentive_Code=MO08R&RE=1&EE=1 andhttp://www.dsireusa.org/incentives/incentive.cfm?Incentive_Code=IL04R\.

57. U.S. Energy Information Administration (28 May 2013). Frequently Asked Questions: How much energy is consumed inresidential and commercial buildings in the United States? Retrieved 20 December 2013 from http://www.eia.gov/tools/faqs/faq.cfm?id=86&t=1.

58. E. Schneider, St. Louis Regional Chamber, personal communication, January 17, 2014.

59. Missouri Department of Natural Resources (2002–2012).

60. St. Louis County (2003–2010).

61. Missouri Department of Natural Resources (2012).

62. Fullerton, Don, and Sarah Miller (2010). Waste and Recycling in Illinois: Illinois Communities Cope with Waste in Different Ways. Retrieved 18 December 2013 from http://igpa.uillinois.edu/IR_2010/PDF/pg70-80z_Waste&Recycling.pdf.

63. United States Environmental Protection Agency (December 2011). Municipal Solid Waste Generation, Recycling, and Disposal in the United States: Facts and Figures for 2010. Retrieved 9 July 2014 from http://www.epa.gov/wastes/nonhaz/municipal/pubs/msw_2010_rev_factsheet.pdf.

64. Traxler, Anthony (April 1, 2014). City of Maplewood Municipal Parking Lot Trash and Recycling Consolidation Composting for Restaurants, PowerPoint presentation at the Earth Day Symposium, St. Louis, MO.

65. M. Corcoran and A. Traxler, city of Maplewood, personal communication, July 2, 2014.

66. Illinois State Board of Education and Missouri Department of Elementary & Secondary Education (2008–2014).

67. Rado, Diane, and Alex Richards (31 October 2013). Illinois Grade School Test Scores Plunge—Especially in Poor Communities. *Chicago Tribune*. Retrieved 5 February 2014 from http://articles.chicagotribune.com/2013-10-31/news/ct-metschool-report-card-scores-20131031_1_isats-test-scores-illinois-standards-achievement.

68. Illinois State Board of Education (2008—2014). Illinois State Report Card Data.

69. Hernandez, Donald (2012). Double Jeopardy: How Third-Grade Reading Skills and Poverty Influence High School Graduation, Annie E. Casey Foundation. Retrieved 4 February 2014 from http://gradelevelreading.net/wpcontent/uploads/2012/01/Double-Jeopardy-Report-030812-for-web1.pdf.

70. Illinois State Board of Education (2011–2014). Illinois State Report Card Data; Missouri Department of Elementary & Secondary Education (2011–2014).

71. Ibid.

72. U.S. Census Bureau (2000); U.S. Census Bureau (2009–2011), American Community Survey.

73. Illinois State Board of Elections; Missouri Office of the Secretary of State (2006–2012).

74. Corporation for National & Community Service (2004–2013). Volunteering and Civic Life in America.

75. Americans for the Arts (2010), Local Arts Index; R. Kushner, Muhlenberg College, personal communication, August 29, 2013.

76. City of Maryland Heights (June 2014). Newsletter. Retrieved 9 July 2014 fromhttp://www.marylandheights.com/modules/showdocument.aspx?documentid=9316.

About the Authors

Mary Rocchio is the manager of regional policy research at East-West Gateway Council of Governments. She received a master's degree in public policy administration from the University of Missouri–St. Louis and a bachelor's degree in sociology from Missouri State University. Since joining EWG in 2007, Mary has prepared multiple reports, technical memoranda, and other information products to communicate research findings and policy analysis to audiences as varied as local and state elected officials, citizen groups, the private sector, and transportation and social service providers.

Medora Kealy is a policy analyst at the East-West Gateway Council of Governments. She works on developing and analyzing the performance measures for the regional plan for sustainable development, OneSTL, and the *Where We Stand* reports on the competitiveness of the St. Louis region. For her master's capstone project she contributed to the Sustainability Progress Report for the city of Dubuque, Iowa. The project won the 2013 AICP Student Project Award for Contribution of Planning to Contemporary Issues. She holds a master's degree in urban and regional planning from the University of Iowa and a bachelor's degree in sociology and general science from Grinnell College.

ST. LOUIS
CURRENTS

Tomorrow's Diversity

When St. Louis (like other American cities) was bursting at the seams with social activity and commerce a century ago, it was a city of immigrants. Frequently, discussions of diversity focus on race. However, diversity in the twenty-first century must include the role of immigrants. Just as the economy and the climate bring global matters close to home, immigration is changing the face of the region.

Dr. Onésimo Sandoval examines the region's demographic trends and points to the region's future as a "mosaic" of many faces and peoples. He raises a critical point: that natural population growth may be coming to an end for St. Louis if younger families reproduce at a rate that cannot offset the eventual decline in the baby-boomer population. The population growth of the future will come from immigration and the diversity of the region will transform.

It is imperative that leaders know the profile of immigrant populations as well as the settlement patterns in order to build the strongest possible region for the twenty-first century and celebrate the vigor and culture that these populations contribute. *Laissez faire* is not a choice.

A Demographic Portrait of a Mosaic Immigrant Population in the St. Louis Region

J.S. Onésimo Sandoval, Ph.D.

Introduction

St. Louis is an iconic American city and its historical impact will be enshrined in the urban studies canon of academic literature. However, the importance of St. Louis has been diminished in recent decades, partly due to the large decline in the city's population since 1950. This decline in the population coupled with stagnant population growth for the metropolitan region has started conversations among business and community leaders to develop a plan for a strong, sustainable social and economic future for the city and region.

Although St. Louis city continues to lose residents, the St. Louis Metropolitan Statistical Area (MSA) remains in the top twenty most-populated metropolitan regions.[1] However, being in the top 20 most populated regions does not mean that the St. Louis metropolitan region does not face demographic challenges. Case in point: the daunting fact that the St. Louis metropolitan region only has 122,891 immigrants, which is ranked 45th among metropolitan regions in the U.S.[2] Only 4% of the population in the St. Louis metropolitan region is composed of immigrants.

Given these demographic facts, one is left to wonder why so few immigrants make the greater St. Louis region their home. One clue that could help explain this demographic trend for immigrants, is that the academic literature regarding the life of immigrants in St. Louis city and more broadly the St. Louis metropolitan region is small and undeveloped when compared to Chicago, New York, Miami, and Los Angeles.[3] There are only a handful of studies related to the immigrant experience in St. Louis.[4] Therefore, the positive stories (e.g., how immigrants shape the cultural and economic spaces in St. Louis) are rarely told in academic conferences or shared with students or the media. This area of immigrant scholarship for St. Louis needs to be developed, especially as it relates to the cultural, social, economic, and political impacts that immigrants have in the city and region. In recent years, scholars have tried to fill this gap in knowledge with articles that describe how immigrants adapt to the socioeconomic environment in St. Louis, or they describe the impact that immigrants have on the economic conditions of the region.[5]

Understanding the demographic profile and trends of immigrants and their settlement patterns will help St. Louis leaders understand its future. The demographic writing is on the wall for many American cities. Natural population growth may be coming to an end. Many countries are already experiencing natural population decline (i.e., Japan, Russia, and Germany).[6] This population decline is typically offset with an increase in immigrants. As new immigrants arrive they bring valuable cultural, symbolic, and economic capital that invigorates a local economy by creating jobs, raising wages, and reducing home vacancies.[7] As St. Louis tries to reinvent itself as a major global and cosmopolitan city that will be attractive to immigrants and international capital, the internal structure and migration patterns of the foreign-born population will have to change.

Complicating matters, the inflow of immigrants to the U.S. may be in jeopardy after 2050. The 2050 milestone is an important year for demographers, because many projections point to a possible decline in the world population.[8] Whether the world's population declines or continues to nudge up each year is not important for St. Louis. The important point, from a demographic perspective, is that we are in the end stages of significant population growth. What does this mean for cities across the U.S.? The one constant demographic resource that cities could rely on—constant population growth—is in peril. Cities across the U.S., especially cities like St. Louis that have been losing their population base to the suburbs, need to shore up their population if and when natural population declines can no longer be erased by national immigration policies. This is an important point because immigration is a key demographic lever that the U.S. uses to mitigate potential population drops and declining fertility rates. The U.S. is now competing with other countries to attract highly skilled immigrants.

Many people may view thirty-five years as plenty of time to solve the immigration challenge for the St. Louis region. However, demographic transitions do not happen overnight unless there is a major demographic shock (e.g., Hurricane Katrina) that triggers immediate out-migration or in-migration of populations. During the next thirty-five years (just like the U.S. is competing with other nations for skilled immigrants) U.S. cities will be competing with each other to attract immigrants from all walks of life to replenish the population stock, as well as foster innovation and creativity in the private sector, universities, and government. St. Louis, Baltimore, Detroit, Louisville, just to name a few cities, have started to compete with each other, with different welcoming initiatives for immigrants.

In this essay, I explore the historical trends of the foreign-born population in the city of St. Louis and the metropolitan region to provide a more accurate assessment of the immigrant demographic transitions taking place within the city and across the region. The next section describes the social and economic diversity within the foreign-born population. The third section portrays the geographic settlement patterns of the foreign-born population. The final section explores the St. Louis Mosaic Project, which is designed to foster an environment that is conducive to promoting a promising path to welcoming more immigrants to the St. Louis region.

History of Immigration in St. Louis

Today's demographic profile of the immigrant population in St. Louis offers a glimpse into the future cultural and social fabric of the city of St. Louis and the region. To understand and appreciate the diversity of the current immigrant residents, it would be useful to understand the past demographic transitions of the immigrant population in St. Louis. The dearth of immigrant residents living in St. Louis today was not the norm. Data from the U.S. census to 1850 showed that half (50.5%) of the population in St. Louis County was foreign-born[9] (See Table 1). Although the percent foreign-born population declined from 1850 until 1870, the number of foreign-born residents more than doubled from 1850 until 1870. This is remarkable given that there were only two metropolitan regions in 2012 that had a larger percent foreign-born population compared to the 1870 foreign-born population in St. Louis, which was 35%: Miami–Fort Lauderdale had 38% and San Jose–Sunnyvale–Santa Clara had 36%. To get a sense of the density of the foreign-born population in St. Louis in 1870, one has only to compare the numbers to the Los Angeles–Long Beach–Santa Ana metro area, where 34% of the population was foreign-born in 2012.

Beginning in 1880, the U.S. census started to report data for the city of St. Louis and St. Louis County separately. Table 2 shows the foreign-born trends. The foreign-born population in the city of St. Louis peaked in 1910 with 125,706 foreign-born residents. The percent foreign-born population for the city peaked in 1880. The demographic storyline for St. Louis County is different—the number of foreign-born residents has continued to grow since 1880. However, the zenith of the percentage of foreign-born residents in St. Louis County was in 1880. Beginning in 2000, the demographic outlook of the immigrant numbers changed in St. Louis city and county. Figures 1 and 2 illustrate that immigrants are once again making the St. Louis region their home. The 2010 percent foreign-born population for the city brings the percentage back in line with the 1940 percentage, and the 2010 percent foreign-born population for the county brings the percentage roughly back in line with the 1930 percentage.

The U-shaped trends represent an important demographic hurdle that both the city and county have jumped over. The enormous loss of immigrants can be truly felt in the city of St. Louis. The data for the St. Louis metropolitan region points to a demographic reality check—St. Louis County and the surrounding suburbs, in the greater part of St. Louis, are now home to four out of five immigrant residents (82%) (see Table 3). Although the general population grew faster for the region than the foreign-born population, the St. Louis metropolitan region has jumped over the demographic hurdle as well and the percent foreign-born continues to increase.

Social and Economic Diversity

Figures 3 and 4 show the changing demographic transitions from 1980 through 2010 for the foreign-born population by region of the world for the city of St. Louis and St. Louis County, respectively. The net growth of the foreign-born population for the city of St. Louis can be attributed to immigrants from Asia and the Americas. There has been a net loss of immigrants from Europe during the past thirty years. The Asian immigrant population is now the largest population in the city, followed by European immigrants and immigrants from the Americas. Given the current trends, the immigrants from the Americas will surpass the immigrants from Europe, becoming the second-largest immigrant group in the city.

The trends for St. Louis County are slightly different. Asian immigrants, by far, are the largest population in the county. However, European immigrants are the second-largest group, and, more importantly, the growth of European immigrants has rebounded in 2000 and 2010 after a loss of population from 1980 through 1990. There were slightly more than 3,000 European immigrants in 2010 compared to 1980. Immigrants from the Americas and Africa have increased in every decennial year in the county.

Hidden within Figures 3 and 4 is the immense geographical diversity within each region of the world. The 2008–2012 ACS identified 129 countries that were home to the foreign-born population living in the St. Louis metropolitan region.[10] The largest foreign-born population is from Mexico (15,417), followed by India (11,615), Bosnia and Herzegovina (9,409), China (7,679),[11] and Vietnam (5,036). These five countries represented only 40% of the foreign-born population.

Coupled with the range in country of birth, the diversity of immigrants can be explored through citizenship status and year of entry into the U.S. First, slightly more than half of the immigrants were non-citizens (54%). Second, slightly more than half came to the U.S. before 2000 (56%). However, when the two trends were combined, interesting demographic patterns emerged. Fifty percent of the foreign-born population that was classified as naturalized citizens arrived in the U.S. prior to 1990. This compares to 1% of the foreign-born citizens who arrived after 2010. In contrast, only 10% of the foreign-born population who were classified as non-U.S. citizens arrived to the U.S. prior to 1990. This compares to 8% of the non-citizens who arrived after 2010.

Another way to examine these data is to measure what percent of the foreign-born population that arrived after 2010 were citizens and non-citizens. Nine out of ten immigrants (94%) who live in the St. Louis metropolitan region and arrived in the U.S. after 2010 were non-citizens.

This compares to two out of ten immigrants (19%) who arrived prior to 1990 and were non-citizens. The data clearly show that the citizen composition of the foreign-born population has dramatically changed since 1980.

Table 4 provides detailed demographic data for the St. Louis metropolitan region for native-born residents and foreign-born residents by citizenship status. There are several important findings from these data. First, foreign-born non-citizens were more likely to be younger, male, and Hispanic compared to foreign-born citizens, who were more likely to be older, female, and white non-Hispanic. Second, the foreign-born residents were more likely to be married (63.0%) compared to native-born residents (48.7%). Third, foreign-born citizens (44.1%) and non-citizens (43.3%) were more likely to have a bachelor's degree or higher compared to native-born citizens (29.3%). Most of the difference in educational attainment can be attributed to the percentage of foreign-born residents that have a graduate or professional degree. It is important to note that at the other end of the educational distribution, foreign-born citizens (13.1%) and non-citizens (21.9%) were more likely to have not completed high school compared to native-born citizens (10.2%). Fourth, foreign-born citizens (28.2%) were twice as likely to speak only English at home compared to foreign-born non-citizens (14%). Moreover, a little less than half (46.6%) of the foreign-born non-citizens reported that they speak English less than "very well," compared to 30.8% of foreign-born citizens. Fifth, foreign-born males were the only demographic group that earned more money ($55,420) than their native-born counterparts ($52,585).

Perhaps one of the most surprising findings was the difference between foreign-born citizens and non-citizens regarding social security and retirement income. Foreign-born citizens were more likely to receive social security (27.1%) and retirement (15.9%) income compared to foreign-born non-citizens, 6.0% and 2.4%, respectively. The reliance on social security and retirement income for foreign-born citizens reflects that this population is significantly older compared to the foreign-born non-citizens. The last major finding is related to poverty. In general, foreign-born citizens were economically better off, which shields many of them from the exposure of poverty. However, their non-citizen counterparts' exposure to poverty was higher, especially for vulnerable populations like the youth and seniors.

To understand and appreciate the immigrant population in the St. Louis metropolitan region, it is necessary to recognize the social and economic diversity of the population. Oftentimes, the narratives of social, cultural, and economic characteristics of the immigrants frame policy and demographic trends that describe immigrants as a homogenous population. In the case of St. Louis, the rich diversity of the immigrant population is lost when generic and homogenous narratives are used. The social and economic data presented in this section demonstrate the rich mosaic fabric of the foreign-born population in St. Louis. The next section of the essay adds a layer of complexity to the social and economic demographic transitions, in that most of the immigrants live in the suburbs.

The Geography of Immigrant Enclaves

The cities, suburbs, and neighborhoods that make up the St. Louis metropolitan region provide unique elements to the social, economic, political, and cultural fabric of the region. One of the unique aspects of immigrant residential settlement patterns throughout many cities in the U.S. is the cultural, economic, and symbolic impact that immigrant neighborhoods have on the region.[12] Immigrant enclaves create an urban space of opportunity for new immigrants as they begin the process of cultural and social adaptation to their new home.[13] The academic literature has traditionally defined an immigrant enclave a section of a city that has a higher percentage of foreign-born residents compared to the national average.[14] These immigrant enclaves are important points of entry into a region for new immigrants. Immigrant enclaves typically are home to stores, churches, restaurants, community-based organizations, and family networks that are important to the daily lives of newly arrived immigrants.

It is often assumed that new immigrant enclaves have not emerged in St. Louis because of the low number of foreign-born residents at the regional level. However, immigrant enclaves do exist in the region. Using the latest data from the U.S. census, the St. Louis metropolitan region is home to nine immigrant suburban enclaves (see Figure 5). To be defined as an immigrant enclave, a census designated place[15] must have a percentage of immigrants greater than the national percentage of immigrants (i.e., 12.9%). Most people are surprised to discover that immigrant enclaves exist in St. Louis, given the low number of immigrants. These immigrant enclaves are listed in Table 5. Of the nine enclaves, two are located in Illinois and seven are located in Missouri. The percent foreign-born ranges from a high of 39% (Fairmont City Village, Illinois) to a low of 14% (Edmundson City, Missouri).

There is no general demographic pattern that describes these enclaves. Some enclaves like Fairmont City Village, Illinois, Royal Lakes Village, Illinois, and Edmundson City, Missouri, have a high percentage of non-citizens, whereas the majority of the immigrants in Bella Villa, Missouri, are naturalized citizens. There is no clear pattern by year of entry among the immigrants for these enclaves that explains why they have emerged. Of the nine enclaves, only three have a population larger than 15,000 people (Mehlville CDP, Missouri, [28,615]; Maryland Heights City, Missouri, [27,418]; and Creve Coeur, MO [17,777]). In three of the enclaves (Bella Villa, Marlborough Village, and Mehlville CDP), the largest immigrant population was born in Bosnia and Herzegovina. In two of the enclaves (Fairmont City and Edmundson City), the largest immigrant population was born in Mexico. In two additional enclaves (Maryland Heights and Creve Coeur), the largest immigrant population was born in India. Finally, the largest immigrant population in Olivette City was born in China,[16] and the largest immigrant population in Royal Lakes Village was from West Africa.

Although the city of St. Louis has a low probability of becoming an immigrant enclave by 2050, there are many municipalities, villages, and census designated places that have a good chance to become one. As immigrants continue to make the suburbs their home, the emergence of small immigrant enclaves will continue to shape the cultural, social, and political landscape in these suburban places. The findings from this section of the essay reinforce one of the major themes in this essay—the immigrant population in St. Louis is diverse. In these nine immigrant enclaves, five different ethnic groups represent the largest share of the foreign-born population. Furthermore, in only three of the immigrant enclaves (Fairmont City Village, Royal Lakes Village, and Edmundson City) does the largest foreign-born population represent more than half of the foreign-born population. The remaining immigrant enclaves represent what I call pan-immigrant places. For example, in Olivette City, the foreign-born population from China only represents 27% of the foreign-born population. The next four largest foreign-born populations (Mexico [15%], Ethiopia [8%], India [8%], and Poland [6%]) only account for 37% of the remaining foreign-born population. Therefore, it is safe to say that Olivette is a pan-immigrant city.

A Mosaic Immigrant Population

The demographic future of the city of St. Louis and more broadly the St. Louis metropolitan region will be defined by the potential growth of new immigrants making St. Louis their home. A *laissez faire* attitude that immigrants will come to St. Louis can no longer be the unstated policy. In recent years, business and community leaders have recognized that they have to step forward and develop a short-term and long-term plan to recruit a diverse immigrant population to the St. Louis metropolitan region. Recent data point to positive signs that the region has started to experience a net gain in the immigrant population. Demographically speaking, a net gain of the population is a small victory for St. Louis as the region tries to attract immigrants.

Frankly speaking, the St. Louis metropolitan region will not be a major gateway destination like Chicago, Miami, or New York. However, the St. Louis metropolitan region has the potential to become a secondary destination for immigrants who are relocating from New York, Chicago, and Los Angeles in search of their American dream, which may include a better quality of life, affordable housing, and educational and entrepreneurial opportunities. Unlike birth and death demographic transitions, which are typically viewed as natural transitions related to economic development and increased education, migration demographic transitions are greatly affected by social policy and economic opportunity. In other words, continuing to foster a *laissez faire* policy that immigrants will continue to make St. Louis their home is a recipe for a demographic disaster, given that many cities around the U.S. have become proactive in their recruitment of immigrants.

A recent initiative called the St. Louis Mosaic Project[17] is creating a social, economic, and political environment to foster an awareness of the importance of immigrants to the cultural, social, and economic fabric of the city of St. Louis and the region. The birth of this initiative came from a report by Jack Strauss (2012), which empirically showed that the sluggish economic profile of the St. Louis metropolitan region was associated with the low number of immigrants living in St. Louis. The report was important for three reasons. First, it highlighted the economic costs and benefits associated with the inflows and outflows of immigrants in the region. For example, the report found that immigrants have a direct impact on housing values, vacancies, and household income. Moreover, the report suggested that if the demographic trends continue and there is no change in the immigrant trend line, the St. Louis metropolitan region will no longer remain in the top 20 most populated regions in the U.S. The conclusion was clear: if St. Louis wants to remain in the top 20 most populated regions in the U.S., it will have to increase its immigrant population.

Second, the report made important comparisons to other comparable regions to St. Louis. The report clearly articulated that the *laissez faire* policy embedded throughout the St. Louis metropolitan region was in contrast to proactive city-based immigrant policies that were designed to recruit and welcome a diverse group of immigrant workers, students, and residents.

Third (and probably the most important reason), the report galvanized business and community leaders to come together and reflect on the challenges and opportunities in the region to recruit immigrants. This reflection and community dialogue to develop a shared vision of the region and develop proactive immigrant policies was the impetus to create the St. Louis Mosaic Project.

Since its inception in 2012, the St. Louis Mosaic Project has been a visible advocate in the region to bring attention to the importance of immigrants to the regional economy and social and cultural fabric of St. Louis. Although the St. Louis Mosaic Project is "managed by St. Louis Economic Development Partnership, World Trade Center St. Louis, and a 22-member committee,"[18] it has reached out to universities, community leaders, and immigrant entrepreneurs for support, advice, and assistance in marketing St. Louis as an immigrant-friendly region.

One of the stated goals of the St. Louis Mosaic Project is "to be a cultural mosaic because this community believes that immigrants invigorate our region, drive innovation and take us back to our roots." It continues, "The St. Louis Mosaic Project's goal is to transform St. Louis into the fastest growing metropolitan area for immigration by 2020 and promote regional prosperity through immigration and innovation." To achieve this goal, the St. Louis Mosaic Project has developed six priorities as part of its strategic plan to grow the immigrant population.

(1) Communication	(2) Business and Government Affairs	(3) Pathways	(4) Analysis	(5) University Engagement	(6) Infrastructure
"Develop marketing strategies to reinforce a regional community-wide culture of inclusion and dispel myths about immigration."	"Foster leadership development opportunities for immigrants in and with regional businesses, nonprofits, and academic institutions."	"Create unique and supportive pathways for people who choose to live in the St. Louis region including those on visas, visiting with passports, permanent residents, and those on a path to citizenship."	"Comprehensive internal gap analysis and external best practices assessment to document current environment and develop consensus for future initiatives."	"Attract and support international students for earlier and deeper integration into the community."	"Reinforce a St. Louis advantage by developing ideal services: legal, health, finance, housing, transportation safety, and faith."

Source: 2015 Strategic Priorities and Action Plans—Original May 2014, Updated January 2015. Illustration provided by the author.

Although the St. Louis Mosaic Project has had considerable success in promoting a regional vision for immigration policy, the it faces fierce competition from similar immigrant welcoming initiatives across the U.S. (e.g., Global Detroit,[19] RISE in Louisville, Kentucky,[20] BIC in North Carolina[21]) to attract immigrants. The success of the St. Louis Mosaic Project to promote the St. Louis region as a place for immigrants to call home will rely on the magnitude of immigrant integration into the local economy and cultural and civic life. Government, business, and nonprofit leaders, as well as academics, have started a conversation with immigrant leaders to work on a comprehensive plan that fosters a conducive environment for immigrant integration and that contributes to the social and economic success of the region.

Summary

The city of St. Louis and the St. Louis metropolitan region are at a crucial demographic crossroads. There are many factors at play that shape demographic transitions, and hopefully the St. Louis Mosaic Project represents an important shift in proactive immigration policy that will augment the projected growth of immigrants for the city and region. The demographic and economic future of the region and the city rests in the trends of continued growth of immigrants and immigrant entrepreneurs. The diversity from the immigrants will continue to add to the rich and cultural fabric of the region and transform the region into a global and cosmopolitan city that will attract new immigrants, especially new immigrant entrepreneurs.

In this essay, I have made two points. First, a large number of immigrants living in St. Louis was the norm a century ago. These immigrants had a significant impact on the city and the region, as they greatly contributed to early cultural, social, economic, and political institutions. As St. Louis makes plans to attract new immigrants to the region, leaders should reflect on its immigration history to promote St. Louis as an immigrant-friendly city that is devoted to diversity and inclusion.

Second, although the immigration numbers for the region are below average for the size of the metropolitan region, there are many strengths that can be built on from the current immigrant population. The most important strength from the immigrant population living in St. Louis is its ethnic diversity. The diversity of the immigrant population will reinforce the image that the U.S. population is composed of immigrants from all over the world, and with continued growth in immigration the region will grow in diversity and benefit from the gifts that immigrants bring with them. Because of the unique institutions in St. Louis for refugee resettlement and the growing pan-Latino population, St. Louis is in a great situation to market itself as a pan-immigrant region that is committed to diversity and inclusion.

Although the city of St. Louis has suffered a significant decline in population since 1950, brighter days are ahead for the city and region. Much of this optimism rests on the empirical data presented in this essay, which shows that the city, St. Louis County (the largest county in the region), and the metropolitan region have been able to reverse the downward immigrant demographic trends that have historically fostered low levels of immigrant settlement. As immigrants continue to find their way to St. Louis, the city and region will once again be viewed and recognized as a great place for immigrants. The journey to create a vibrant mosaic immigrant population will be long, but rest assured that the city of St. Louis and the greater metropolitan region will be greatly rewarded with the energy and dreams of the new immigrants.

During the next thirty-five years, there will be many challenges and opportunities that the St. Louis region will have to embrace. One of the biggest challenges is to develop sustainable policies to attract and grow the immigrant population. The creation of the St. Louis Mosaic Project was a brilliant move to stimulate different pro-immigration policies within the private sector, universities, and government. Attracting immigrants is a regional effort that will require hard work and commitment from businesses, government, universities, and community leaders. If the demographic trends continue upwards for the foreign-born population, the region will continue to benefit from its new immigrant residents. With every challenge, there is an opportunity. The opportunity for St. Louis is to leverage the diversity of the pan-immigrant population as leaders recruit new immigrants to the region. The immigrant numbers may be small, but one of the strengths of the relatively small immigrant population is the immense sociocultural diversity within the population.

As a major urbanized region, St. Louis has many features to offer new immigrants: good neighborhoods, educational opportunities, good housing, etc. And immigrants have many gifts they can offer to the region. The test of the region's capacity to attract new immigrants is creating permanent spaces that foster dialogue and reflection on the different potential demographic trends facing St. Louis and the work that will be required to achieve the desired outcome. Alternatively, sitting back and taking a *laissez faire* approach to regional immigrant policy will surely doom the region and the city to the second tier or third tier. And all the hard work to create the St. Louis Mosaic Project will be viewed as an ephemeral exercise so leaders can at least say we tried.

It is my hope that the leaders of St. Louis, with efforts like the St. Louis Mosaic Project, will overcome the tenacity of the *laissez faire* attitude in the region regarding immigrants and recognize the economic, social, cultural, and symbolic power of immigrants. Immigrants are leaving traditional gateway cities to find the new American dream. Let's hope that by 2050 scholars will describe St. Louis as an exceptional gateway destination that promotes diversity and inclusion for all residents, especially immigrants, as a place to work, play, live, and retire.

Endnotes

1. According to the 2008–2012 American Community Survey (ACS), US Census Bureau, 2012. The St. Louis Metropolitan Statistical Area (MSA) had 2,810,367 residents according to the 2008–2012 ACS estimates. The St. Louis MSA is the 18th largest MSA.
2. US Census Bureau, 2012.
3. Sandoval, 2013.
4. See Rynerson; Mormino, 1982; Ling, 2005; Anderson, 2008.
5. See Jennings and Sandoval, 2012; Sandoval and Jennings, 2012; Sandoval, Jennings et al., 2012; Strauss 2012; Strauss, Tranel et al., 2013.
6. See Longman, 2004; Pearce 2010; Last, 2013.
7. See Strauss, 2012.
8. See Kotlikoff and Burns, 2004; Longman, 2004; Wattenberg, 2004; Kotkin, 2010; Pearce, 2010; Last 2013.
9. The city of St. Louis and St. Louis County were part of St. Louis County until the great divorce of 1876.
10. The 129 regions reported by the U.S. census is an underestimate. In that number, there is an "other" category that the U.S. census uses to summarize the immigrant populations that have low numbers, or immigrants who did not specify a country of birth but listed a region of the world.
11. This number excludes immigrants from Hong Kong (n = 292) and Taiwan (n = 1,519).
12. See Portes and Manning, 1986; Bartel, 1989; Logan, Alba et al., 2002; Barry and Miller, 2005.
13. See Iceland, 2009.
14. See Benton-Short and Price, 2008.
15. According to the U.S. census, "Census Designated Places (CDPs) are the statistical counterparts of incorporated places, and are delineated to provide data for settled concentrations of population that are identifiable by name but are not legally incorporated under the laws of the state in which they are located. The boundaries usually are defined in cooperation with local or tribal officials and generally updated prior to each decennial census. These boundaries, which usually coincide with visible features or the boundary of an adjacent incorporated place or another legal entity boundary, have no legal status, nor do these places have officials elected to serve traditional municipal functions. CDP boundaries may change from one decennial census to the next with changes in the settlement pattern; a CDP with the same name as in an earlier census does not necessarily have the same boundary. CDPs must be contained within a single state and may not extend into an incorporated place. There are no population size requirements for CDPs."
16. The number for China includes 37 immigrants from Hong Kong.
17. More information about the St. Louis Mosaic Project can be found at: http://www.stlmosaicproject.org/.
18. The 22 members represent 22 different organizations.
19. More information about Global Detroit can be found at: http://www.globaldetroit.com/.
20. RISE stands for Refugees and Immigrants Succeeding in Entrepreneurship. More information about RISE can be found at: http://riselouisville.com/.
21. BIC stands for Building Integrated Communities. More information about BIC can be found at: http://migration.unc.edu/programs/bic/.

Bibliography

Anderson, Kristen L. "German Americans, African Americans, and the Republican Party in St. Louis, 1865–1872." *Journal of American Ethnic History* (2008): 34–51.

Barry, R., and Paul W. Miller. "Do Enclaves Matter in Immigrant Adjustment?." *City & Community* 4(1) (2005): 5–35.

Bartel, Ann P. "Where Do the New US Immigrants Live?." *Journal of Labor Economics* (1989): 371–391

Benton-Short, L., and M. Price. *Migrants to the Metropolis: The Rise of Immigrant Gateway Cities*. Syracuse, NY, Syracuse University Press: 2008.

Iceland, John. *Where We Live Now: Immigration and Race in the United States*. Berkeley, CA, University of California Press, 2009.

Jennings, Joel. and J. S. O. Sandoval. "Evaluating the Role of Latinidad and the Latino Threat in the Show Me State." Great Plains Research 22(2) (2012): 123–135.

Kotkin, Joel. *The Next Hundred Million: America in 2050*. New York; The Penguin Press, 2010.

Kotlikoff, Laurence J., ed. *The Coming Generational Storm: What You Need to Know about America's Economic Future*. Cambridge, Mass., The MIT Press, 2005.

Last, Jonathan V. *What to Expect When No One's Expecting: America's Coming Demographic Disaster*. New York: Encounter Books, 2013.

Ling, Huping. "Reconceptualizing Chinese American Community in St. Louis: From Chinatown to Cultural Community." *Journal of American Ethnic History* (2005): 65–101.

Logan, John R., Wenquan Zhang, and Richard D. Alba. "Immigrant Enclaves and Ethnic Communities in New York and Los Angeles." *American Sociological Review* (2002): 299–322.

Longman, Phillip. *The Empty Cradle: How Falling Birthrates Threaten World Prosperity*. New York, Basic Books, 2004.

Mormino, Gary Ross. "The Playing Fields of St. Louis: Italian Immigrants and Sport." *Journal of Sport History* 9(2) (1982).

Pearce, Fred. *The Coming Population Crash: and Our Planet's Surprising Future*. Boston: Beacon Press, 2010.

Portes, Alejandro, and Robert D. Manning. "The Immigrant Enclave: Theory and Empirical Examples." *Comparative Ethnic Relations*, Academic Press (1986): 47–68.

Rynearson, Ann. "Social Convergence and Cultural Diversity among Immigrants and Refugees." In David W. Haines and Carol A. Mortland, editors, Manifest Destinies: Americanizing Immigrants and Internationalizing Americans. Westport, Conn.: Praeger, 2001.

Sandoval, J. S. Onésimo. "Understanding the Demographic Hurdles to Revitalize St. Louis." *St. Louis University Public Law Review* 33 (2013): 161–182.

Sandoval, Juan Simón Onésimo, and Joel Jennings. "Latino Civic Participation: Evaluating Indicators of Immigrant Engagement in a Midwestern City." *Latino Studies* 10(4) (2012): 523–545.

Sandoval, J. S. O., et al. "Engaging Latinos in Access to Counseling and Education (EnLACE): An Applied Research Project to Understand Quality of Life among Latino Immigrants in St. Louis, MO." *Journal of Applied Social Science* 7(1) (2012): 24_41.

Strauss, Jack. "The Economic Impact of Immigration on St. Louis." *St. Louis University* (2012): 4.

Strauss, Jake, et al. "Immigration Recommendations for St. Louis Region: How Can We Jump-Start Growth?" St. Louis, MO; The William T. Kemper Foundation, Commerce Bank Trustee (2013).

U.S. Census Bureau. "2008-2012 American Community Survey" (2012).

Wattenberg, Ben J. *Fewer: How the New Demography of Depopulation Will Shape Our Future*. Chicago, Ivan R. Dee, 2004.

About the Author

J.S. Onésimo Sandoval, Ph.D., is associate professor and director of the sociology program at Saint Louis University. He currently teaches several courses in urban sociology, demography, and geospatial science and spatial analytics. Professor Sandoval has research interests in urban sociology, demography, spatial statistics, spatial criminology, spatial inequality, racial stratification, Latino sociology, and social-environmental synthesis. As part of his research activities, Professor Sandoval sits on the board of directors for the Saint Louis Metropolitan Research Exchange and Kingdom House, and he is the chair of NCERA 216—Latinos and Immigrants in Midwestern Communities—which is one of the largest research consortia related to immigrants and Latinos in the United States Professor Sandoval is currently working on several projects, including a book manuscript that examines neighborhood racial diversity and racial segregation from 1980 through 2010 for metropolitan statistical areas larger than 500,000 residents.

Unbuilding and Rebuilding a Neighborhood

The St. Louis region often displays the scars from its lengthy history. Look in all directions of downtown for many miles, and you will see the way the city has built, demolished, rebuilt, and even re-demolished. The design of various developments is based on whatever the values were of the moment, and these values are sometimes inconsistent with historical context or long-term need.

Patty Heyda takes an informed and careful look at the experience of the McRee Town neighborhood, as well as the adjacent Shaw neighborhood and the Missouri Botanical Garden. This neighborhood has long been the subject of attention—mostly for its troubles. There have been multiple attempts to improve the neighborhood. However, not all of this can be considered a success.

Heyda gives us an intriguing perspective on how to move forward with future development by paying careful attention to context—inviting us to go deeper than the clear-and-rebuild approach that was employed for decades.

Unbuilding and Rebuilding St. Louis

Patty Heyda, M.Arch., LEED AP

"Urbanism" is as much about un-building or erasing neighborhoods as it is about the building of new social spaces. *Unbuilding* creates separations between processes driving redevelopment and their various outcomes. This separation happens through practices of urban erasure that literally cut off or remove constituents and their histories from their urban contexts. Distinguishing redevelopment's unbuilding alongside rebuilding is important in a political and economic context where project-specific lenses focus on discrete metrics of the rebuilt—aesthetic, economic, or demographic—as measures of success. I argue that these metrics represent a limited conceptualization of redevelopment since they do not take into account the constitutive *processes* of urban change—economic, political, social—that equally, or perhaps more impactfully, shape space. Through the narrative of McRee Town's ongoing transformation, I examine these "separations" that enable urbanism as "unbuilding." I then illustrate how criteria of "improvement" become a variable concept, mobilized differently according to contrasting visions of desired outcomes. In the case in McRee, design and aesthetics become malleable mechanisms for serving different visions with convergent political and market-driven agendas. This chapter argues for a critical understanding of redevelopment as a cumulative project, in order to expose practices of erasure as physical, political, and historical separation. By considering urbanism in this more connected sense, designers will gain a more robust capacity to measure and assess redevelopment "outcomes."

The redevelopment story examined here is simultaneously unique and typical. The McRee Town neighborhood in St. Louis became, by the 1990s, a crime-plagued space that was transformed over two decades into a "new" neighborhood christened Botanical Heights. Rename an area is typical of other processes of urban decay and revitalization (or some might say gentrification) and as such, is perhaps unremarkable. Yet it is unique, I suggest, in that in more recent times—and in the wake of politically charged recent urban renewal practices—designers became more closely involved in redevelopment efforts.

In 2014, an era now considered by most practitioners and scholars to be a "post-urban renewal" era, vectors shaping redevelopment are meant to be heavily influenced by community-driven ground-up processes. The trajectory of McRee Town's transformations highlights multiple incidences of contemporary urban erasure as "redevelopment" in St. Louis. Yet following on this extreme model, a slower incremental paradigm is emergent, coincident with the general economic slowdown of the great recession of 2008. Whether intended or not, this incremental model of urbanism has proved a dynamic, contextual redevelopment process, one that recalibrates urban values toward longer-term asset building.

The name itself indexes the kinds of shifts under way: from the stigma of "McRee" (recognized by many St. Louisans as a synonym of danger and crime) and the poverty of "Town," to the stable anchor of "Botanical" (tied to the nearby Missouri Botanical Garden and the region's emerging science- and research- based development cluster) and the upwardly mobile aspiration of "Heights." A subset of this area is now known as the green-minded "Grove." What were the tactics and paradigms deployed in the un-building of McRee Town and the rebuilding of Botanical Heights to Botanical Grove? What are the design implications of this story? Should this dual recognition—of urbanism as unbuilding/rebuilding—impact how we measure "success" when we evaluate outcomes of various urban redevelopments? In this context, I seek to illustrate how design becomes a malleable tool for constructing the redevelopment narrative, in the appropriation and misappropriation of aesthetics and formal languages.

McRee's story highlights the complexity of achieving—and constructing narratives for—change, since ultimately redevelopment efforts are cumulative constructions, not isolated events. The aesthetic and social outcomes of McRee's later redevelopment builds on values already present in the neighborhood, something the prior redevelopment process left out. But it also builds on demographic changes that prior efforts already set in motion. The outcomes reinforce that gaps exist in how we measure successes of rebuilding, since a city's richest assets may not always be measured in dollar figures (quantitative terms), but on physical, aesthetic, cultural, and environmental (qualitative) terms. The outcomes also reinforce how we define terms like preservation, which in McRee has multiple facets. Where preservation refers commonly to the building stock of cities, the redevelopments in McRee also illustrate the need for a broader conceptualization of historic preservation where it includes demographic and cultural history.

Building an Urban Neighborhood 1.0

Shaw was an early 1900s elite "garden-suburb" development that emerged west of St. Louis's central core and riverfront (Figure 1). It grew as a neighborhood anchored by two exquisite open spaces: the large, classically laid out Tower Grove Park and the Missouri Botanical Garden, both remarkable landscape and garden preserves founded in the 1850s by the businessman turned philanthropist Henry Shaw. Homes surrounding the park and garden—including Henry Shaw's large estate—were grand brick structures on lush tree-lined streets interwoven with commercial venues on the corners and main avenues. As the anchor institution (Missouri Botanical Garden) grew, so too did Shaw, through some of the garden's own development efforts. It was an early public-private model collaboration, building the neighborhood along civic-minded philanthropic ideals.

Figure 1. McRee Neighborhood/Botanical Heights Area

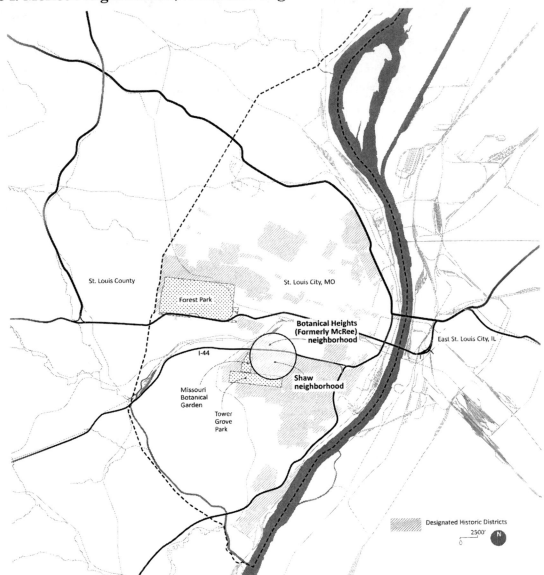

A block north of the garden, the McRee neighborhood was established as a working-class extension of Shaw (Figure 2). Here the homes were more modest in scale, more densely arrayed, yet still designed in brick, with rich architectural detailing and generously high ceilings to ventilate the summer heat. The McRee residential district emerged as the Liggett and Myers Tobacco Company (located on McRee's northern side) grew its operations and workforce. In 1900, over 50% of McRee's employed residents worked for Liggett and Myers or the affiliated box factory.[1] At that time, many residents were immigrants from Germany or Ireland. During the Depression years, this demographic transitioned to include more emigrants from Appalachia and rural Missouri, to the point that the district became referred to as "Hoosier City."[2] The neighborhood was a lively mixed-use area, although bounded on three sides by a wide rail corridor to the north of the large factory, and two major streets on either side east and west. Even as it grew and filled in as a neighborhood, McRee maintained an identity as the working-class and minority section of Shaw. The meaning of space was already inscribed by class divisions between the wealthier Shaw neighborhood and the laboring Hoosier city of McRee Town.

Figure 2: McRee Neighborhood/Botanical Heights Map

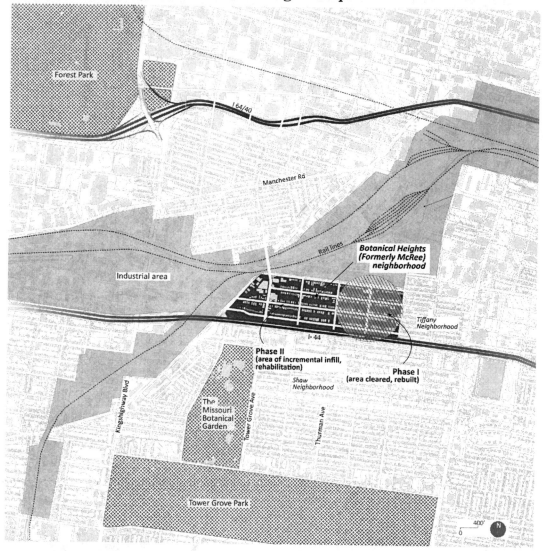

By the 1950s, St. Louis was experiencing the flight of its industrial economy out of the urban core to the growing periphery.[3] As jobs left the city, so too did residents who left for new homes in the emerging suburbs. These homes were made affordable through federal housing incentives, and were laid out in lower densities on lots following curvilinear street and block patterns. The new suburbs were made accessible by miles of new highway being built from the downtown outwards. Accessibility was not universal, however. Racially-fueled redlining real estate sales and development practices in St. Louis prevented African Americans from freely moving to other neighborhoods, unlike many of their whiter peers.[4] Most lower-income St. Louis downtown neighborhoods, including McRee (which by this point had long been absorbed into city lines), became majority African American districts in the city. What had been an enclave of stable labor with stable employment slowly emerged as a racially marked space, a reality that fast led to new stigmas during a time of pronounced racial tensions.

Unbuilding an Urban Neighborhood

A paradigm of urbanism that grew on explicit and implicit separations—first of class, then of race—was exacerbated in 1973 with construction of the massive Interstate 44 across McRee's southern edge. The push to urban flight had the redoubling effect of separating an already isolated district even further from the rest of the city. Indeed, these were effects experienced by many U.S. urban neighborhoods under the federal urban renewal program, a mid-century planning and design agenda that resulted in the clearing of dense, poorer downtown residential areas (perceived as blighted and unsanitary) for new highways and high-rise typologies deemed to bring efficiencies of access and healthy lifestyles to the city.

The highway construction itself marked the first moment of unbuilding, erasing six blocks of Shaw/McRee and filling the gap with a wall along the southern edge of McRee, one block north of the Botanical Garden. The growth imperative that defined a city expanding outward justified this infrastructure spending as it justified cleaning up a troubled minority space. While the Shaw neighborhood on the side of the Botanical Garden also lost population and suffered disinvestment at midcentury, it rebounded somewhat with help from the garden, which continued improvements to its campus, having spin-off effects in the surrounding area.[5] While urban planners of the time might have viewed the highway plan as a powerful "connector," by our modern notions it is apparent that this device only deeply disconnected, as it undermined values of other types of *locally scaled* urban accessibility (Figure 3).

Figure 3: Separation of Shaw and McRee Neighborhoods

The model of separation and enclosure deepened as McRee was confined between the rail to the north and the interstate to its south, with only two places to pass under the highway to Shaw: along Tower Grove Avenue and Thurman Avenue. The Thurman Avenue connection was closed just a few years later in 1976.[6] Boxed in, and without the same proximity to the garden as Shaw benefited from, the McRee neighborhood fell into a predictable pattern of neglect. Homes were unimproved or left abandoned, or lots sat vacant and the streets became sites for drug trading and violent crimes. The downfall speaks to the relative power of long-standing (wealthy) institutions in a city, like the Botanical Garden, which seems to have lost affiliation with McRee after the highway was constructed. This would have reflected a general ideology at the time, whereby many institutions intentionally walled themselves off from potential detracting neighborhoods.

By the 1990s, McRee was the de facto center for drug trade in St. Louis. It was referred to by locals as "the dark side" because of its downtrodden trajectory but also because many simple urban services like streetlights were perpetually in disrepair and the streets were literally dark.[7] McRee was considered one of the most undesirable neighborhoods in St. Louis to inhabit, " . . . a last resort for the poorest of St. Louis" poor, many of whom had been displaced by other neighborhood redevelopment efforts over the years."[8] The urban clearing and highway building that had been purported to lower the city's congestion only enabled the exodus of the city's middle class, who used it to flee to the suburbs. Neighborhoods like McRee that most needed a helping political hand only worsened.

Rebuilding as Unbuilding an Urban Neighborhood

In 1998, with McRee in severe physical, social, and economic decline, the Missouri Botanical Garden in Shaw realized the addressing McRee was essential. At this time, the general attitudes of institutions toward their urban contexts were changing in U.S. cities as governing boards realized helping their broader communities could have mutual benefits. Yet "helping" can as easily entail "transforming" or "removing" as it can facilitating the reproduction of existing communities. The garden mobilized a commission to aid the area that the institutions had helped to build one hundred years prior, but which now was detached and detracting values of the blocks around it. The McRee Town Redevelopment Corporation was formed with members from the area neighborhood associations appointed by a board that included representatives from the Botanical Garden. (As another point of erasure and renaming, this body was later renamed the Garden District Commission.) The improvement plan (Phase I) that emerged from the commission's planning process was one that called for the demolition and leveling of six entire blocks of McRee east of Thurman Avenue. The process for rebuilding would once again rely on demolition, this time not to enable flows of residents and capital outward from the city center, but clearing to encourage flows of a new kind of population back to the city center.

The strategy was considered a way to make the area feasible and attractive to outside developers who had avoided it until now since its reputation had become simply unmarketable and costs to transform it unaffordable.[9] Development sites without existing buildings or residents, much like greenfield sites outside city limits, are usually favored by banks and business people, since contingencies have been removed, leaving fewer risks for costly delays or environmental unknowns. Unlike the urban renewal projects of the 1960s, this project was not federally funded or driven by a federal policy. But it was enabled through a legislative city vote approving the site as blighted, allowing the redevelopment corporation to acquire land invoking powers of eminent domain. Much of the land was already owned by the city. Fifty-six percent of the properties were vacant or considered to be of dilapidated or blighted quality.[10] Other houses were still occupied, in varying states of stability or disrepair. As had occurred during the urban renewal era, owners had to sell their properties and move, regardless of their willingness or interest. Tenants were given relocation money, and owners were compensated for their properties. While some felt the relocation funds were a positive form of support to enable families to finally afford to leave a dire area, others felt compensation was inadequate. These sentiments echoed those of the urban renewal era in St. Louis forty years before, when people similarly witnessed buyouts, demolitions, and clearing under the calls for "progress."

The blocks cleared had been listed on the National Register of Historic Districts in 1987 as part of the Tiffany district, including blocks in the Tiffany neighborhood just east of McRee.[11] Ironically, the historic preservation movement in the U.S. had emerged as a direct response to the urban renewal era extremes of redevelopment, to protect treasured older building stock in cities like St. Louis from being further demolished. As a result of the movement, federal and local authorities began offering tax breaks to encourage the renovation and rehabilitation of old buildings, recognizing that this would save the character of cities while encouraging new investments. In St. Louis the historic tax credit program was introduced in 1998 to help builders with 25% of rehabilitation costs. It went on to be considered a valued program for the city, if not a model program for other cities.[12] In 2004 a request was made to "decrease" the 1987 National Historic Register boundary of the Tiffany Historic District so as to exclude the McRee portion. This scenario was never formally approved. Instead the entire district's historic status was revoked.[13] (And the six blocks within McRee were torn down.) For the development team involved in rehabilitation, it was more important to have a clean slate to build from than call attention to the fabric that was there, despite the fact that tax breaks existed explicitly to make it cost effective to keep and reuse old buildings. The rebuilding narrative in the early 2000s was about building a new neighborhood, not rebuilding the one that was there.

On June 7, 2004, when the bulldozers arrived in McRee to begin work, city officials gathered for the demolition's groundbreaking, marking the official start of the Phase I clearings. On this day, the McRee neighborhood name was also officially "cleared" and its new name, Botanical Heights, launched.[14] The renaming was a strategic rebranding. The famously downtrodden "McRee" became "Botanical," reaffiliating with the stable, long-standing Missouri Botanical Garden institution, with the aspirational "Heights." The neighborhood was now reconnecting with its original anchor institution, but only after it had fallen apart to the point of disappearing, untethered to its anchor for decades.

Building an Un-Urban Neighborhood

After the vast area was cleared and regraded, 143 new homes, all market rate and priced up to $400,000 were built on the six vacant blocks.[15] Formally and aesthetically, the new houses were an eclectic mix of pseudo-historic-looking suburban homes. The developer of the six Phase I blocks was McBride & Sons, a major homebuilder in the region whose primary market until this project had focused on building replicable houses in the suburban periphery outside the city. As a result, many of the new Botanical Heights homes were built with an aesthetic, scale, and typology of the familiar white middle class McMansions found around suburban and exurban cul-de-sacs around the U.S. (Figures 4 and 5). A few smaller homes made reference to the typologies that had existed in McRee before, but even these were detailed with suburban features. Rebuilding was about a construction of narratives staging the return to the city with the aesthetic allure and implicit safety and scale of suburbia.

Figure 4: Botanical Heights Cul-de-Sac

Photograph: Patty Heyda, 2014

Figure 5: Botanical Heights: Typical House

Photograph: Patty Heyda, 2014

Despite real or projected ambitions, the new houses were not built by the same urbanistic rules or aesthetic integrity of the historical blocks. The homes ranged in size with some almost double in area of their historic predecessors and on slightly wider lots. The gaps between the houses were larger than the original high-density, closely packed historic homes. As a result, these gaps broke the continuous-feeling "street wall" that closely packed house facades typically define in urban street corridors. The new blocks maintained a template that had a back service alley, except in some cases the two-car garages were attached to the house instead of lining the alley. A common trait of the suburban tract home, like one that might be found in Chesterfield, an outlying suburb of St. Louis, is the attached two-car garage.[16] Although in the more recently built suburbs, the garages typically connect through the front of the house. Styles of many of the new homes looked markedly suburban with their mix of references to different periods of architectural history. There were houses that had Colonial-inspired symmetry and oval windows and others that had Arts and Crafts type nested gabled roofs, white picket-styled railings, then a mix of smaller sized windows and thin eaves. Many of these kinds of elements featured on the homes evoked patterns and styles found in suburban neighborhoods all over the U.S..[17] As the St. Louis Real Estate Society news blog reported, "Botanical Heights is proof of our lack of imagination."[18] Rebuilding was not about rebuilding within a fabric but about importing new fabrics. Was this an aesthetic maneuver that imagined itself as remaking a dangerous urban neighborhood into something approximating the largely white security of St. Louis suburbia?

Critiques of suburban type developments in design schools usually revolve around the lack of authenticity these formulaic models offer. If the same styles and typologies of building are used in multiple neighborhoods across a vastly varied city region, then the result is an increasingly homogenous landscape. Worse, this translates into a placelessness where all neighborhoods begin to feel and look alike, lacking any unique character and identity. To counter this effect, McBride & Sons homebuilders created the City Series and Heritage Series of houses to mix into the overall development. Of these two types, the City Series evoked most closely the character of the existing (prior) fabric, as they looked (vaguely) like their historic predecessors, although with Colonial undertones[19] (Figure 6). The facades were made of brick, the houses were set back and raised up off the street a few feet, and ground floor rooms had ten-foot ceilings and arched doorways. The problem with these gestures, though, is that some were carried out with little integrity in the construction methods. For example, the bricks were applied as a thin-looking veneer and interior arches were disproportioned, making them appear more decorative than necessary from a load-bearing perspective. There were transom windows above the doors, which let additional light in, but these windows did not necessarily open as original transoms did to ventilate cross breezes through the length of the house while keeping doors locked.

Figure 6: Botanical Heights City Series House-type

Photograph: Patty Heyda, 2014

Few of the City Series homes had the iconic flat roof of the historic 1900s homes but instead used the suburban gable. At the time of the original neighborhood development, bricks were the standard construction material because they were produced locally and were affordable. Brick walls were structural, resulting in a weighty appearance. Air conditioning did not exist, so homes needed to breathe via air circulation through their lengths. In design circles, literal imitation is seldom heralded as an appropriate aesthetic response, since building technologies, materials, and economies of scale change so radically over the years. Yet the Botanical Heights project that unfolded in the space of the old did not solve a design problem so much as create new ones. Rebuilding was forgetting about erasures, or pretending they never happened, by (mis)appropriating the aesthetics of the former place. Aspirations for design might have created a forward-looking series of homes by building on the literal fabric that was there before, yet with relevant language (as tied to building material and technologies) of the current day. Instead a backward looking "city" series of homes were built as a pretend version of the neighborhood that was there before.

Design, of course, is inherently as formal and spatial as it is aesthetic. The phenomenon of rebuilding the new district with a superficial nod to the aesthetics of the old one is not only a matter of *looks* in this case: in urban design, the arrangement of space and massing of buildings are an intentional construction—a highly designed order tied to goals of framing spaces for healthy, happy inhabitation, both inside and outside of buildings. A designer's challenge is to resolve constraints while making spaces conducive to public and private life, at the scale of the block and street just as at the scale of the room and detail. Controlling the mundane platting, the distances between buildings from each other and from the road, and heights and density are ways in which space is shaped to impact use and perceptions of form. Houses that are separated from each other convey a sense of private precinct, where houses with open porches in alignment and in proximity convey social interaction. The new blocks sold quickly, highlighting the inherent disconnect between designers' views of quality and market realities. They targeted middle-class market preferences, but the size and spacing of the homes, with their meaningless design features and their relationship to big cul-de-sac-ending streets (that fenced off connections to and jogged axial alignments to the remaining fabric's sidewalks and streets), resulted in a shallow urbanism that has notably not rebuilt the city in terms of its potential for social diversity and robust urban life.

Rebuilding How We Measure Rebuilding

What happened to McRee's redevelopment over the decades reflects how policy and markets influence design efforts that shape urban spaces per middle-class preferences. In the 1960s, this meant constructing highways downtown to aid the growth of new upwardly mobile neighborhoods outside the city. Today, this includes redesigning neighborhoods as rebranding, to attract the primary and stable middle-class demographic back to the city. This follows market trends nationally that resound, "No McMansions [no suburbs] for Millennials."[20] Young Gen-Y and empty nesters do not want to live far out in the suburbs where they grew up, but are interested in walkable, vibrant urban neighborhoods again.[21] Yet the downtown urban/suburban Phase I project styles point to the fact that this demographic is still attracted to some of the aesthetic comforts of suburbia. During the earlier era of highway redevelopment in this area, the real demographic in need in McRee was *displaced* from the site of improvement, not included in it. Rebuilding has consistently followed paradigms of the more lucrative markets. Of course, other deeper structural factors are compounding the existence of urban poverty, making neighborhood improvement challenging. These factors include urban public school performance and jobs, which are becoming more and more high-skilled as the economic base in the city shifts toward technology and science and medical sectors. High-skilled jobs require adequate schooling, thus entering a cycle that is difficult to overcome without additional welfare-type policy shifts. Fundamentally, though, residents left McRee and could not afford the new market rate replacement homes to be able to return. American municipalities need revenue, and rebuilding becomes about attracting stability of income through increased land values. In this case, redevelopment goals are mostly economic, where design integrity and social implications become secondary.

The redevelopment erasures in McRee were considered successful since all the new homes were sold, and at market rate.[22] Who profited? Despite this commercial success, some attitudes and general public sentiment toward the Garden District Commission remained resentful. Many saw contradictions in the wasteful tearing down of well-built, reusable buildings by a commission partnered with an institution (the Botanical Garden) that promoted sustainability and the environment. Father Gerald Kleba told the *Riverfront Times*, "Their [the Botanical Garden's] signs in the geo-dome say the two keys to an alive planet are recycling and biodiversity. But they can't think we could recycle a house, or that black, poor or elderly people are an aspect of biodiversity that would enhance the garden because it would enhance the world at their doorstep."[23] Carolyn Hewes Toft, the then-executive director of the Landmarks Association of St. Louis, a historic preservation organization, said, "This is an incredibly lost opportunity. Building materials [for new houses] have to be mined and manufactured. Renovation puts more people to work and it costs less."[24] When metrics measuring success are limited entirely to economic terms, projects do not fulfill the performance standards they might otherwise have been capable of achieving. The design world measures projects on qualitative and performative terms, not only quantitative ones. A project is well designed when it creatively solves multiple challenging issues or constraints simultaneously. In these terms, a good project would responsibly meet budget restrictions, but might also reduce its environmental impact, support urban public life, and retain a neighborhood's character while bringing new life with aesthetics relevant to the current day and to the place where it locates.

Building an Urban Neighborhood 2.0

Phase II of the new Botanical Heights redevelopment project proceeded in 2006. By this time McBride & Sons did not exercise its option to participate in the project. Not insignificantly, there was a looming economic recession and imminent collapse of the real estate market in the United States. A husband and wife pair of architects, Brent Crittenden and Sarah Gibson, purchased one of the vacant, run-down corner buildings in the yet uncleared side of Botanical Heights west of Thurman Street. The couple updated and renovated the historic building, moved into the apartment upstairs with their young children, and opened an architecture and construction contractor's office called Urban Improvement Company (UIC) on the ground floor with shop-front windows open to the street. As new resident stakeholders to the area, but also perhaps as an ambitious fledgling business, UIC became involved in the Phase II redevelopment.

The approach derived by the commission working with UIC was incremental. Some of the old existing buildings would be rehabilitated where possible and new models developed for infill housing on the vacant lots in between. Inspired by the constraints of the recession, not compromised by them, UIC designed cost-efficient, environmentally minded "green" homes for the empty lots, branded "Live Green StL."[25] The new house layouts tightly adhered to the reigning typological organization of the older buildings extant in the neighborhood. This meant they followed the same dimensional envelope, lot coverage, setbacks, proportions, and materiality of McRee's historic building stock. The new buildings were pared down stylistically, but their formal massing and spacing illustrated the ability of design, from an ordering sense, to mediate and respect the historic context in which a building sits, while still meeting aspirational contemporary standards of healthy living (Figure 7).

Figure 7: UIC Live Green STL Home in Botanical Heights, Phase II

Photograph: Patty Heyda, 2014

"Healthy living" also brought noteworthy additional metrics to the development table: the project introduced environmental savings into the pro forma. This fact marks an important aspect of the Phase II redevelopment, where quality became part of the decision making. The first block of Phase II included infill houses made with locally sourced "green" materials and geothermal heat pumps that would reduce operating costs to amounts as low as 50% that of a typical new home, while also cutting CO_2 emissions to about 50% of the typical output generated by natural gas–powered systems.[26] Houses also included options for solar arrays and other sustainable building features. This portion of Botanical Heights was named Botanical Grove. Now from "Heights" came another shift to the green-minded "Grove," with a connection to a smaller, more intimately scaled community of trees.

UIC's commitment to preserving the context of the existing neighborhood meant they would not replicate the products of an era one hundred years ago. In fact, most of UIC's projects—whether new construction or the interiors of renovations—were unapologetically contemporary. The primary aesthetic design components were simple, with clean, minimalistic details emphasizing the spatial connections between rooms and between the inside and outside. The exteriors were also modernistic in shape, but drawn from a close analysis of the texture and materiality of the existing buildings. The formal expression of the renovated buildings amplified existing architectural components through the use of color. New buildings related to old through subtle design features that tied to neighboring buildings in the material sense. For example, the houses were faced with a mix of bricks that were varied slightly in tone and color. This gave them a rustic, irregular appearance that blended with the weathered brick on the old adjacent buildings. In places, brick was wrapped around the sides of the house a few feet, conveying thickness but also playing with the language of the thin materiality of a contemporary façade, reading as an overlapping of brick over the siding. The result created a blend of new and old that neither stands out nor entirely fits in, but establishes a dialogue with the past, enriching the character of the existing place. At the same time, the aesthetics skillfully restake the territory; this time as a modern, green district—although still targeting a trendy Gen X and Gen Y socially conscious, "creative class" of young innovators (the group returning to cities for the entrepreneurial high-skilled jobs.)[27]

The 2008 economic recession, which virtually halted real estate financing to riskier (unprecedented) real estate development projects, coincided with Phase II. Slower speed change resulted in a more dynamic process; not a stagnating one, but one that allowed for adjustments along the way. Existing houses could be assessed one by one, and empty lots could be filled a few at a time. Moreover, UIC was located in the neighborhood. Design could unfold in real time, as the architects learned of stories and needs for the neighborhood or as they befriended business owners or residents who could communicate their desires during redevelopment efforts, not solely before or after. Rebuilding was still an economic equation, subject to market slowdowns when the recession made the economics of rebuilding along traditional paradigms more difficult, design proved relevant.

The design and development team recognized that housing alone cannot make a real community thrive. Like in the original McRee and Shaw neighborhoods, a mix of institutions and commercial uses were needed to support urban life. So while the residential infill and home rehabilitations were shoring up the secondary streets, UIC and others helped recruit two new institutional and commercial magnets to anchor the reviving neighborhood's main road, Tower Grove Avenue: A City Garden charter elementary school and a local wine bar and restaurant, Olio and Elaia among a few other shops. The bar and restaurant occupied the old gas station and adjacent house at the corner of McRee and Tower Grove Avenues, rehabilitated by the young couple's firm. The school building was also located on the prominent Tower Grove Avenue, the north-south gateway to the neighborhood. The school occupied a renovated warehouse, with a design also championed by UIC, which helped secure financing for the project through an aggressive combination of tax credit programs and their own creative design economies that specified inexpensive materials, and innovatively left exposed some of the existing industrial aesthetic of the historic warehouse. These buildings brought investment confidence to a transitional area without necessitating erasures to do so. On the one hand, this confidence brought high-end dining and a pastry shop, and could be critiqued as aiding gentrification in the neighborhood; on the other hand, it is complex to pinpoint sources of gentrification since most of the existing residents had already left as a product of the earlier Phase I redevelopment. In this context, the new school served as an interesting counterpoint to these critiques of gentrification, since it brought residents the good-quality training that local schools were lacking before. The new anchors were added elements to begin regrowth of a healthier neighborhood, the school contributing not just from a physical standpoint but from a structural one.[28]

The result of this latest phase of redevelopment in Botanical Heights is a neighborhood still in transition but one that remains relatively intact, in an aesthetic and material sense. While some new buildings look different, their varied styles are in fact consistent overall with historical patterns. Botanical Grove, despite the renaming, maintains an authenticity of physical character of the original McRee Town because the original blocks and houses remain, some now repaired and restored. This second redevelopment leveraged existing housing stock not only for design quality but also for economic benefit from the historic tax credit incentives. A handful of residents remained, but by the time of Phase II the number of people still living there was extremely low.[29] So while the rebuilding here followed a "preservationist" approach, what exactly "preservation" means and how exactly success is measured, is not as straightforward. With such low resident numbers it is hard to determine if the demographic fabric will (or can) be preserved as equally as the material fabric has. It is always a challenge to rebuild within an existing population. And it is true of the new infill housing of Phase II, that while homes are still cheaper than the units developed by McBride & Sons, they remain outside of low income brackets. In this case, it is important to recognize that the Phase II rebuilding of McRee/Botanical Heights shares benefits enjoyed by Phase I, in that it was practically able to start over from a blank (social) slate. "Preservation" in this case works as an incomplete concept, referring to a restored building fabric, but not to a returned or restored demographic fabric.

In St. Louis, an immigrant, then minority enclave is transformed multiple times through rebuilding efforts that follow paradigms of neglect and middle-class separation and flight to the suburbs, followed by paradigms of returning to the city, justifying erasures to remake the city with aesthetics familiar to the suburbs. And finally, it gets rebuilt once more through a paradigm of building *on* the city, but on a city that had already been largely deconstructed. Rebuilding marks and remarks space through paradigms of *unbuilding* as equally and importantly as through rebuilding, and aesthetics are the malleable vehicle for various and changing rhetorical political goals over time that in actuality follow economic markets. In McRee, these paradigms of building or unbuilding are part of cumulative and complex (not discrete) political and economic processes. When redevelopment's urban design and planning choices are measured on a continuum rather than through isolated snapshots that focus on *quantitative* metrics, the debates over what is "successful" are more meaningful and issues of urban equitability are more transparent. In our current era, illuminated most recently by the events in Ferguson where the city and the world have been made blatantly aware of the structural inequalities plaguing much of the region, the case for transparency—for inclusion, not separation—in how and for whom urban affairs are conducted becomes paramount.[30] Investing in "degrowth"—that is, the kinds of urban design and architecture that foremost serve the environment and residents—can form the basis for how we recognize processes of building and rebuilding as a cumulative project, as yet one more variable to measure along with other metrics determining success.[31]

(Essay illustrations provided by the author.)

Endnotes

1. From the registration form of the National Register of Historic Places, United States Department of the Interior, National Park Service, for the Liggett & Myers Historic District, dated May 4, 2009, p. 78.

2. From the registration form of the National Register of Historic Places, United States Department of the Interior, National Park Service, for the Liggett & Myers Historic District, dated May 4, 2009, p. 75.

3. See Joseph Heathcott, Malre Agnes Murphy, "Corridors of Flight, Zones of Renewal: Industry, Planning and Policy in the Making of Metropolitan St. Louis, 1940–1980," *Journal of Urban History* 31, January 2005, pp. 151–189.

4. See Colin Gordon, *Mapping Decline, St. Louis and the Fate of the American City* (Philadelphia: University of Pennsylvania Press, 2008).

5. Jeff Janson, "Shaw from 1945–1970: Prosperity and Decline," *Micah Program Virtual Book*, 1998, revised 2004, accessed June 2014, http://www.slu.edu/outreach/micah/Virtual%20Book/janson.htm.

6. Shelley Smithson, "The Greening of McRee Town," *Riverfront Times*, October 8, 2003.

7. Local church volunteer John Minner is quoted in the *Riverfront Times* describing his church as the only source of "light" in McRee: "You know, this neighborhood is known as the dark side." McRee resident Jackie Ingram says: "It's so black here at night you can't see nothing. They shoot out the streetlights and as soon as they come and fix them, they shoot them out again." From Shelley Smithson, "The Greening of McRee Town," *Riverfront Times*, October 8, 2003.

8. Shelley Smithson, "The Greening of McRee Town," *Riverfront Times*, October 8, 2003.

9. Eddie Roth, then president of the Redevelopment Commission told the *Riverfront Times*: "To attract resources the people with this kind of dough—there had to be a new-housing element. . . . That had to be at the core of remaking McRee Town." George Robnett, Garden District Commission's executive director: "We have to increase home-ownership—people with a vested interest in the neighborhood. New housing is the best way to do that." From Shelley Smithson, "The Greening of McRee Town," *Riverfront Times*, October 8, 2003.

10. Facts as listed on the Missouri Botanical Garden website, "Botanical Heights" information/narrative web page. Accessed May 2014, http://www.missouribotanicalgarden.org/media/fact-pages/botanical-heights.aspx.

11. National Register of Historic Places, United States Department of the Interior, National Park Service, for the Liggett & Myers Historic District, dated May 4, 2009.

12. Scott Ogilve, St. Louis Board of Aldermen, 24th Ward, "Why Capping Missouri's Tax Credits Would Hurt St. Louis." Next City blog, March 22, 2013, accessed March 2013, http://nextcity.org/daily/entry/why-capping missouris-historic-tax-credits-would-hurt-st.-louis.

13. National Register of Historic Places, United States Department of the Interior, National Park Service, for the Liggett & Myers Historic District, dated May 4, 2009; p. 83.

14. "From McRee Town to Botanical Heights," Homes & Communities, Missouri News, U.S. Department of Housing and Urban Development website, June 2004, accessed March 2014, www.hud.gov/local/mo/news/botanical-heights2004.cfm.

15. Facts as listed on the Missouri Botanical Garden website, "Botanical Heights" information/narrative web page. Accessed May, 2014, http://www.missouribotanicalgarden.org/media/fact-pages/botanical-heights.aspx.

16. This was pointed out in a blog written by Matt Kastner on the St. Louis Real Estate Society web news, "Botanical Heights Is Proof of Our Lack of Imagination," December 11, 2007, accessed June 2014 http://stlresociety.com/43/botanical-heights-is-proof-of-our-lack-of-imagination/.

17. These are phrases mentioned by non-designers in conversations with the author about suburban styled homes, various dates.

18. Matt Kastner, "Botanical Heights Is Proof of Our Lack of Imagination." St Louis Real Estate Society, December 11, 2007, accessed June, 2014, http://stlresociety.com/43/botanical-heights-is-proof-of-our-lack-of imagination/.

19. Circa Properties, pamphlet from 4012 Blaine home listing for sale, picked up by author, July 2014.

20. S. Mitra Kalita and Robbie Whelan, "No McMansions for Millennials," *Wall Street Journal*, January 13, 2011.

21. Ibid.

22. See James Nicholson, "Botanical Heights: McRee Town lifts itself to HIGHER GROUND," *RCGA St. Louis Commerce Magazine*, November, 2004, archives accessed June, 2014, www.stlcommercemagazine.com/archives/november2004/heights.html

23. Shelley Smithson, "The Greening of McRee Town," *Riverfront Times*, October 8, 2003.

24. Ibid.

25. "Green Machines," Livegreenstl web blog, April 14, 2004, accessed July 2014, http://livegreenstl.com/blog.html.

26. Ibid.

27. See Richard Florida, *The Rise of the Creative Class* (New York; Basic Books, 2002).

28. See Elisa Crouch, "City Garden Charter School's Success Boosts City Neighborhoods," *St. Louis Post Dispatch*, February 17, 2013.

29. As told informally to author in conversations with Brent Crittenden on December 3, 2013.

30. Events in Ferguson, Missouri were launched in August 2014, when an unarmed black teenager was shot and killed by the police. Months of investigations and protests ensued, sounding a broader, universal call for equity in urban affairs and amenities (and treatment of citizens) across the St. Louis region and other U.S. cities.

31. See *Degrowth: A Vocabulary for a New Era*, Giacomo D'Alisa, Federico Demaria, and Giorgos Kallis, editors (Routledge, 2014).

Patty Heyda, M.Arch., LEED AP, is assistant professor of urban design in the Sam Fox School of Design & Visual Arts at Washington University in St. Louis. Her teaching and research focuses on the politics and spaces of urban re-development in globalizing contexts. She has a master of architecture II (Distinction) from Harvard University and a bachelor of architecture/ master of architecture from Tulane University. Heyda's current book, provisionally titled *Rebuilding the American City* (Routledge Press, forthcoming 2015) elaborates paradigms and particularities of American downtown redevelopment in the first decades of the new millennium (co-author D. Gamble). Heyda's other research and design projects explore spatial and social impacts of the political economy in areas of St. Louis, Missouri, and other sites. Heyda's professional experiences include several years dedicated to the Zlaty Andel project in Prague with the Pritzker Prize–winning firm Architectures Jean Nouvel in Paris, and competition design work with Atelier 8000 in the Czech Republic. In the United States, her professional work focused on multi-scalar riverfront framework plans in Washington, D.C., and St. Louis.

ST. LOUIS
CURRENTS

CPSIA information can be obtained
at www.ICGtesting.com
Printed in the USA
FFOW02n0150010216
20817FF